Probiotic Allies

How to maximise the health benefits of your microflora

Peter Cartwright

Published by
Prentice Publishing
PO Box 1704
Ilford IG5 0WN
United Kingdom
Tel/fax: +44 (0)20 8551 6192
mail@prentice-publishing.co.uk
www.prentice-publishing.co.uk

Copyright © Prentice Publishing 2011

All rights reserved
No part of this publication may
be reproduced, stored in a retrieval
system, or transmitted in any form or
by any means, electronic, mechanical,
photocopying, recording or otherwise
without the prior permission
of the copyright holders

A CIP record for this publication
is available from the British Library

ISBN 978-0-9544438-1-8

Prentice Publishing

Contents

- § **Acknowledgements** vi
- § **Foreword (by Prof. Seppo Salminen)** vii
- § **Preface** ix
    - ❖ Why should you read this book?
    - ❖ The general approach
    - ❖ Structure of the book

Part I – The Human Microflora

1 Creatures with Whom We Live 2
- ❖ The body's defence systems
- ❖ Symbiosis
- ❖ Human symbiotic relationships
- ❖ The microflora can be disturbed

2 Our Microflora 8
- ❖ The naming system
- ❖ General characteristics of the microflora
- ❖ The skin
- ❖ The nose, throat and windpipe
- ❖ The mouth
- ❖ The female reproductive system

3 The Gut Microflora 25
- ❖ The stomach
- ❖ The small intestine
- ❖ The large intestine
- ❖ What are the benefits of the intestinal microflora?
- ❖ How does the microflora defend against pathogens?
- ❖ Disturbance of the gut microflora

4 The Immune System and the Microflora 40
- ❖ The importance of the microflora-immune system relationship
- ❖ Outline of the body's immune system (IS)
- ❖ The innate immune system
- ❖ The adaptive immune system
- ❖ Influences of the gut flora on the IS
- ❖ The potential of probiotics

Part II – The Essentials of Probiotics

5 A History of Probiotics 52
- ❖ Fermented drinks and foods
- ❖ Microbes first identified
- ❖ The large bowel: fermenting or putrefying?
- ❖ Metchnikoff and Bulgarian peasants
- ❖ Decline of early popularity
- ❖ Early commercial products
- ❖ Probiotics for animals
- ❖ Probiotics become fashionable again
- ❖ The cause of stomach ulcers

6 Probiotic Benefits for the Intestine 62
- ❖ Infectious diarrhoea
- ❖ Antibiotic-associated diarrhoea
- ❖ Constipation
- ❖ Irritable bowel syndrome (IBS)
- ❖ Inflammatory bowel disease (IBD)
- ❖ Lactose intolerance
- ❖ Gastritis and stomach ulcers

7 Probiotic Benefits for Other Parts of the Body 79
- ❖ The systemic immune system
- ❖ Allergies
- ❖ Female urogenital infections
- ❖ The mouth
- ❖ Upper respiratory tract
- ❖ The skin

8 Safety 93
- Infection risks
- Spread of antibiotic resistance
- The immunocompromised person
- The unborn child
- A final thought

Part III – Practical Questions and Solutions

9 Choosing a Good Probiotic Product 104
- Milk-based or freeze-dried
- Multi-strain probiotics
- Types of probiotic microbes
- Evidence of health benefits
- Total number of microbes in a product

10 Types of Probiotic Microbes 117
- Genus *Lactobacillus*
- Genus *Bifidobacterium*: early colonisers
- The model microbes
- *Escherichia coli*
- *Bacillus subtilis*
- *Saccharomyces cerevisiae*
- Major microfloral genera
- *Clostridium butyricum*

11 What are *Prebiotics*? 130
- The background to prebiotics
- Non-digestible oligosaccharides (NDOs)
- Boosting numbers of beneficial bacteria
- NDOs as food
- Galacto-oligosaccharides (GOS)
- Fructo-oligosaccharides (FOS)
- Inulin
- Lactulose
- Other prebiotics
- Advantages of prebiotics
- Disadvantages of prebiotics
- Synbiotics
- Clinical studies using prebiotics

12 Young and Old 143
- ❖ *Children*
  - ♦ Birth by caesarean section
  - ♦ Antibiotics in the early months
  - ♦ Formula feeding
  - ♦ Pre-term infants
  - ♦ Giving probiotics to children
  - ♦ Cow's milk allergy
  - ♦ Dosage for children
- ❖ The elderly
  - ♦ Altered microflora
  - ♦ Reduced stomach acid secretion
  - ♦ Constipation in the elderly
  - ♦ Diarrhoea caused by medications
  - ♦ Development of diverticula

13 Future Developments 153
- ❖ An ideal microflora?
- ❖ The effects of stress
- ❖ The choice of antibiotics
- ❖ Additional conditions to benefit from probiotics
  - ♦ Colo-rectal cancer
  - ♦ Radiation-induced diarrhoea
  - ♦ Obesity
  - ♦ Various other conditions
- ❖ Surgery
- ❖ Unusual approaches to probiotics
  - ♦ Bacteriophages
  - ♦ Faecal enemas
  - ♦ Worm therapy

§ **References** 167
§ **Bibliography** 187
§ **Index** 189
§ **About the Author** 193

Illustrations

Preface
- Figure 1: Probiotic products exist in a range of forms

Chapter 1: Creatures with Whom We Live
- Figure 2: African buffalo
- Figure 3: Examples of bacterial parasites

Chapter 2: Our Microflora
- Figure 4: The microflora of the human body
- Figure 5: Coccus-shaped and rod-shaped bacteria
- Figure 6: The structure of the human skin
- Figure 7: The upper respiratory tract
- Figure 8: Parts of the mouth
- Figure 9: The female reproductive system

Chapter 3: The Gut Microflora
- Figure 10: The microflora of the intestinal tract
- Figure 11: The small intestine
- Figure 12: The large intestine

Chapter 4: The Immune System and the Microflora
- Figure 13: A phagocyte engulfing and destroying a pathogen
- Figure 14: Early stages of inflammation
- Figure 15: The close relationship between gut microbes and mucosal immune cells

Chapter 5: A History of Probiotics
- Figure 16: Fermented foods and drinks

Chapter 6: Probiotic Benefits for the Intestine
- Figure 17: The gastro-intestinal tract
- Figure 18: Helicobacter pylori
- Figure 19: A summary of evidence of benefit from probiotics

Chapter 7: Probiotic Benefits for Other Parts of the Body
- Figure 20: The urinary system
- Figure 21: The upper respiratory tract

Chapter 8: Safety
- Figure 22: Chromosome and plasmids within a bacterium

Chapter 10: Types of Probiotic Microbes
- Figure 23: A bacterium
- Figure 24: Bifidobacteria
- Figure 25: A Bacillus bacterium with a spore forming inside
- Figure 26: Saccharomyces boulardii

Chapter 11: What are *Prebiotics*?
- Figure 27: *Prebiotic* foods

Chapter 12: Young and Old
- Figure 28: Diverticula in a section of the colon

Chapter 13: Future Developments
- Figure 29: A bacteriophage
- Figure 30: Helminthic worms

Acknowledgements

Although I take full responsibility for the content of this book, it is important to recognise assistance received from a range of colleagues and friends.

Professionally, I would like to thank the medical journalist Sara Bernstein for her astute editing suggestions, Doig Simmonds for his clear illustrations, Gillian Oliver for Figure 1, Jennifer Browett for the cover design, George Mann for the layout and production, and Jonathan Sowler and Lizzie Hardy for their sales and marketing advice.

Thanks also to Professor Torkel Wadström of Lund University, Sweden, for his comments on parts of the text.

Among friends, I would like to acknowledge Alan Bolding for his consistent interest in my writings, Pete and Sue Wright and Trevor Bridle for their inspiration, and of course my wife Yvonne who has been my greatest supporter.

Peter Cartwright

Foreword

by Professor Seppo Salminen

Probiotics are "live microorganisms with a demonstrated health benefit on the host." Prebiotics, on the other hand, are nondigestible food ingredients, mostly carbohydrate components, that selectively stimulate the growth and/or activity of beneficial microorganisms in the human gut. When probiotics and prebiotics are mixed together, they form a **synbiotic**. All probiotics are unique in their properties and thus combining probiotics is also a challenge – this challenge should be handled in a scientific manner.

The science of probiotics and prebiotics has expanded fast and there are, already, probiotics in foods, fermented milks, oat-based products, drinks, and dietary supplements (for example, capsules, tablets, and powders) and in some other product forms as well. Examples of foods containing probiotics are yoghurts, fermented and unfermented milks, sauerkraut, miso, tempeh, and some juices and soy beverages. How does a consumer ensure that he or she gets the right probiotic strain for herself?

The most common probiotics are lactic acid bacteria and bifidobacteria, and sometimes there are combinations. How does the consumer know that there are health benefits from a particular strain or species? Changes in legislation in Europe (and elsewhere in the world) are helping to ensure that more accurate health claims are made on labels and in advertising. It is not easy, however, to obtain reliable and clear background information on probiotics, and this is where a book like the one you have here is very useful.

The help often comes in a very practical form in terms of types of uses, concentration estimates and viable probiotics and, of course, the scientific documentation for particular causes. Here the author has chosen a simple but efficient way to describe the probiotics, their properties and application as well as potential uses at home and in the hospital. Those practical terms and applications are especially important now that the role of fermented foods in total diet has decreased.

The book is clearly written, and the short titles are informative. It takes you through the steps of assessing different probiotics, choosing the right ones and considering the scientific data backing current probiotics. This way one can make informed choices and hopefully enjoy the health benefits of specific probiotics and prebiotics.

Seppo Salminen
Director
Functional Foods Forum
University of Turku
Finland

Preface

What are probiotics? They are living microbes that can improve your health, and are available in a range of different products. Twenty years ago, the general public may not have heard of probiotics. Today, a large number of people are aware of the 'friendly bacteria' found in yoghurts. This change has been brought about, not only by increased advertising, but also by greater awareness in the scientific community of the concept of benefits from these probiotic allies.

Here are some examples of the results that led to this increase in scientific awareness:

- Infants born prematurely or of low birthweight, had their risk of developing a dangerous disease (necrotising enterocolitis) reduced by two-thirds, and their risk of death reduced by more than half when they were given probiotics [1].
- A group of women with diagnosed irritable bowel syndrome (IBS) had symptoms reduced by more than 20% (compared with a placebo/blank group) [2].
- A group of elderly people who consumed a probiotic cheese for 16 weeks reduced the risk of developing a yeast infection of the mouth by three-quarters, compared with those consuming the ordinary cheese [3].

More examples are found in chapters 6 and 7.

Why should you read this book?

This book describes an aspect of your body that you may never have considered – how human beings have evolved in symbiosis (close association) with microscopic living creatures, and how the way the symbiosis operates has a major impact on our health. An understanding of that symbiosis is valuable in recognising when the relationship is out-of-kilter and how you can help it to return to a desirable state.

I want you to enjoy reading this book, rather than finding it a dutiful burden. Everything in this book is focussed on explaining things clearly, and you should be able to absorb the information easily and decide how much is relevant to you. Sometimes when complicated information is simplified, the meaning becomes distorted. I have worked hard to ensure that the message has remained accurate.

The general approach

The subtitle of this book is *How to Maximise the Health Benefits of Your Microflora*. From this, it would be reasonable to assume that I am providing a sort of 'health recipe', such as "for goal Z, do actions A, plus B, plus C". I am not using the 'health recipe' approach, for several reasons.

Firstly, to be effective in improving your health, you need some background knowledge, in the same way that a good cook needs some basic knowledge about food and cooking methods. You are less likely to make a mistake.

Secondly, with such basic knowledge you will be in a better position to judge whether the advice you are receiving makes sense. Instead of being a passive receiver of advice, you can become an active participant in your own health improvement. You can engage in a dialogue.

Thirdly, current information on the microflora and on probiotics is only partial, although it is increasing rapidly. If you understand the basic principles set forth in this book, it will be possible to interpret new information in a sound context. Instructions that are too specific may be superceded by new research. A recipe written in the nineteenth century can still be very successful in producing an excellent meal; a probiotic 'recipe' now may work quite well, but in the near future it is likely to be adjusted and produce a much better result.

If, on reading this book, you conclude that probiotics are worth trying, I would suggest that you inform your doctor. This is because, although probiotics are very safe, it is always advisable to keep your doctor fully in the picture. Furthermore, many doctors are becoming increasingly interested in probiotics, because of the growing scientific evidence of benefit and because the underlying concept is increasingly convincing. Most doctors are very interested to receive feedback from their patients, especially when a relatively new approach is being used.

Structure of the book

There are three main parts to this book: on the Microflora, on Probiotics and on Practical Solutions. The individual chapters have been written so that the ideas and information build up from one chapter to another. There is, however, no reason why you should not dip in and out of the book as you wish, selecting those chapters that are of particular interest to you. Each chapter can be read on its own.

Within the text you will see an occasional number, which refers to an original document from which the information was sourced. These references are found in the References section at the back of the book. As a general reader, you do not need to be bothered with such references (unless you are especially keen), but they will be of interest to your doctor or other relevant health professionals. If your doctor is interested in the subject of this book, the references will reassure him/her that the information is scientifically based.

Health professionals may also find the book of interest as a 'quick read' to familiarise themselves with the main aspects of the subject.

Summary of main points

❖ Probiotics are 'friendly' microbes that provide health benefits.
❖ There is growing scientific evidence of such benefits.
❖ This book is aimed at helping the general reader become better informed, so that he/she can be a more active participant in the improvement of their own health.

Fig 1: Probiotic products exist in a range of forms

Part I

THE HUMAN MICROFLORA

Creatures With Whom We Live

Our Microflora

The Gut Microflora

The Immune System and the Microflora

~~~

1
Creatures With Whom We Live

One of the reasons that probiotics have become popular in recent years is to offset the inadequacies of antibiotics.

Antibiotic drugs were introduced towards the end of the Second World War and their effect against dangerous and troublesome bacterial disease was immediate and powerful. There was such elation at the potential to control infectious disease that, for a while, it was thought that all disease could be conquered within a relatively short time.

Together with the development of vaccination and improvements in sanitation and hygiene, antibiotics caused the death rate for infants to fall dramatically and life expectancy for adults to steadily increase. Despite these major advances, by the end of the twentieth century less progress had been made in conquering disease than had been anticipated at the middle of that century.

Bacteria resistant to the effects of specific antibiotics arose and were consistently present in certain environments, especially hospitals. Initially, there was little concern, because many different classes of antibiotic drug were being developed, and it was thought we would always be at least one step ahead of the pathogens (disease-causing germs). Over time, however, some bacteria became resistant to several different classes of antibiotic. Such multiply-resistant bacteria became sufficiently common that a fear arose that bacteria resistant to all types of antibiotic might appear.

The body's defence systems

The threat to the effectiveness of antibiotics prompted the medical profession to question whether its approach to treating disease might be flawed. It was recognised that antibiotics did not kill pathogenic bacteria outright, but rather they reduced the number of pathogens sufficiently for the body's natural defence systems to take over and finish the job.

This led scientists to look afresh at the body's defence systems, such as the immune system, and consider how we might enhance it rather than undermine it. There was a fresh appreciation of the value of vaccination in harnessing cells of the immune system.

The other major consequence of looking again at the body's defence systems was to recognise, perhaps for the first time, how valuable are the various microflora living on and in our body surfaces. Microflora are communities of different microbes - miniscule single-cell living creatures too small for the naked eye to see. Most of the microbes in our microflora are bacteria, and they live with us in a mutually-beneficial life-long relationship.

Recognition of the value of our microflora coincided with the rise of the science of ecology; the study of the relationships between living organisms and their environments. An important aspect of ecology is consideration of the way different species interact with each other. As human power to dominate microbes was faltering, a more subtle and ecological approach to infectious disease became attractive.

Our microflora might be supported by the consumption of 'friendly' bacteria (probiotics) and by consuming foods to improve the microflora (*pre*biotics). This book looks at this fundamental shift in attitude, and considers how such an idea can have a major impact on improving your health.

Understanding probiotics and the microflora is greatly aided by looking at the process of symbiosis; how organisms live together.

Symbiosis

The planet Earth is teaming with life and, in addition to microbes, there are animals, plants and other types of organisms. Each species (type of organism) tends to congregate together, due to a preference for certain environments and also as a factor in reproduction.

All species do, however, also interact with some other species. A regular interaction between two different species is known as a symbiosis ('living together'). Symbioses take three main forms:

- ❖ Parasitic or predatory – one species gaining at the expense of the other species. [A parasite is usually smaller than its host and usually does not kill the host. By keeping the host alive, the parasite continues to have a ready source of food. A predator is a type of parasite, but aims to kill its prey and eat all or most of it.]

❖ Commensal – one species benefits and the other is unharmed.
❖ Mutual – both species benefit.

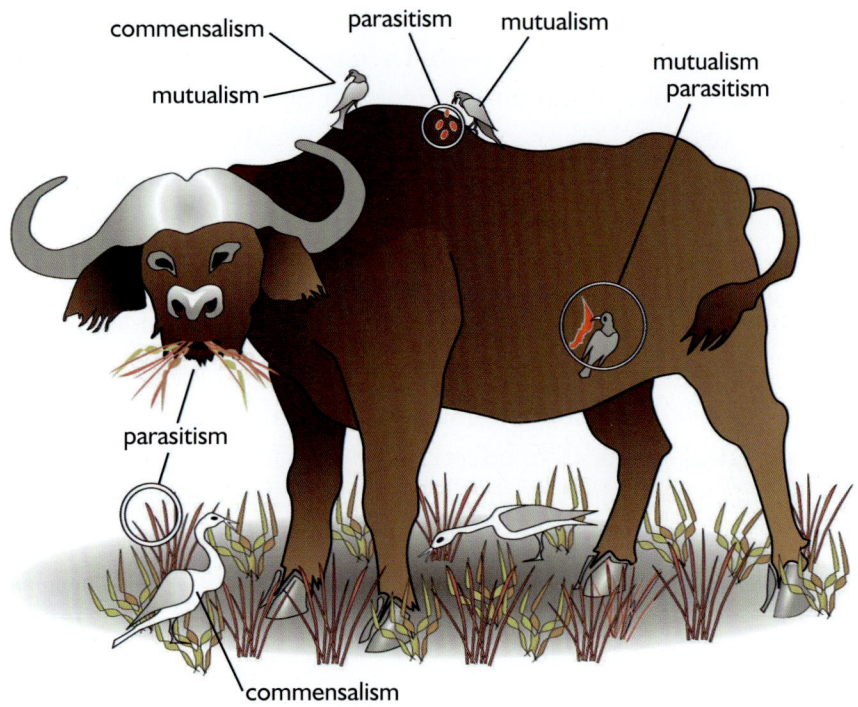

Fig 2: An African buffalo illustrates symbioses

The buffalo eats grass (parasitism). Ticks suck the buffalo's blood (parasitism). Oxpecker birds feed on the ticks (mutualism). Oxpeckers eat fly larvae in wounds (mutualism), or peck open wounds to suck the buffalo's blood (parasitism). Oxpeckers perch on the buffalo's back and feed on small flies hovering above the buffalo (mutualism). From their buffalo perch, oxpeckers issue alarm calls, which warn other oxpeckers and sometimes the buffalo, depending on the type of danger (commensalism or mutualism). The egret bird feeds on grasshoppers disturbed by the buffalo (commensalism).

Human symbiotic relationships

There are several types of tiny creatures, barely visible to the unaided eye, which live on the surface of our bodies. There are fleas and lice, which live by sucking blood through the skin. There are also mites that live off tissue, dead cells and oil from the skin. All these surface parasites can cause irritation, but with increasingly clean and dry homes, fewer human beings are bothered by such creatures.

The cavities (spaces) within the human body, such as the nose, the windpipe, the vagina and the intestine, are more attractive to parasites than the skin surface. This is because cavities are less accessible to attack and are consistently warm and damp.

The digestive tract, running from mouth to anus, is especially attractive to parasites, because it receives a regular supply of food. There are multicellular parasites such as tapeworms, roundworms, hookworms and threadworms. They can remain in the intestine for many years, causing diarrhoea, poor absorption of nutrients and anaemia. These infections are common in environments with poor sanitation, but as more parts of the world obtain reliable water supplies and sound sewerage, such internal parasites become less common.

Microbial parasites of humans

Microbial parasites of humans, including bacteria, fungi and viruses, cause a range of diseases. Examples of bacterial parasites are listed in the table below.

Bacterium	Disease	Part of body affected
Staphylococcus aureus	Impetigo	Skin
Propionibacterium acnes	Acne	Skin
Chlamydia trachomatis	Conjunctivitis	Eye
Neisseria meningitidis	Meningitis	Brain
Clostridium tetani	Tetanus	Nervous system
Mycobacterium leprae	Leprosy	Nerves and skin
Streptococcus pyogenes	Pharyngitis	Throat
Streptococcus pneumoniae	Pneumonia	Lungs
Streptococcus mutans	Dental caries	Teeth
Shigella species	Dysentery	Intestine
Salmonella enterica	Gastroenteritis	Intestine
Vibrio cholerae	Cholera	Intestine
Campylobacter jejuni	Gastroenteritis	Intestine
Helicobacter pylori	Gastric ulcers	Stomach
Escherichia coli	Cystitis	Bladder
Neisseria gonorrhoeae	Gonorrhea	Genitals
Treponema pallidum	Syphilis	Genitals/systemic

Fig 3: Examples of bacterial parasites

There are, of course, many more human diseases caused by microbes. Despite this wide range of pathogens (disease-causing germs), however, humans in developed countries are only occasionally infected to such a degree that symptoms are experienced. A crucial factor in our relatively good health is the consumption of adequate amounts of nutrients, so that the body functions properly, especially the body's defence systems. The commensal and mutual bacteria of our microflora are an important part of such defences.

Human commensal and mutual bacteria

There are bacteria resident on most human body surfaces and cavities, with the mouth, the intestine and the vagina being the most heavily populated. Each of these resident communities of bacteria is known as a microflora. The different microbes in a microflora are either commensal or mutual in their symbiotic relations with their human host. The combined effect of the whole microflora is mutual, with the bacteria resident in the intestines living off undigested food passing through the gut. In return, they offer two main benefits to their human host. They make the local environment unwelcoming to newly-arrived harmful germs, and improve the human body's defences.

An evolutionary perspective

An understanding of our various microflora and their symbiotic relations with us can be advanced by considering how such host-microbe relations evolved.

Life on Earth started about 4 billion years ago, and it is estimated that for the next 2.5 billion years or so, all living organisms were unicellular (single cell creatures) [1]. Members of the same species may have grouped together, but each cell was capable of living as a separate entity.

Then multicellular organisms appeared and the process was probably as follows. As cells divided, they kept together and developed slightly different roles and structures. This distinguishing of cells (differentiation) meant that they became increasingly dependent on each other, and on the combined activity of all the cells together. Over the next 1 billion years, such early multicellular organisms evolved into a very diverse range of organisms, including plants and animals [2].

Each organism prospered when living arrangements enabled their growth and reproduction. Sometimes, that desirable arrangement meant that the organism co-operated with another organism, and in other circumstances competition and exploitation was more suitable.

We humans do not consciously decide to cooperate with bacteria, and nor do our bacteria consciously decide to cooperate with us. It is an arrangement that occurs naturally; all parties having evolved together.

The microflora can be disturbed

Pathogens sometimes overwhelm the microflora through sheer numbers or through being of an unusually virulent type. Stress can disturb the mixture of bacteria in the microflora; and antibiotics can harm the gut microflora as a secondary consequence of taking a drug to treat a harmful infection.

Probiotic products are valuable in such circumstances, as they undertake some of the positive activities that would otherwise have been undertaken by the missing microflora bacteria. Probiotics can also be taken as a preventative against illness, by bolstering the microflora before a disease takes hold. Furthermore, probiotics can directly influence the body's immune system so that it functions more effectively in its defence against pathogens and harmful substances.

With the greater appreciation of the ecology of the human body, the medical profession became more sympathetic to the concept of working with the microflora through probiotics.

Summary of main points

- ❖ Limitations to the effectiveness of antibiotics has led to an increased appreciation of the benefits of our microflora
- ❖ The microflora are communities of bacteria that live in close association (symbiosis) with particular parts of your body.
- ❖ The gut microflora gains food from the human intestine, and protects us from pathogens.
- ❖ The microflora of humans can be disturbed and, in such circumstances, probiotic products can help repair the damage.

2

Our Microflora

There are two main routes through which probiotics improve human health. They bolster our immune system (considered in chapter 4) and they support our microflora.

Our microflora, are found on the following parts of the body:

- ❖ the skin
- ❖ the nose, throat and windpipe
- ❖ the mouth
- ❖ the female reproductive system
- ❖ the intestines.

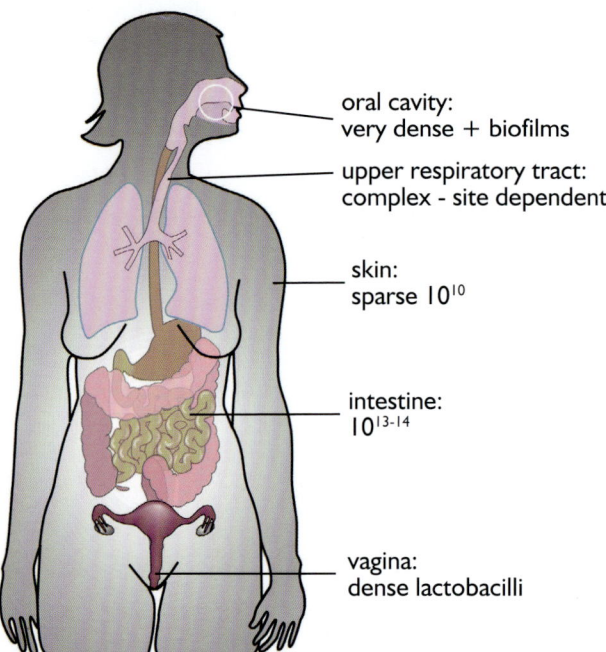

oral cavity: very dense + biofilms

upper respiratory tract: complex - site dependent

skin: sparse 10^{10}

intestine: 10^{13-14}

vagina: dense lactobacilli

Fig 4: The microflora of the human body

In this chapter we look at the microflora in all these places, except the intestines, which is covered in the next chapter. By having a better understanding of your various microflora, you should be in a good position to judge whether and where probiotics may play a useful role in your body.

The naming system

Before considering our microflora, it is helpful to know how microbes are classified; that is, how they are grouped and named.

Just as many of us have a family name and two personal names, so scientists have given bacteria three names.

Rather like the Chinese naming system where the family name comes first the bacterial family name, known as the genus, comes first. The two genus names that constitute the majority of probiotics are *Lactobacillus* and *Bifidobacterium*. Genera (the plural of genus) are formed on the basis of certain shared characteristics, for example, shape, behaviour, genes.

The second part of the name is called the species. A well-known probiotic species is 'acidophilus'. Because some microbes have the same species name, but belong to a different genus, a species name is never properly used except with its genus name. Thus *Lactobacillus acidophilus* is a proper species name (sometimes abbreviated to *L. acidophilus*).

The third part of the name is the strain (or variety). Bacterial strains differ in small ways from other strains of the same species. These small differences can sometimes mean major differences in their behaviour. For example, the bacterium species *Escherichia coli* (often abbreviated to *E. coli*) has strains that differ in their relationship to human beings. The great majority of *E. coli* strains are benign towards human beings. In fact, *E. coli* is a natural resident of the human intestine. There are, however, a number of disease-causing *E. coli* strains, and there are also some probiotic strains.

On yoghurt pots and on probiotic capsule boxes, you will see names of the microbes contained within. There will be species names, and sometimes strain identification will also be given. The strain name comes after the genus and species name and can be letters, numbers or occasionally a word or name.

General characteristics of the microflora

The microflora resident on and in different parts of the human body have certain characteristics in common.

Almost all are bacteria

The microbes living on humans are almost all bacteria. Bacteria are single-celled organisms that are mainly either rod-shaped (bacilli) or spherical (cocci). Their width differs between species, but is usually about 1 micrometer (a thousandth of a millimetre) or one forty-thousandth of an inch.

Although such small sizes are hard to imagine, it is useful to note that bacteria are rarely present as single cells. They reproduce by dividing in half and therefore they tend to cluster together in colonies. In some circumstances, the number of bacteria in a colony can get so large that it is possible to see the colony with the naked eye.

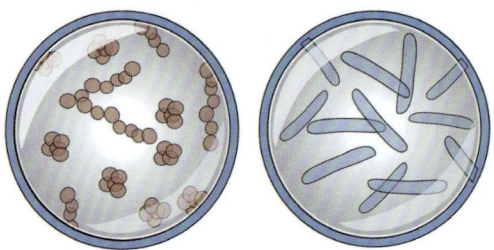

Fig 5: Coccus-shaped and rod-shaped bacteria

Microflora and humans have a long history

The microflora are different in different parts of the body. For example, there is a different mixture of species present in the nose compared with the intestines. This is because each part of the body provides a different living environment for the microbes. Different environments favour different bacteria.

However, within a particular part of the body, such as the skin, the species there are found on humans all over the world, irrespective of geography, climate and racial group. Furthermore, the microflora of other vertebrates are related to, but distinct from those in humans [1]. These factors suggest that the relationship between the microbes and their human hosts has evolved over a long period of time, and is acceptable to both parties. In other words, under normal circumstances the skin microbes either benefit humans or are harmless to them.

A relationship under tension

While the microflora of humans are usually well-established and stable, it is a relationship that is under some stress.

It is unimaginable that humans could have avoided interaction with microbes, because they are everywhere, and consequently the relationship would have been forced on humans. As a species, we may have been in an ongoing adjustment of our relationship with microbes, so that the benefits are maximised and the drawbacks are minimised for both parties.

Microfloral bacteria do place stress on their host, and this is demonstrated in germ-free mice. These mice live in laboratories under conditions where there are absolutely no microbes, and it has been found that they live about 30% longer than normal mice with microflora [2,3]. Clearly, the absence of microflora in the germ-free mice has relieved them from some life pressure. It may be that resident bacteria in normal mice place demands on their immune systems, as it is necessary to check whether these bacteria are harmful or not. This continual demand may shorten the mouse's life.

Another drawback of the microflora is that occasionally they act in a disease-causing (parasitic) manner, under certain circumstances. For example, the microflora of the nose includes *Staphylococcus aureus*, which occasionally changes its behaviour and causes disease. Such microbes are sometimes referred to as opportunistic pathogens.

This should not be surprising, because mutual, commensal and parasitic behaviour (as described in the first chapter) is not fixed or static. Each behaviour is part of a dynamic relationship. A symbiosis may alter under changed circumstances. For example, the African buffalo has a symbiotic relationship with the oxpecker bird. The bird eats insects and larvae on and around the buffalo's body, and from this the bird gains food and the buffalo is protected from irritants and potential disease. But occasionally, the oxpecker bird will act parasitically by picking at a scab on the buffalo's hide, opening a wound and drinking the blood.

It is not clear under what circumstances the oxpecker bird changes its behaviour, but it is known that microbes resident in humans become parasitic when they sense that the human has been weakened in some way. For example, if the microflora have been damaged, or the body's immune system weakened.

Despite these tensions in a symbiotic relationship, it would not continue in a stable way unless it was overwhelmingly satisfactory to all parties. Those benefits are described in the next chapter on gut microflora. In the meantime, current knowledge of the microflora found in other parts of the body is set out below.

The skin

The skin consists of three layers: the epidermis (surface), the dermis (middle layer) and the hypodermis (fatty basal layer). There are two major structures within these layers: sweat glands and hair follicles. The microflora of the skin is found in just two places: near the surface of the epidermis, and within hair follicles.

Under the microscope, the surface of the human skin has a flaky appearance. These flakes are dead skin cells full of keratin, which is a tough fibrous substance that is the same material that makes up hair and nails. This rough surface of the skin is dry, salty and slightly acidic and, as such, is not a particularly attractive environment for microbes [4]. The bacteria that live there are usually found just below the surface, among the flakes of dead cells.

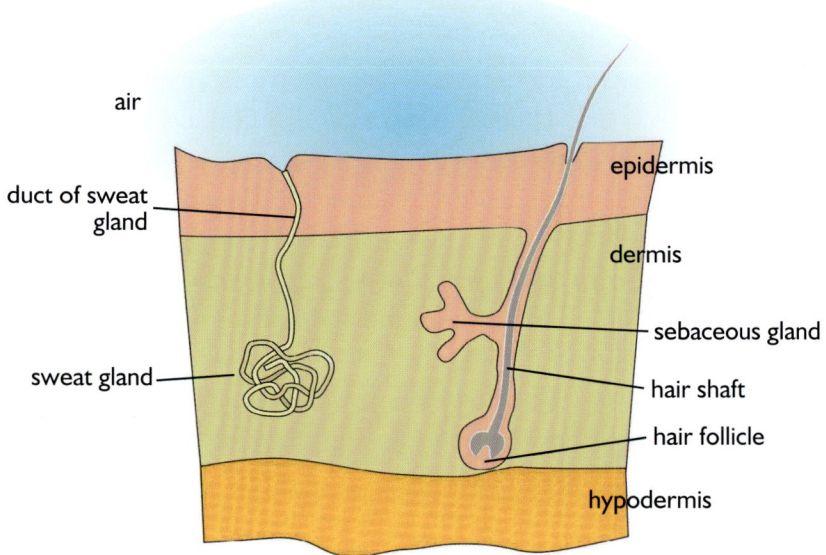

Fig 6: The structure of the human skin

Bacteria need water to thrive, and therefore do better in sweaty areas of the body. The numbers of microfloral bacteria will, therefore, be much greater where skin does not have access to the air and sweat has difficulty evaporating, such as the armpit, the groin and within any creases.

The other places in the skin where the resident microflora can be found are the hair follicles. A follicle is a tiny channel within the skin in which a hair is rooted. Bacteria in the follicles feed on sebum, which is an oil secreted by the sebaceous gland. The sebum keeps the hair from drying, keeps skin soft and acts as a barrier to harmful substances and microbes entering the body.

A rough estimate for the numbers of microbes over the whole of a person's skin, is ten billion [3,4,5]. This is a large number, but as the surface area of skin covering a human being is about 1.7 square metres (5½ square feet), the resident microbes are spread sparsely compared with other human microflora.

Types of bacteria

The microbes living on and in the human skin are a mixture of bacillus and coccus shapes, with a mixture of aerobic and anaerobic living processes. For the record, the main genera of resident skin bacteria in humans are *Corynebacterium*, *Propionibacterium* and *Staphylococcus* [6,7], but there are also other types represented, including the yeast *Malassezia*.

One of the more deeply studied species is *Staphylococcus epidermidis*, which produces certain proteins that have antibacterial properties. These antibacterial proteins work against competing bacteria, such as *Staphylococcus aureus*, which has a tendency to cause disease [4,8]. *S. epidermidis* also influences the immune cells within the skin so that they are 'primed' to be more alert and responsive to the presence of pathogens [9].

Although the species in the skin microflora are either beneficial or neutral towards its human host, some of these microbes act as opportunistic pathogens under certain circumstances. This is demonstrated in the case of two types of infection.

Catheter infections

About half of all hospitalised patients are given an intravascular catheter (delivery tube into a vein) during their stay, and some patients develop an infection from resident skin bacteria entering the bloodstream. In the majority of cases, such an infection is caused by *S. epidermidis*, which as described above is normally a beneficial member of the skin microflora.

The catheter-associated infection is difficult to treat, because the *Staphylococcus* bacterium forms a biofilm, feeding on blood and tissue near the entry-point of the catheter into the skin. The biofilm, with its sticky consistency, is resistant to the body's defence systems and to antimicrobial drugs, including antibiotics. Preventing and treating catheter infections is a continuing problem for hospitals.

Acne

Acne is a skin condition in which numerous red pimples appear as a consequence of inflamed sebaceous glands. The glands produce sebum, which is an oily substance released into hair follicles. The cause of acne is not fully understood, but it seems to involve the thickening of the follicle opening and increased sebum production. The trapped sebum leads to increased bacterial numbers, which in turn triggers an immune defence response involving inflammation of the local area.

Standard medical treatment involves the use of antibiotics, and the resultant fall in the numbers of skin bacteria reduces the condition. A relatively recent difficulty has been that the long-term use (for months or even years) of antibiotics for acne, causes strains of bacteria resistant to the antibiotic to become predominant. This makes the antibiotic less effective in treating acne. The main skin bacterium associated with acne is *Propionibacterium acnes*. Under normal circumstances, it is a harmless microbe to humans.

Body odour

Species of *Brevibacterium* produce a cheese-like odour as a natural consequence of their biochemical processes (metabolism). The odour is produced through the bacterium releasing sulphur compounds from proteins within sweat. Brevibacteria have not been studied enough to identify any possible benefits of their presence.

The nose, throat and windpipe

The respiratory system is a collection of tubes for transporting air to the bloodstream so that oxygen is added to the body and carbon dioxide is removed. Air gets to the lungs from the nose and the mouth, the throat (pharynx) and the windpipe (trachea).

As air contains microbes (riding on dust particles) and an adult human inhales and exhales approximately 10,000 litres of air a day, there is potential for microbes to be present in the respiratory system. Such microbes might be disease-causing and so there is good reason for the respiratory system to have a protective microflora.

In fact, the lungs are usually microbe-free (sterile), while the nose, throat and windpipe do have a microflora. [The microflora of the mouth is considered under a separate section, as the primary function of the mouth is digestion of food rather than transport of air.]

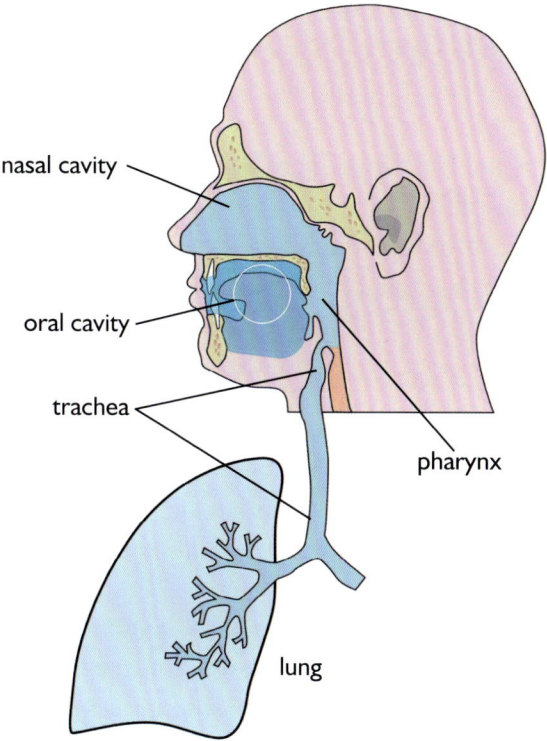

Fig 7: The upper respiratory tract

Within the nose there are hairs to trap large particles from the air and sticky mucus to trap smaller particles.

2: Our Microflora ~ 15

The windpipe connects the throat to the lungs. The throat and the windpipe are lined with many hair-like vibrating structures (cilia) that move mucus towards the mouth and the gullet. The hairs of the nose and the cilia of the throat and windpipe are physical ways of stopping potentially harmful matter from entering the lungs and causing an infection.

The species present

A wide range of species make up the microflora of the respiratory tract, including those of *Streptococcus*, *Neisseria*, *Haemophilus*, *Staphylococcus*, *Corynebacterium*, *Propionibacterium*, *Prevotella*, *Mycoplasma* and *Porphyromonas*.

This is a wider range than found on the skin, probably because respiratory surfaces are damp and of a more stable temperature. Also, the food available, in the form of secretions such as mucus, is more complex in its molecular content and likely to satisfy a wider range of bacterial types.

The point at which the throat meets the mouth (oropharynx) has the most complex and variable of the respiratory microflora. Not only does the area receive secretions from the nose, but also saliva and some food from the mouth, all of which is likely to contain bacteria. In comparison, the windpipe has very few bacteria in its microflora, because the efficient cilia force bacteria upwards to the throat. Most of the windpipe microflora will have dribbled down from the throat.

Are there benefits from the respiratory tract microflora?

Laboratory experiments have shown that species of the respiratory tract microflora produce substances that are anti-microbial, such as bacteriocins, fatty acids and hydrogen peroxide. This has led to research into whether such resident species are able to prevent respiratory tract infections.

People with higher levels of a particular type of streptococcus (viridans group) in their microflora tend to have low levels of certain disease-causing bacteria, such as *Streptococcus pyogenes* (causing pharyngitis, sinusitis and tonsillitis) and *Streptococcus pneumoniae* (causing bronchitis and pneumonia). Also, people with low-levels of such viridans streptococci are more prone to respiratory tract infections. This suggests that the viridans group in the microflora inhibits the growth of potentially pathogenic species [10]. Other members of the respiratory tract microflora, such as *Prevotella* species, have also been associated with low levels of pathogens.

Furthermore, a serious pathogenic bacterium is found in the throats of 5-10% of the population without causing disease. *Neisseria meningitidis* causes meningitis, a dangerous infection of the brain and spinal cord. This pathogen is present in human throats at levels that are too low to cause disease, and it is reasonable to presume that the other bacteria in the throat microflora are keeping it in check [11]. Without the throat microflora, the incidence of meningitis might be much higher.

The mouth

The mouth is the beginning of the digestive tract, but as it has a very large and complex microflora, it is being considered separately from the rest of the digestive tract. The soft parts of the mouth have a significantly different microflora from that of the teeth.

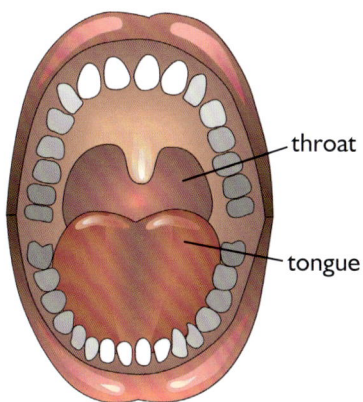

Fig 8: Parts of the mouth

Soft tissues

The soft tissues of the mouth consist of the cheeks, the palates and the tongue. Compared to the teeth (see below), the soft tissues are not especially conducive to the formation of a microflora, for three reasons. Firstly, when food is placed in the mouth, it is bitten and chewed, and the tongue manipulates it into a shape for swallowing. This movement has the effect of dislodging microbes from surfaces within the mouth.

Secondly, saliva (which lubricates the passage of food, and starts the digestive process) contains antibacterial substances, which undermine the formation of microbial colonies.

Thirdly, many of the surfaces available for colonisation by microbes within the mouth are covered by a mucus gel. The mucus helps to protect the soft tissues from damage by hard food, but also acts as a barrier to microbes. Furthermore, surface cells are regularly shed from the soft tissues, so that a complete layer of surface cells changes every two days. The cells lost from the surface of soft tissues carry with them attached colonies of microbes.

Of the soft tissues within the mouth, the tongue has the largest number and widest range of microbes in its microflora. The reason is that, unlike the soft and hard palates and the cheeks, which are relatively smooth, the upper surface of the tongue has many small undulations. Bacteria are better able to hide within the crevices of the relatively rough surface.

Although the microflora on the tongue appears to be mostly commensal or mutualistic, it is associated with bad breath (halitosis). About 90% of cases of halitosis are caused by mucus in the nasal passages at the back of the nose flowing down onto the rear upper surface of the tongue. This movement of mucus is known as nasal drip. Bacteria on the tongue digest the nasal mucus and in some cases the by-products of the digestion are foul-smelling [12]. A comparison of people with and without halitosis found a substantial difference in bacteria on the tongue. For example, in people with odour-free breath, *Streptococcus salivarius* was by far the predominant species, while in people with halitosis *S. salivarius* was typically absent [13]. In other words, halitosis occurs when the normal microflora of the tongue is disturbed. It is not known, however, what are the main causes of such disturbance to the tongue microflora.

Although saliva has some antibacterial characteristics, this does not stop it from carrying many microbes that have been shed from the tongue, cheeks and elsewhere in the mouth. One millilitre of saliva contains about one million bacteria [5,14]. The microbes do not grow in the saliva, but are transported by this liquid to lower parts of the digestive tract [15].

The teeth

A tooth is composed mainly of a bone-like material known as dentine. This living material is hard because its cells are full of minerals. The dentine is covered by an even harder mineralised substance known as enamel, which is the hardest substance in the body. Below the gum-line, dentine is covered by a thin layer of cementum, a substance similar in strength to enamel.

Bacteria colonising the teeth are able to survive much better than bacteria in other parts of the mouth. This is because enamel (and cementum) does not shed its surface and so the bacteria have a more permanent surface on which to attach and establish colonies.

When the density of such microbes has reached a certain level, a biofilm (plaque) will start to form. This provides the colonies with protection from harmful substances and enables a stronger attachment to the tooth. The biofilm is formed by the microbes increasing in numbers very rapidly, secreting sticky substances and then slowing their growth. The amount of oxygen within the biofilm diminishes and this encourages other species to join the biofilm. As more species join, a greater range of by-products are produced which attracts even further species. Bacterial species prone to pathogenic behaviour, such as *Porphyromonas gingivalis* (involved in gum disease), tend to appear late in the development of plaque biofilms [16]. The microbial population of dental plaque is very dense, calculated at about 100 billion cells per gram [5,14].

Plaque forms on teeth above the gum-line. Although there is a wide range of bacterial species in plaque, the predominant types on all areas of the teeth are streptococci and actinomycetes. The diet of the host can affect the composition of plaque communities. For example, a diet high in sugar makes plaque more acidic and stimulates streptococci numbers, while a diet high in dairy products reduces streptococci numbers.

Plaque in the crevices between tooth and gum has a greater species diversity than plaque found on the rest of the tooth. This greater range of species may appear because the plaque is less disturbed as it is more difficult to reach by brushing.

A wide range of microbial species has been identified within the mouth; most of them attached to the teeth. About 700 different species have been detected. In each person, however, the number of resident species will be much less; perhaps about 100 species. Why do we not see the same dominant species in each person? This is not clear, but it may be that each person's mouth is slightly different and suits a slightly different mixture of microbes. Also, the species that became established early in a person's life may alter the oral environment slightly to consolidate their colonies.

Are the mouth microflora beneficial?

The mouth microflora, in the form of plaque, is involved in the development of tooth decay (dental caries) and gum disease (gingivitis). But modern diets rather than the microflora might be seen as the chief cause of tooth and gum disease. Dental caries is caused by acid, produced by the microflora, wearing away tooth enamel. The centre of the tooth becomes exposed and infection occurs. Such infection causes severe pain because the centre of the tooth houses nerves. There is also a danger that infection will spread to other parts of the body via the tooth's blood vessels. If, however, the person's diet is changed so that less sugar is consumed, then the microflora will produce less acid and the teeth will be less likely to rot.

Similarly, with gum disease, if there is less sugar then plaque will be less developed, the immune cells in the gums will be less provoked and inflammation will be reduced. By reducing gum inflammation, the root of the tooth is less exposed to attack by microbes.

It cannot be denied, though, that dental microflora is an essential element in such widespread disease. Studies with germ-free rodents (without any microbes) show that adding individual bacterial species causes tooth decay, especially *Streptococcus mutans* [17].

This exceptional situation, in which the microflora is a consistent cause of disease, may be due to the unique characteristics of teeth. They provide a surface which is so stable as to allow the development of biofilms that protect and house bacteria, some of which are harmful to their host.

On the other hand, given the large numbers of bacteria living in the mouth, it could be argued that there is relatively little disease and the mouth microflora is providing some protection. This debate has not yet been resolved.

The female reproductive system

The female reproductive system consists of ovaries, Fallopian tubes, uterus, cervix, vagina and vulva. Only the cervix, vagina and vulva have a microflora. The other parts are normally sterile.

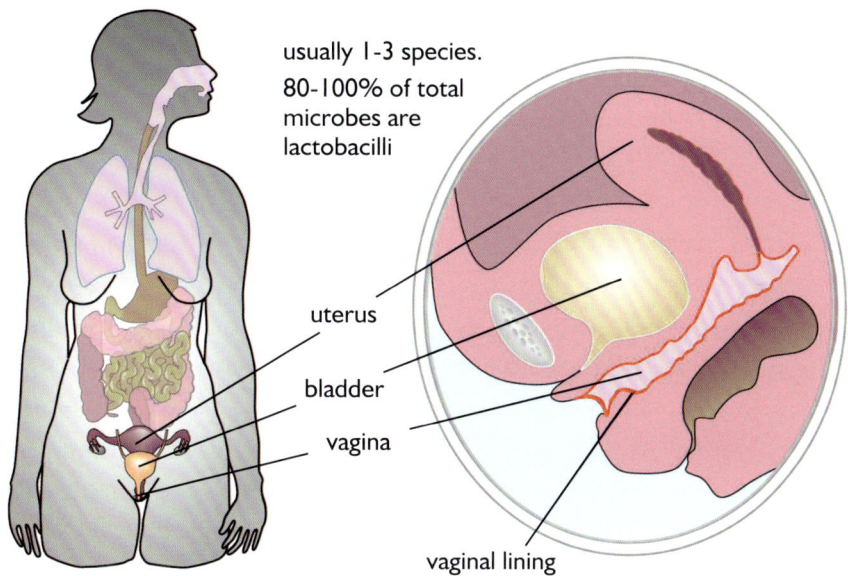

Fig 9: The female reproductive system

The vagina receives the male penis during sexual intercourse. Consequently, there is a higher risk of infection than in other parts of the female reproductive system, because the penis might be carrying microbes that are pathogenic. Furthermore, the vaginal opening is relatively close to the anus and, as such, can easily receive intestinal microbes.

It is, therefore, not surprising that a vaginal microflora has evolved. On the mucus-laden surface of the vagina, there are approximately 10 million microbes per millilitre of mucus [5].

Species in the vagina

The microflora of the vagina consists of a range of different species, but unlike the microflora in other parts of the body, there is a clearly dominant type of bacterium, the *Lactobacillus*. This is particularly interesting, because lactobacilli are the most commonly used bacteria in probiotic products. In most women only a single species of *Lactobacillus* is present. In about 15% of women, one or two additional

Lactobacillus species may be present.

The species of *Lactobacillus* bacteria most often found in the vagina of healthy women are *L. crispatus, L. gasseri, L. jensenii* and *L. iners* [18]. They create an environment that is unattractive to pathogens by the following methods:

- ❖ Producing various acids as by-products of their metabolism. Pathogens tend to dislike acidic environments, and some of the acids produced by lactobacilli, such as lactic and acetic acid, have specific anti-microbial effects on a wide range of species.
- ❖ Some of the *Lactobacillus* species found in the vagina, such as *L. crispatus* and *L. jensenii*, also produce hydrogen peroxide, which is toxic to many microbes.
- ❖ Other lactobacilli produce biosurfactants, substances that can interfere with the attachment of pathogens to the vaginal wall, and even detach bacteria already living on the vaginal wall.
- ❖ Some lactobacilli produce antibiotic-type substances that are active against one of the most common pathogens found in the vagina, *Gardnerella vaginalis*.

The cervix has a microflora that is similar to that of the vagina, while the vulva has a mixture of vaginal and intestinal microbes.

Contraceptive methods

The use of oral contraceptive pills has little effect on the vaginal microflora, nor does the use of condoms. Of other contraceptive methods, the diaphragm with spermicide and the cervical cap are associated with increases in the pathogenic versions of *Escherichia coli* (*E. coli*) and *Enterococcus* species. There are two likely explanations for this. A commonly-used spermicide (nonoxynol-9) inhibits or kills lactobacilli, and a fall in the numbers of lactobacilli makes it easier for pathogens to get established. Also, both the diaphragm and the cervical cap increase the oxygen content of the vagina, making it a more attractive environment for aerobic bacteria such as *E. coli*.

The use of the copper-releasing intra-uterine device (IUD) for at least three years increases the diversity of the cervical microflora. Some of the increased genera, such as *Bacteroides* and *Fusobacterium*, are associated with a serious condition, pelvic inflammatory disease.

Microflora or pathogens?

There are some microbes frequently found in the vagina whose status is unclear. The yeast *Candida albicans* and the bacterium *Gardnerella vaginalis* might be part of the normal microflora that occasionally cause disease, or they might be pathogens that are usually controlled by the vaginal microflora. Whatever the correct classification, both can cause disease if there is a change in the numbers and types of lactobacilli [19].

Other changes

The microflora of the vagina is influenced by a number of factors, such as sexual activity and pregnancy, although a clear picture has yet to emerge. Better information is available on post-menopausal women. In such women, the numbers of lactobacilli fall, but they still remain the dominant type within the microflora. There is also a fall in the numbers of those microbes that are sometimes pathogenic, such as *Candida albicans* and *Gardnerella vaginalis*. The significance of these changes for vaginal health is currently not clear.

Summary of main points

- Microflora exist on the skin, the nose, throat and windpipe, the mouth, the vagina and the intestines.
- The mixture of bacteria in a particular part of the body differs from those in another part of the body.
- The microflora in a particular part of the body tends to be very similar in people throughout the world. This suggests that the symbiosis between microbes and humans has evolved over a long period of time.
- On the skin, resident microbes are found in the surface layer and within hair follicles.
- Within the respiratory tract, the lungs are normally free of microbes, but the nose, throat and windpipe have microflora.
- Most of the mouth microflora is found on the teeth and the crevice between the teeth and gums. Some bacteria also grow on the tongue.
- *Lactobacillus* species dominate the vaginal microflora, but there may be other species present.
- The vaginal microflora keeps a range of pathogens at bay, including the yeast *Candida albicans* and the bacterium *Gardnerella vaginalis*.

3
The Gut Microflora

Within the human intestine there is a section that is very highly populated with microbes; the most densely-populated microflora of any part of the body. Also, a high proportion of human infectious diseases are initiated in the intestine. This also is where the best evidence of the benefits from probiotics is found.

The intestine, also known as the gut, is part of the digestive tract. It starts at the end of the stomach and finishes at the anus. From the mouth, food passes into the stomach via the oesophagus (gullet). The main function of the stomach is to hold food from a meal, so that it can be released into the intestine in small regular amounts that are easier to digest. To this end, the stomach is bag-shaped and holds food for two to three hours, during which time a protein-digesting enzyme is released together with hydrochloric acid. The ingredients are mixed by muscular churning of the stomach wall, making them more liquid and easier to pass into the intestine.

The intestine consists of two main parts, the small intestine and the large intestine, both of which are in the abdominal cavity (tummy area). The main functions of the small intestine are to complete the digestion of food and to absorb nutrients into the body. The main functions of the large intestine are to aid the absorption of water and minerals into the body and to store solid digestive waste until such time as it is convenient to be excreted. The large intestine also provides an environment for the microflora to digest food that human enzymes have failed to digest. Such bacterial digestion releases a range of nutrients that can be absorbed and used by the human body.

The number of microbes in the digestive tract increases along the digestive tube. In the stomach there are very few and in the large intestine there are very many. On average, the numbers of bacteria are approximately:

- ❖ Stomach – 1,000 per gram of content
- ❖ Small intestine
  - ◆ Duodenum – 10,000 per millilitre (ml) of content
  - ◆ Jejunum – 100,000 per ml
  - ◆ Ileum – 10,000,000 per ml
- ❖ Large intestine – 100,000,000,000 per gm

[Note: You will see that the figures above refer to numbers per gram (gm.) or per millilitre (ml.). These are equivalent, because the contents of the intestine are mostly water, and a millilitre of water weighs one gram.]

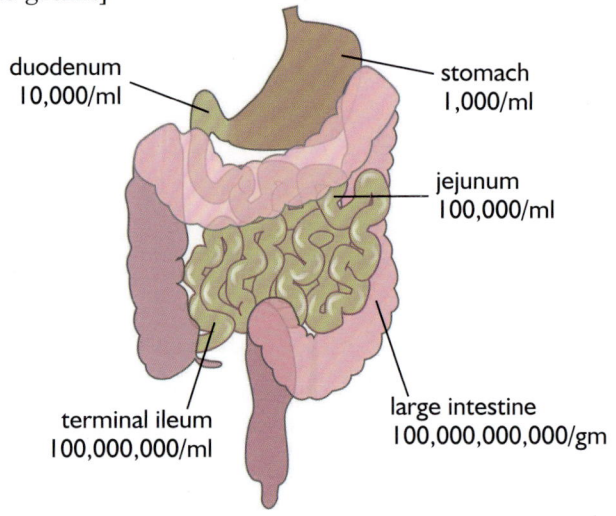

Fig 10: The microflora of the intestinal tract

The stomach

The microbes in the stomach are mostly types that live in the mouth and throat, especially those that are aerobic as oxygen is present in the stomach. The mouth and throat are areas with high bacterial populations, so why are there so few bacteria living in the stomach? The reason is that hydrochloric acid in the stomach kills the majority of bacteria that enter it [1]. There is some variation between individuals as to the degree of acidity in the stomach, but in general the stomach is very acidic when empty of food (pH 1.5-3.5) and less acidic when food is present (pH 4-5).

When the stomach is full of food, there are about 10,000 bacteria per gram of contents, but only about 100 per gram when the stomach is nearly empty [2,3]. This is either because the original meal contained bacteria, or the food collected bacteria from the mouth and throat as it was moved about by the teeth and tongue, and swallowed [4]. Also, food contains substances, mostly proteins, which reduce the effect of acid. The substances are known as buffers and they help to keep food neutral, neither acidic nor alkaline.

After about an hour within the stomach, food starts to become acidic. This is because the stomach wall continues to pump hydrochloric acid into the space of the stomach and this acid eventually overwhelms the buffers. By the time that most of the food from a meal has left the stomach for the small intestine, the stomach will have become very acidic (pH 1-2) and almost all of the bacteria left behind in the stomach will have been killed.

After the addition of stomach enzymes and acid to the food, the churning creates a thick soup-like substance known as chyme (pronounced 'kaime'). This chyme is released into the small intestine in small amounts.

The small intestine

The small intestine (also known as the small bowel) is a tube about 6 metres (20 feet) long running from the stomach to the large intestine. The tube is tightly-packed within the abdominal cavity and has many turns and curves so that the whole length fits within the space available. Although the external appearance of the small intestine is similar along its whole length, it is usually described as having three sections; the duodenum, the jejunum and the ileum, reflecting slightly different functions.

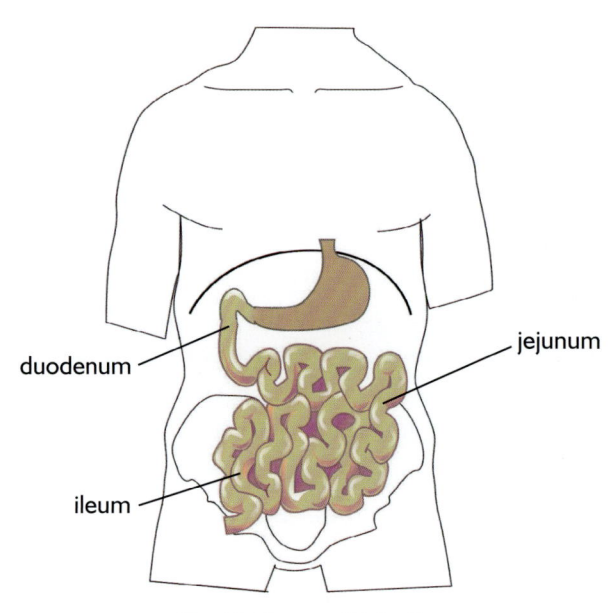

Fig 11: The small intestine

The duodenum is the first 25 centimeters (10 inches) of intestine running from the stomach. Most of the chyme (partly-digested food) released into the duodenum is acidic, as a consequence of the hydrochloric acid present in the stomach. The acid is neutralised by secretions released into the duodenum from nearby organs (pancreas and gall bladder). The secretions contain enzymes for digesting proteins and carbohydrates, as well as bile to process fats.

The next section of the small intestine is the jejunum, which is about 2.5 metres (8 feet) in length. It is along the jejunum that most digested food is absorbed across the intestinal wall into the bloodstream and body tissues. The final section of the small intestine is the ileum, which is about 3.5 metres (12 feet) in length. Some of the digested food is absorbed along the ileum, where bile molecules are reabsorbed for recycling to the gall bladder via the liver. The end of the ileum is the place where an important vitamin, B12, is absorbed.

Food travels quite quickly along the small intestine, usually taking two to three hours to travel all 6 metres. The food is moved by the sequential contraction of muscles of the intestinal wall, a process known as peristalsis. Rapid transit of contents is aided by the large amounts of fluid that are released into the small intestine.

Microflora of the small intestine

The microflora of the small intestine is the least well understood of all human microflora. This is because the small bowel is relatively inaccessible to study. The available evidence suggests that the numbers and types of microbes increase as the chyme travels along the small intestine [5].

Initially, small numbers of microbes enter the duodenum from the stomach. These are mostly types normally found in the mouth [6], especially those which are acid-resistant, such as lactobacilli, streptococci and the yeast *Candida* [7]. Estimates of the numbers of bacteria in the duodenum are similar to those of the stomach, in that the empty duodenum has about 100 bacteria per millilitre, and this increases to about 10,000 per millilitre when food arrives [8]. Unlike the stomach, however, food tends to enter the duodenum in small regular amounts and therefore at any one time there is likely to be a more dense population of bacteria than in the stomach.

The limited evidence available suggests that the numbers of microbes in the jejunum gradually increase along its length, perhaps by ten-fold [7]. By the standards of bacterial reproduction, this is not a large increase. It might be thought that, with stomach acid being neutralised in the duodenum, microbes would be less inhibited and start to increase substantially in number. There are two likely reasons why this does not occur. Firstly, there is a high level of digestive enzymes in the upper small intestine and this provides an environment that is generally not conducive to microfloral growth. Secondly, the quick transport of food along the small intestine gives little opportunity for bacteria growing in chyme to attach to the lining of the intestine and form a colony. Those that do attach risk being flushed away by the fast-flowing contents.

There may be an increase in the numbers of microbes in the upper small intestine if there is a lot of food further down the small bowel, in the ileum. Through a feedback process, a message is sent from the ileum so that the muscles of the duodenum and jejunum slow their contractions [9] and consequently the movement of chyme slows.

Although much of the small intestine is unfavourable to bacterial growth, the latter part of the ileum (terminal ileum) does host a large and diverse microflora. This is partly because movement within the small intestine slows at the terminal ileum, with contents backing up from the valve (sphincter) that controls passage from the ileum to the caecum (first part of the large intestine). Also, many of the substances harmful to bacteria, such as human enzymes, will have been absorbed back into the body by the time that the chyme reaches the terminal ileum.

The ileum microflora is better understood than the jejunum microflora, because the ileum is more accessible. The concentration of bacteria in the ileum is approximately 10 million per millilitre of contents, with levels reaching 100 million per millilitre in the terminal ileum [7,10]. The type of microbes in the terminal ileum is closer to those found in the large intestine, consisting mostly of anaerobes.

The large intestine

The large intestine (or large bowel) follows on from the small intestine. It gets its name because the bore (diameter) of the tube of the large intestine (6 centimeters or 2½ inches) is wider than that of the small intestine (3.5 cm or 1½ inches). The large intestine has, however, a much shorter length (at 1.5 metres or 5 feet) than the small intestine. The large bowel receives the remains of food that have not been digested by the enzymes secreted higher up the digestive tract. The chyme, on entering the large intestine, is renamed faeces.

The entire large intestine is positioned in the abdomen as a rectangle that frames the small intestine. There are three distinct parts of the large intestine; the caecum, the colon and the rectum.

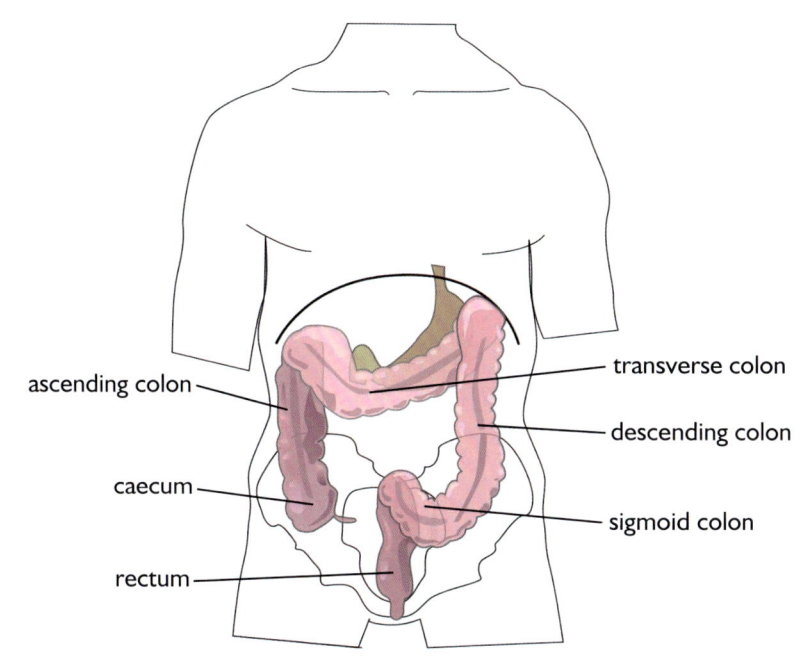

Fig 12: The large intestine

The caecum is the first part of the large intestine, and is found in the lower-right quarter of the abdomen. It is a cul-de-sac pouch where faeces collect before moving into and along the colon. The colon is the main part of the large intestine. It runs upwards (ascending colon) towards the upper-right quarter of the abdomen, across the upper abdomen from right to left (transverse colon) and downwards (descending colon) from the upper to the lower left of the abdomen. Finally, the colon forms an S-shape (sigmoid colon) towards the centre of the lower abdomen, where it joins the rectum.

The contents in the large intestine are a porridge-like liquid at the beginning (caecum) and a soft-solid at the end (rectum). The amount of time it takes for faeces to travel the whole length of the large intestine varies a lot between individuals, but the average time is about two days. This is very slow compared with the transport time of food from mouth through the stomach to the end of the small intestine, which takes only about five hours.

The reason it takes so long for the content of the large intestine to travel its full length is that the muscular contractions of the colon are different from those of the small intestine. The colonic content is moved backwards and forwards over a small section of the colon, to provide more time for water to be withdrawn into the body. Occasionally, there is a strong muscular push forward to move the content to another section of the colon, where it will stay and continue the forwards-and-backwards movements.

The long time that the contents of the large intestine take to move forwards provides a more stable environment for bacterial numbers to increase. There are also fewer human digestive enzymes present. These two factors are the reason why the large intestine has a microflora consisting of huge numbers of bacteria.

The microflora of the large intestine

Using a variety of methods of measurement and identification, estimates of the number of bacteria in the intestinal microflora have been produced. The large intestine of adults contains approximately 200 billion bacteria per gram of content [11,12]. With a Western diet, there is on average about 250 grams of content in the large intestine at any one time [13,14]. This means that each person is carrying about 50 trillion bacteria in their large intestine.

Fifty trillion is a very large number to imagine. It is about 8,000-times greater than the total number of human beings on earth. It is also, very roughly, the same as the number of human cells that make up the human body [4,15,16]. The reason we are not conscious of the vast numbers of bacteria in the large intestine is because bacterial cells are much smaller than human cells (on average about 4,000-times smaller, by volume).

About 1,100 different species of microbes are able to live in the large intestine [17,18,19,20]. In each individual, on average, about 250 different species are present in the large bowel [21]. A very wide range of metabolic activities by the microbes are taking place. Such a wide range of chemical reactions are likely to have a wide range of influences on the human body.

The large intestine is an unusual environment, because there is almost no oxygen present. The bacteria living there are therefore mostly anaerobes. About two-thirds of the colonic bacteria have not been cultured (grown in the laboratory) [11,12], probably because the microbes have very specific nutrient requirements and these nutrients have not yet been identified and prepared for laboratory use. Many of these non-cultured bacteria have been viewed under the microscope, but without growing them it is difficult to identify their living characteristics.

It has, however, been possible to learn some things about these non-cultured microbes. By analysing a particular gene from the DNA in all the microbes within a sample, it is possible to get a picture of the range of different types of bacteria living in the large intestine.

By combining the information derived from cultured microbes and from gene analysis, it has been discovered that about 95% of the microflora of the large bowel are from three major groups, which exhibit a very wide range of characteristics [11,12]. Within these three groups there are bacteria from many genera (classification level associated with species names) [22]. The more common genera include *Bacteroides*, *Clostridium*, *Eubacterium*, *Lachnospira*, *Roseburia*, *Faecalibacterium* and *Ruminococcus* [21].

There are also smaller numbers of bacteria from outside the three main groups, such as *Escherichia*, *Lactobacillus*, *Bifidobacterium* and *Enterococcus* [11,12,13]. Some of the non-cultured bacteria have assemblies of genes that are not easy to classify and consequently do not have an allocated species identity. They are also likely to exhibit a wider range of characteristics.

Whatever mixture of microbe species make up the large bowel microflora, the species tend to remain in the gut unchanged for lengthy periods [7,23]. If the microflora is disturbed by some outside factor, the original microbial mixture usually returns after about two weeks [11].

This stability may be influenced by the presence of biofilms on the surface of food particles and the lining of the intestine. As with plaque in the mouth, such biofilms provide a secure and protective environment for communities of established bacteria [13,14].

Also, each human being has a unique bacterial community in the large intestine [11]. Although the mixture of species in each individual tends to differ from other individuals, the combined metabolic activity is similar between individuals.

Microbial nutrition in the large bowel

Intestinal bacteria live partly on secretions released into the intestinal tube from the human body, but mainly on food that remains wholly or partly undigested after travelling through the small intestine. The majority of the molecules that make up the chyme entering the large intestine are carbohydrates. They are undigested because the human enzymes released into the digestive tract were unable to break them down into small enough molecules to be absorbed into the body.

These undigested carbohydrates are known collectively as dietary fibre, mostly coming from the cell walls of plants consumed as food. There are plenty of bacteria in the large intestine that have the ability to break down the cell-wall carbohydrates into smaller molecules. Such 'saccharolytic' bacteria are especially active in the caecum, where the faeces remain for about one third of the time spent in the large intestine [24].

The range of undigested carbohydrates is very wide because each plant will have a range of complex molecules that will not be digested. Furthermore, the range of foods in most people's diet in developed countries is very wide. Not only will there be carbohydrates, but also proteins and fats. It is no wonder that there is such diversity of microbes in the human gut, because there is such a range of foods to suit all types of specialist bacteria.

As the large intestine has almost no oxygen within it, the bacteria living in the large intestine do so anaerobically. Anaerobic metabolism, also known as fermentation, does not release as much energy or useful molecules for the microbe as does aerobic metabolism. Consequently, anaerobic bacteria release quite a lot of unrequired by-products, some of which are used by other gut bacteria.

The bacteria that live off the left-overs of other microbes constitute a further source of bacterial diversity in the gut. Examples of such activities are:

- ❖ Lactic acid produced by bacteria, such as bifidobacteria, enterococci, streptococci and lactobacilli, is utilised by other bacteria, including bacteroides and clostridia.
- ❖ Hydrogen produced in large quantities by many gut species is used by certain other bacteria in their living processes, giving in turn their own by-products (of methane or hydrogen sulphide).
- ❖ Protein-degrading bacteria, such as peptococci and eubacteria, make available amino acids that other bacteria use for energy and growth.

What are the benefits of the intestinal bacteria?

There appear to be three main benefits of the gut microflora: extra nutrition, direct protection against pathogens, and strengthening the body's immune system.

Extra nutrition

One of these benefits is the provision of extra nutrition to the body of the mammal. A comparison found that the rats with a normal microflora obtained about 11% more nutrition from the food they ate than germ-free rats. This is probably due to the resident microbes digesting food that human enzymes had failed to digest. While some of the digested nutrients are used by the microflora, much of it is absorbed by the mammalian host [25,26,27].

Furthermore, the gut microbes produce vitamin K and several B vitamins, which are also taken up by the body.

Defence against pathogens

A second benefit has repeatedly been shown by pathogenic bacteria becoming established in germ-free rodents, but being unable to do so (or to a much reduced extent) in rodents with a normal gut microflora [28,29,30,31,32]. This protective effect has been demonstrated with a range of pathogens, including *Listeria cytogenes*, *Clostridium botulinum* and *Cryptosporidium parvum*. Two studies have shown that mice with an intestinal microflora are about 200,000-times less likely to die from an infection of *Salmonella enteritidis* than germ-free mice [33,34].

How does the microflora defend against pathogens?

There appears to be two main routes by which the microflora defends against pathogens:
- by providing a hostile environment
- by strengthening the defences of the human body.

A hostile environment for pathogens

Bacteria take large complex molecules and break them into smaller molecules. The smaller molecules are absorbed into the bacterial cell and these are broken down further to release energy and provide nutrients to enable repair and growth within the bacterium. Different species of bacteria may be competing for the same nutrients, and those that are most efficient at acquiring them will dominate. This has been demonstrated in laboratory-based artificial models of the large bowel. Competition for carbohydrate has suppressed the growth of *Escherichia coli* and *Clostridium difficile*, both of which have pathogenic versions.

Microbes are able to attach to the surface (epithelial) cells of the intestine. They do this by the linking of molecules protruding from the surfaces of the bacterium and the epithelial cell. Once attached, a bacterium can divide and form a colony from its relatively secure situation. There are only so many attachment places on the inner surface of the intestine and therefore, in theory at least, the established colony reduces the opportunities available to pathogens to attach. Evidence for this is limited, however, due to technical difficulties in studying the natural lining of the intestine.

The microflora can also produce anti-bacterial substances that will discourage pathogens. Some of these, such as lactic acid and hydrogen peroxide, are by-products of metabolism. Others are specifically-targeted substances, known as bacteriocins, which harm competing microbes.

The microflora also stimulates peristalsis (muscle contractions) so that gut contents are moved more quickly, which makes it more difficult for newly-arrived pathogens to become established [35].

Strengthening the body's defences

The intestine has a complicated task. It has to let food molecules pass into the body and, at the same time, bar the entry of microbes (and toxins) that might cause disease. Key elements in this process are the immune (defence) tissues of the intestinal wall and the layer of epithelial cells that line the intestine.

The epithelial cells of the intestinal wall are made healthier by taking up a microbial by-product called butyrate. A healthier epithelial cell is better able to control which substances and cells pass through into the body.

The gut microflora also helps to make the immune system work more effectively, and a fuller picture of such processes is described in the next chapter. One of these benefits is the stimulation of immune cells into a greater state of readiness to act [36]. Consequently, pathogens and their toxins are dealt with more effectively.

Disturbance to the gut microflora

The gut microflora may be disturbed by a range of factors, such as intestinal infections and severe stress. Two other important influences on the gut microflora are diet and antibiotics.

Diet and the microflora

A wide range of undigested food molecules enter the large intestine and a wide range of bacterial species live there also. This association suggests that diet plays a role in the type of microbes living in the gut.

This assumption has been supported by a number of studies in mice that have shown changes in the microflora arising from a change in diet [35]. Human studies have been less successful in finding major microfloral changes through diet [37,38]. This is probably because the methods of measuring species were not subtle enough to measure the change [37,39,40].

Also, in some cases, the behaviour of species alter with the circumstances. For example, some bacteria can digest both carbohydrates and proteins. In the presence of carbohydrates, their metabolism will be saccharolytic (carbohydrate digestion), and in the presence of proteins their metabolism switches to proteolytic (protein-digesting) behaviour [24]. The effect of such changes in metabolism is that different by-products are produced and secreted by the bacteria.

The balance of current evidence suggests that the gut microflora does not usually undergo a dramatic alteration in species mixture in response to diet change [23]. When the mixture of species change, it is most likely to occur through an extreme alteration of diet, such as removing meat and dairy products or by adding a substance (*prebiotic*) targeted at particular microbes. *Pre*biotics are discussed in chapter 11. It also may be that a long-term change in diet is needed before well-established species are changed.

Antibiotics and the microflora

Despite the wonderful improvements to human health achieved by antibiotics, the very power of those drugs has some negative consequences. Antibiotic drugs are used to control infections by bacterial pathogens, but other bacteria are usually also harmed. Most of this 'collateral damage' will be against the gut microflora. A disturbed microflora is less able to resist new infections, including the overgrowth of intestinal pathogens such as *Clostridium difficile* and *Candida albicans* [41,42,43].

Doctors became quickly aware of the destructive effect of antibiotics on the microflora. Even in 1956, members of the American Clinical and Climatological Association discussed 'secondary infections' of the mouth/throat and of the bowel in patients undergoing treatment with antibiotics. There was also concern expressed at the use of antibiotics prior to intestinal surgery. This was felt to have increased, rather than decreased, the risk of post-operative infection in patients [34].

In general, all antibotics tend to reduce the number of species within the microflora. The degree to which an antibiotic disturbs the gut microflora is influenced by a number of factors, including:

- the dose and duration of the drug
- the proportion of the antibiotic that stays within the intestine [44], rather than being absorbed into the body
- the range of microbes attacked by the antibiotic (e.g. broad-spectrum or narrow-spectrum).

With such a range of factors affecting the disruption of the microflora, it is not surprising to find that different antibiotics have different effects. For example, penicillin has only minor effects on the gut microflora, but ampicillin (a derivative of penicillin) causes major disturbance. The latter tends to cause dramatic reductions in the numbers of bacteroides, bifidobacteria, lactobacilli and anaerobic cocci. Furthermore, the same antibiotic can have different effects on different individuals. Each person has a different state of health and a unique microflora.

Most antibiotics are taken orally (by mouth), but some are given intravenously (directly into a blood vessel) and this latter type may also disturb the microflora. An intravenous antibiotic may travel from blood vessels, via the liver, into bile, which is then secreted into the upper small intestine [45].

With so many factors involved in whether an antibiotic will cause a major disturbance to a person's microflora, it is not easy to predict whether a secondary infection will occur. Increasingly, doctors and patients are considering whether probiotics, which can aid the recovery of the microflora, are suitable to take after or at the same time as antibiotics, to reduce the risk of disease arising from microfloral disturbance.

Summary of main points

- The numbers of microflora bacteria are greater in the large intestine than the small intestine.
- Undigested food entering the large intestine takes about two days to travel the 1.5 metre length, which is a much slower pace than the 2-3 hours taken by food to travel all six metres of the small bowel. The slow transit in the large intestine provides a suitable environment for microbes to form colonies.
- Undigested food (faeces) contain many molecules, especially carbohydrates, that human enzymes could not digest. Microbes in the large bowel produce a different range of enzymes, which are able to digest the faeces, and so are able to increase in numbers.
- Some by-products of bacterial metabolism are used by other microbes. The gut microflora is therefore especially complex.
- Almost all the microbes in the large bowel are anaerobes, with a wide range of species represented, particularly *Bacteroides* and *Clostridium*.
- Each person has a unique mixture of species in their large bowel, and these tend to remain broadly unchanged, unless an external factor disturbs the microflora.
- Although each person's microflora is unique, the combined metabolism (cell chemical reactions) of all the microbes tends to be similar between individuals.
- The main benefit of the gut microflora is in protecting the host from infection. This is achieved by developing an environment within the intestine that is hostile to pathogens. The microflora also plays a role in strengthening the defences of the human body.
- The microflora also produce nutrients that can be used by the body.
- Antibiotics tend to disturb the gut microflora.

4

The Immune System and the Microflora

The importance of the microflora-immune system relationship

The immune system (IS) is a collection of tissues, cells and molecules found throughout the human body, that have the function of defending the body from potentially deadly attack by pathogenic microbes.

The microflora that live on surfaces of the human body are able to interact with immune cells near those surfaces. This is especially so for the gut microflora, because immune cells are abundant in the gut wall. The gut microflora has four main influences on the IS of the host body:

❖ The state of readiness of the IS

❖ The development of the IS in infants

❖ The tendency to allergic reaction

❖ The tendency to autoimmune disease.

These influences of the microflora on the IS are very important. For example, the speed and effectiveness of the body's defence against an infection is influenced by the state of alertness of the IS. Also, one reason for the rise in the incidence of allergies among people from developed countries may be the way that the IS develops in children.

As the gut microflora influences the proper functioning of the IS, so the use of probiotics may have a role in improving immune function. To understand how probiotics may improve the functioning of the body's IS, it is necessary to have some understanding of that system.

The IS is very complicated. A large range of cells and proteins undertake a variety of tasks and have an impact on each other. There are many different types of pathogens and different ways of causing disease, and the IS needs to be able to combat such threats. An outline of the IS is given below (in the shaded section). If you already have a basic understanding of the IS, you can skip this section and move on to the next, entitled 'Influences of the gut flora on the IS'.

Outline of the body's immune system (IS)

The IS comes into effect if and when the physical barriers fail or are overwhelmed.

Physical barriers

Physical barriers stop the great majority of harmful organisms from entering the body and becoming established. The main barriers are skin and mucus.

The skin is a physical barrier that protects the body from harmful microbes and non-living harmful substances. The protection is provided because skin is comprised of a thick layer of hardened cells.

Another barrier is mucus, which is a sticky substance that lines the digestive, respiratory and reproductive tracts. It traps pathogens and flushes them away when mucus flows from the body surface. An example is mucus on the inside of the nose. This collects microbes when you breathe in air and, if you have a cold, the mucus is produced in large quantities to flush out the virus (a 'runny nose').

There are two other physical barriers, both of which are specific to the intestine: stomach acid and peristalsis. A high proportion of pathogens are killed or weakened by hydrochloric acid when they pass through the stomach. Furthermore, peristalsis (muscle contractions) of the intestine moves food onwards. This makes it difficult for microbes to stay long enough in the intestine to become established and reproduce.

Although the body's physical barriers exclude or remove the great majority of the pathogens, inevitably some will get through and threaten the body, because there are such large numbers of microbes in the environment.

Two parts to the immune system (IS)

Although all parts of the IS are inter-related, it can be understood as consisting of two main parts: the innate and the adaptive immune systems.

The innate immune system

The innate system, also known as the 'non-specific' system, acts very quickly against most pathogens. It is called 'non-specific', because its cells and proteins are targeted at all foreign cells and do not vary according to the particular pathogen.

The main part of the innate IS is the phagocyte, which is a type of white blood cell. Phagocytes engulf and destroy bacteria and other foreign particles. They were first identified by Professor Elie Metchnikoff, promoter of the probiotic Bulgarian lactobacillus (see chapter 5).

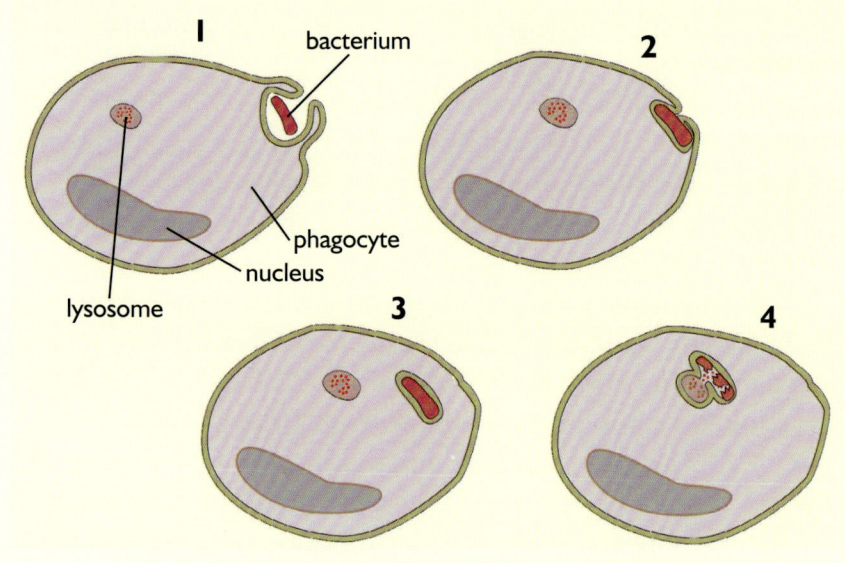

Fig 13: A phagocyte engulfing and destroying a pathogen

Inflammation

Phagocytes are aided in reaching pathogens by the process of inflammation. If microbes enter the body following an injury, such as a splinter piercing the skin, local cells release chemicals that causes inflammation. The inflammatory process involves the flooding of the infected area with blood, so that phagocytes in the blood get close to the pathogens rapidly.

The mechanism of inflammation involves tiny blood vessels (capillaries) dilating so that blood escapes into the tissues. At the same time, other capillaries, that transport blood away from the area, are narrowed to restrict the exit of blood from the infected area. The consequence is that the area of infection is filled with blood and becomes swollen and inflamed (red, hot and tender).

When phagocytes come across pathogens, they immediately attack them. Having successfully engulfed scores of bacteria, a phagocyte will release chemicals that further accelerate the inflammatory process.

The innate immune system, in addition to being a quick and relatively simple method of attacking harmful invaders, also plays an essential role in ensuring that the more complicated adaptive immune system works.

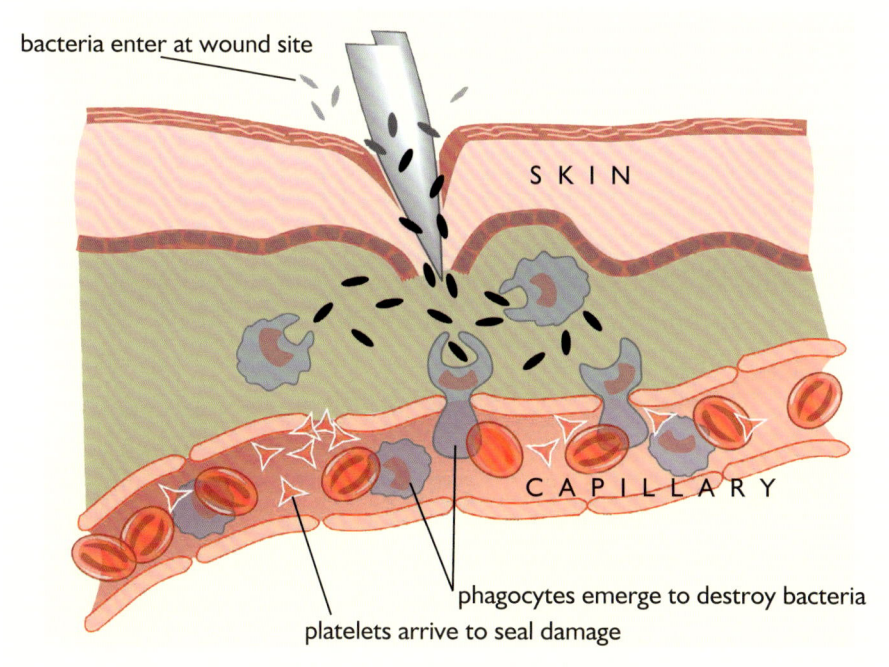

Fig 14: Early stages of inflammation

The adaptive immune system

The system is called adaptive, because the cells and proteins that are produced to attack pathogens differ according to the particular variety of microbe.

While the innate system can deal with most common types of pathogen, the adaptive system can deal with unusual and rare pathogens. The adaptive system also acts as a back-up defence in case the innate immune system is overwhelmed by large numbers of pathogens. The adaptive system is, however, slower to get going than the innate system.

While phagocytes are the major cells of the innate IS, lymphocytes are the major cells of the adaptive IS. Like phagocytes, lymphocytes are white blood cells [1].

Lymphocytes have protein molecules protruding from the surface of their cells, and each lymphocyte has a slightly different protruding molecule from all the other lymphocytes. This means that in each person there are millions of lymphocytes and each one is slightly different. The protruding molecules have the potential to attach to molecules on the surface of a pathogen, with one lymphocyte just right for a particular pathogen. Once such an attachment has taken place, the lymphocyte will duplicate itself into very large numbers, so that the pathogen to which it is matched can be killed.

The lymph system

The lymph system is a network of vessels that runs broadly parallel to blood vessels. There are also lymph tissues where some immune cells congregate. The lymph system has two main functions. Firstly, it acts as a drain for fluid that has leaked from capillaries into tissues. This fluid bathes the tissues, providing them with nutrients. On draining into lymph vessels, the lymph fluid is drawn through the vessels towards the neck, where the fluid rejoins the bloodstream.

The second function of the lymph system is supportive of the adaptive IS. It provides gathering points for lymphocytes where they are more likely to encounter pathogens, and from such encounters the adaptive IS is triggered. The main gathering points in the lymph system are lymph nodes, which are swellings at various points along the lymph vessels.

B and T cells

There are two main types of lymphocyte; one is the B cell which secretes its surface molecules into body fluids, such as blood and lymph. These molecules are known as antibodies. The other type of lymphocyte is a T cell, which holds onto its surface molecules and targets pathogens that have infected human cells, rather than seeking out pathogens in body fluids. Once antibodies and T cells have attached to pathogens or their toxins, the harmful agents are no longer able to attach to and enter human cells to cause disease.

The pathogens that the adaptive IS works against are those

that have avoided the innate IS. These pathogens have, in many cases, fooled phagocytes so that they do not recognise them as being foreign invaders. The important job that B and T cells do is identify harmful agents within the body (microbes, toxins and cancer cells) and distinguish them from healthy human cells. It is important that immune cells and immune chemicals do not attack healthy human cells by mistake. When such a mistake occurs, an autoimmune reaction occurs.

Memory cells

Once the harmful agent has been destroyed, most of the B and T cells die. Enough of them remain, however, to respond if the same pathogen reappears. If the same pathogen does invade again, the remaining B and T cells (now known as memory cells) will go into action and produce masses of antibodies much more quickly than during the original invasion.

This is how people are 'immunised' (protected) against a pathogen once it has initially been defeated by the adaptive immune system. Vaccination against contagious diseases uses this mechanism, by triggering the adaptive response through the use of weakened versions of a virus or bacterium. The vaccine provokes the development of memory cells that are able to respond quickly to a full-blown version of the infection, should it occur.

Summary of IS description

The body's physical barriers stop most harmful microbes from entering the bloodstream. The innate and adaptive immune systems operate together as a highly sophisticated collection of white blood cells, lymph vessels and tissue, antibody proteins, and various inflammatory chemicals to defeat pathogens that manage to enter the body systems.

Influences of the gut flora on the IS

The state of readiness of the IS

With the gut wall containing large numbers of immune cells and molecules, and the intestinal space filled with huge numbers of microfloral bacteria, it would be reasonable to assume that the bacteria would provoke the gut IS into attack mode. But this does not happen. The gut immune tissues tolerate the microflora in the intestine. At the same time, the gut IS is able to recognise pathogens and act against them. The way in which the IS is able to distinguish the good from the bad microbes is not yet clear.

The tolerance of the microflora by the IS enables the microfloral bacteria to be in close proximity with the immune tissues and to have an opportunity to influence the IS. The microflora appears to help the gut IS to function better [2].

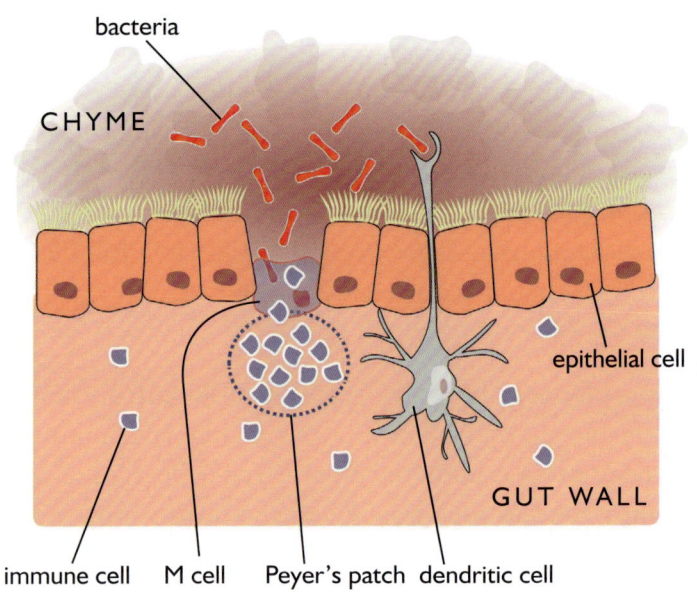

Fig 15: The close relationship between gut microbes and mucosal immune cells

Development of the IS in infants

Not only does the gut microflora improve the functioning of the IS, but it also has a role in developing the IS in infants. When a baby is born, its IS has the main structures (lymphatic tissues and vessels) in place, but is not yet ready to defend the body. The immaturity of an infant's IS is why children are more prone to infection than adults.

Antibodies are not produced for the first 20 weeks of life, and infants have to rely on antibodies supplied by their mothers. Pregnant women produce increased amounts of antibodies during the last ten weeks of pregnancy, and some of these antibodies are transported across the placenta to the child in the womb. Premature babies are at a substantial disadvantage, because they receive fewer maternal antibodies.

It appears that the infant's IS has to be activated in order to work properly, and this activation is undertaken by the gut microflora [2,3,4,5].

It takes about four years for the gut flora of children to develop to a stable state that resembles that of an adult [6]. As the microflora develops, the child's IS matures. It is thought that the mixture of bacterial species in the flora influences how the IS develops [7].

The tendency to allergic reaction

Over the last fifty years, there has been a substantial increase in the incidence of allergic diseases, such as eczema, asthma and hay fever. This increase has been especially noticeable in wealthy developed countries [7]. Allergy is a malfunction of the IS, in which harmless substances are interpreted as being harmful, and the IS reacts incorrectly towards them.

The reasons are not known for this dramatic increase in allergic diseases, but various explanations have been put forward. One that is growing in popularity is that the types of microbes in the human gut play a crucial role. This theory is a development from an earlier idea, known as the 'hygiene hypothesis.'

The hygiene hypothesis proposes that the reduction in incidence of childhood infections is the main explanation for the rise in allergies. Children were not having their immune system provoked often enough in childhood and consequently the IS did not become fully developed [7,8,9,10].

The more hygienic environment of rich countries has had a very positive effect in reducing the rate of infant mortality and reducing the amount of infectious disease. An environment that is relatively free of microbes, however, may also have a negative consequence. If a child's IS is not stimulated sufficiently, the IS may not develop properly or function correctly. In particular, it is thought that T cell lymphocyte behaviour is affected [11].

An association has been found between hepatitis A (virus) infection and lower rates of allergy; and there is some evidence of similar beneficial association with the protozoan parasite *Toxoplasma gondii*. As both these infections start in the intestine, researchers began to focus their attentions on the intestine as a possible source of the 'allergy epidemic'.

In studies comparing children with and without allergic diseases, certain differences in the make-up of the gut flora have been noted. A clear pattern has not yet emerged, but the numbers and species of bifidobacteria appear to be playing a role. There is also growing evidence that different species within the microflora have different effects on the development and maintenance of the gut IS [12].

Furthermore, there is growing evidence of an association between antibiotics and allergic disease. For example, a family doctor practice in Oxfordshire, England found a doubling of the risk of hay fever and eczema among children who had received antibiotics by the age of two years. Use of antibiotics in infants has the potential of interrupting the process of establishing a normal microflora in the intestine, and hence its influence on the gut IS [10].

Evidence pointing to a role for the gut microflora in allergy and immune dysfunction has led to a variation in the hygiene hypothesis, known as the 'old friends hypothesis' (or the 'microbiota hypothesis'). This new explanation suggests that differences in the species present in the gut microflora may be more important in the rise of allergic diseases than the impact of occasional infections [6].

There is some evidence that the microflora in breast-fed infants from developed countries differs from that found in breast-fed infants in less-developed countries. The former may have fewer bifidobacteria and more Gram-negative bacteria [13].

The term 'old friends' refers to microbes that tend to be absent in the intestines of people from rich countries [11]. These missing microbes are not only the probiotic lactobacilli and bifidobacteria, but also microbes associated with unsanitary conditions, such as parasitic intestinal worms (helminths), which are rare in developed countries. Also, bacteria that live off decaying matter (saprophytic mycobacteria) are not common in the gut of people from developed countries, perhaps because food beyond its 'sell-by date' is rarely eaten [8,14]. It is thought that these 'old friend' microbes influence the IS to reduce inflammation and to be more tolerant of microbes and food molecules.

The tendency to autoimmune disease

Other diseases of IS malfunction have also increased in incidence, such as inflammatory bowel disease (Crohn's disease and ulcerative colitis) and automimune diseases. An autoimmune disease occurs when the IS acts against its own body. The IS misreads the body's cells or chemicals as being foreign and attacks them. There is a range of autoimmune diseases, including multiple sclerosis, rheumatoid arthritis and type 1 diabetes [11].

The causes of autoimmune disease are not firmly understood, although it is thought that a combination of factors is involved: genetic, hormonal, environmental and immune [15]. Environmental factors may include a range of influences, including long-term infections by viruses, such as the Eppstein-Barr virus and cytomegalovirus [14]. Although a microbial infection may trigger an autoimmune disease, paradoxically, it appears that the absence of infection in childhood may make a person more prone to autoimmune disease. The 'old friends' hypothesis of allergy is also being applied to autoimmune diseases, based on indications from animal studies [16].

The potential of probiotics

It is not practical to segregate human beings from microbes and other substances that provoke a malfunction of the IS or to reduce public hygiene in developed countries. Alternative approaches are needed, and one of these is the use of probiotics to improve the mixture of species within the gut microflora, and so improve the functioning of the IS [17].

Summary of main points

- ❖ The function of the immune system (IS) is to defend the body from potentially deadly attack by pathogenic microbes and harmful substances.
- ❖ The gut microflora normally provokes the IS into a very mild state of inflammation, so that it is ready to respond rapidly and effectively against pathogens.
- ❖ The gut microflora aids the infant's IS in developing towards a state of maturity, especially during the first year of life.
- ❖ The increase in the incidence of allergy and autoimmune diseases in developed countries may be due to a change in the mixture of species that make up the gut flora.
- ❖ This causal explanation is known as the 'old friends hypothesis', which proposes that the reduction in the number of certain microbes in the gut flora (lactobacilli, bifidobacteria, helminthic worms and saprophytic mycobacteria) reduces the ability of the IS to 'turn off' an inflammatory reaction.
- ❖ If the 'old friends hypothesis' is true, then probiotics may be beneficial in reducing immune-related disease.

Part II

THE ESSENTIALS OF PROBIOTICS

A History of Probiotics

Probiotic Benefits for the Intestine

Probiotic Benefits for Other Parts of the Body

Safety

~~~

5

A History of Probiotics

The probiotic concept of using microbes to improve health is a hundred years old, and the use of fermented foods (which involve microbes) has a much longer history. During the twentieth century, enthusiasm for probiotics rose, fell and rose again, this time with increasing scientific evidence of benefit. By understanding the variation in popularity of probiotics during the previous century, their suitability for modern health challenges is clarified.

Fermented drinks and foods

Microbes have been used in fermented food and drink for thousands of years. Fermentation happens when microbes break down plant and animal material, gaining energy and chemicals that enables them to grow and reproduce. The process of fermentation has been known for centuries, even if the cause and the chemical reactions involved have not been understood until more recently. The type of microbes involved in food and drink fermentation are bacteria and yeasts.

One of the by-products of yeast fermentation is alcohol, and wine is the fermented juice of grapes. The fermentation occurs naturally when yeasts on the grape skin react with the juice when the skin breaks. Organised vine growing and wine production has taken place for more than 5,000 years, apparently starting in South-West Asia [1].

The production of beer also involves a fermentation process and beer has been produced for at least 3,500 years, possibly originating in Mesopotamia (now Iran and Iraq) [2].

Fig 16: Fermented foods and drinks
1. olives, 2. soy sauce, 3. beer, 4. veined cheese, 5. wine, 6. bread, 7. yoghurt, 8. sauerkraut, 9. salami.

Various foods are made using fermentation. For instance, bread rises when the yeast ferments sugars in the dough and carbon dioxide is given off in tiny bubbles. Bacteria that secrete lactic acid are used to ferment sauerkraut (shredded cabbage), table olives, and European hard sausages (e.g. salami) to preserve the food and improve its flavour. Soy sauce, from the Far East, is the product of fermented soya beans.

Many long-standing milk products involve fermentation. For example, there are 'soured milks' called keffir (Russia), mazun (Armenia), gioddu (Sardinia), kumiss (Asia), leben (Egypt), dahi, lassi (India) and yoghurt (the Balkans and Russia).

Traditional butter-making involved the cream being 'soured' before being churned. Cheese was originally developed by microbial fermentation in which the two parts of milk, the curd and the whey, were separated and the more solid curd (protein) formed the cheese. Adding other bacteria that form coloured veins develops flavours.

Humans have therefore used bacteria and yeasts for thousands of years to improve and preserve food. It is likely that these fermented foods were first developed by accident, perhaps by Stone Age humans burying food in the ground for safe-keeping and finding that it was

5: A History of Probiotics ~ 53

preserved as the result of natural fermentation [3].

It has been estimated that 20-40% of foods and beverages consumed in the world are fermented, showing that the processes involved continue to be valued [4].

Microbes first identified

The first person to see bacteria was a Dutch scientist, Antoni van Leeuwenhoek, in the 17th century. He reported to the Royal Society of London how, with the use of an early microscope, he had observed a wide range of 'animalcules' not normally visible to the human eye [5].

But it was not until the middle of the 19th century that experimental methods and laboratory equipment improved sufficiently to enable a proper study of microbes.

During the latter half of the nineteenth century the French chemist Louis Pasteur showed that fermentation, as in wine production, was caused by microbes. He also demonstrated that the decay of food into an inedible form was caused by micro-organisms and that the bad-smelling form of decay, putrefaction, was a type of fermentation.

Pasteur also developed the theory that microbes could cause disease (the germ theory). This was verified by various experiments conducted by other scientists in Europe.

Then, when the important French wine and vinegar industries were suffering from spoilage of their products, Pasteur solved the problem by developing a heat treatment. This process, later known as pasteurisation, killed off harmful bacteria, but did not spoil the product.

The large bowel: fermenting or putrefying?

At the turn of the twentieth century there was a debate in medicine about the significance of the huge numbers of bacteria in the human intestines, particularly the large bowel.

Louis Pasteur thought they might be indispensible, as if an essential beneficial fermentation was taking place in the gut. Other scientists took the opposite view, that the microfloral bacteria were harmful, as if a decaying putrefaction was taking place [6].

One of the supporters of this latter idea was Elie Metchnikoff. He was a Russian zoologist who had gained eminence through his work in discovering phagocytes (cells of the immune system), for which he was awarded the Nobel Prize.

While working at the Pasteur Institute in Paris at the turn of the twentieth century, Metchnikoff proposed that the bacterial population of the intestines could be improved by adding beneficial bacteria.

Metchnikoff's adoption of the idea of beneficial bacteria arose from his enquiries into how old age could be delayed and life prolonged.

Metchnikoff and Bulgarian peasants

In his wide-ranging enquiries Metchnikoff became interested in a population of mountain peasants in Bulgaria who were known for their longevity. He thought that the fermented milk they drank had a role to play in their long life. Metchnikoff reckoned that by consuming similarly soured milk the human microflora could be changed and improved.

He found a bacterium in the peasants' milk, and named it *Bacillus bulgaricus*. Metchnikoff argued that the lactic acid produced by the bacterium reduced the harmful effects of other micro-organisms.

Because of inadequate records, it is not certain which bacterium Metchnikoff identified. It may have been *Lactobacillus delbrueckii* subspecies *bulgaricus*, a strain of bacteria commonly used today in the production of yoghurt.

The fashion for fermented milk products

As a consequence of scientific legitimacy given by Metchnikoff's theory, it became fashionable in the early part of the 20th century in Europe to consume fermented milk products.

One observer commented on the enthusiasm in Britain, "For several months one heard of nothing but the Bulgarian bacillus. The bacillus shared with Lloyd George's budget the honor of monopolizing the conversation at the dinner tables of the great. He [the bacillus] dominated Belgravia, frolicked in Fulham, and bestrode Birmingham and the whole of the British Isles." [7] In his history of bacteriologists, Paul de Kruif wrote in 1926, "The Bulgarian bacillus became a rage, companies were formed, and the directors grew rich off selling these silly bacilli." [8]

It is understandable why fermented milks with their 'good bacteria' became popular. There was a long-standing belief that the contents of the lower intestines were undesirable, which is hardly surprising as solid waste is passed out of the body and may be foul smelling.

This belief was supported by some leading scientists and doctors of the time, who thought that gut bacteria produced toxins that entered the body and caused a range of illnesses.

There was also the romantic idea that rural peasants lived longer lives because of something they ate, and that this food could be brought to urban areas.

Decline of early popularity

The popularity of fermented milk, in the early part of the twentieth century, faded because of several developments.

First, a range of scientific experiments showed that toxins produced in the colon were not responsible for the illnesses that some doctors claimed.

Secondly, Metchnikoff died in 1916 at the age of 71. He had spent his last fifteen years consuming large quantities of soured milk with the Bulgarian bacillus, and many people believed this would extend his life substantially. His death further weakened support for his ideas.

Following Metchnikoff's death, Leo F. Rettger at Yale University investigated the two bacteria used in yoghurt production (*L. bulgaricus* and *Streptococcus thermophilus*). He found that most were killed by stomach acid and intestinal bile salts. He also found that *L. bulgaricus* did not colonise the gut and was therefore a transient bacterium, less likely to affect the intestines [9].

In the 1920s, vitamins were discovered and their importance to health, together with minerals, was established. Scientific opinion assumed that the perceived benefits from fermented milks were the result of the presence of vitamins and minerals, rather than from the activities of lactic acid bacteria.

Later, medical interest in beneficial bacteria waned even further with the development of antibiotic drugs. The focus shifted to the use of antibiotics in controlling infectious diseases, through the inhibition and killing of bacteria. There seemed to be no need for the ingestion of beneficial bacteria when antibiotics could destroy the harmful ones.

With the decline in support from the medical profession, public interest in fermented drinks also fell away. Interest among the general public did not die out completely, however. Some demand for these milks continued, and this made it feasible for companies to maintain commercial production.

Early commercial products

In the United States, the Yale scientist Leo F. Rettger switched his attention away from *L. bulgaricus* towards other lactic-acid bacteria, especially *Lactobacillus acidophilus*. He found that various preparations with this bacterium helped to alleviate constipation and to remedy diarrhoea [10]. Although these two benefits appear contradictory, lactobacilli do have both characteristics. Rettger's work helped the development of commercial products in the U.S.A., such as acidophilus milk (unfermented milk with *L. acidophilus* added).

In 1919, the Danone company was formed in Barcelona, Spain, producing yoghurts. Today this company is a major producer of 'functional foods', that is, foods that have health benefits in addition to normal nutrition [11]. In Europe, Danone produces two major probiotic products: Actimel®, a fermented milk drink, and Bio Activia® yoghurt. Both contain probiotic bacteria (a lactobacillus and a bifidobacterium, respectively).

In Japan in 1930, Dr Minoru Shirota, a microbiologist, identified a lactic acid bacterium resistant to stomach acid, later named *L. casei* Shirota. By 1935 his company had produced a milk drink with the name Yakult. This subsequently proved very popular in Japan and is delivered to workplaces by travelling salespeople known as Yakult Ladies, of whom there are currently more than 50,000. The Yakult company produces many other items, including skin products. It has also expanded, more recently, to Europe and North America.

Not all early probiotic products were milk-based. Some were in freeze-dried form in capsules. Two prominent examples are a probiotic *E. coli* and a probiotic yeast.

During the First World War, a German doctor, Alfred Nissle, was searching for a strain of the bacterium *E. coli* that would attack pathogenic bacteria. As *E. coli* are a natural part of the human intestinal microflora, Nissle looked to find such strains in the stools of people who were especially resistant to intestinal infections. A good source of such bacteria was soldiers in field hospitals. Dysentery and other diarrhoeal diseases were common, and readily spread between soldiers. Those patients who were resistant to such infections were targeted for investigation.

After identifying several strains that had strong anti-pathogen characteristics, Dr Nissle selected one, which was named *E. coli* Nissle. The probiotic strain was incorporated as live cells into a capsule, but later manufacturing involved freeze-dried bacteria. In freeze-drying, the microbes remain alive but dormant; becoming active again when water is added. This product was first manufactured in the 1920s and is still sold today, with growing popularity [12].

Saccharomyces boulardii is a yeast which was discovered in Indochina (now Vietnam) in 1923 by the French scientist Henri Boulard. He had observed that local people used the skins of various tropical fruits, such as lychees and mangosteens, for anti-diarrhoeal purposes. He identified that the active factor in such treatment was a yeast, later named *S. boulardii*. The yeast is closely related to the baker's and brewer's yeast, *Saccharomyces cerevisiae*.

S. boulardii has been produced by a number of European companies for many decades. Almost all the scientific research has been undertaken by a French company, Biocodex, that produces this probiotic under a number of brand names including Ultra-Levure® and Florastor®. It is now sold in more than 90 countries.

These early products were not known as probiotics, but were described by a range of different terms, such as bacteriotherapy [13]. The term probiotic did not start to be used until the early 1990s.

Probiotics for animals

A revival in the popularity of probiotics took place in products for animals before humans, because farmers were interested and veterinarians had greater freedom to recommend such products.

From the early 1970s in the U.K., farmers were banned from using certain antibiotics as growth promoters, making them more open to alternatives for keeping farm animals healthy. There was also concern about the relatively high level of diarrhoea in intensely-farmed animals.

For example, incubator-hatched chickens are much more susceptible to intestinal infection from salmonella bacteria than are free-range chickens. A reasonable explanation for this is that because the incubator-hatched chickens are born and grow in a clean environment, they do not acquire the normal gut flora from their mother. Reconstituting that flora might help to confer resistance to infection.

In 1973, two Finnish veterinarians extracted samples of the intestinal contents of healthy chickens and transferred the samples into the intestines of newly-hatched chicks. Resistance to harmful salmonella bacteria was greater in the treated chicks than in those chicks that did not receive any transferred gut contents [14].

This study strengthened the belief that a well-balanced gut microflora was an important factor in animal health, and led to a search to identify which bacteria in the normal microflora were the important ones in providing protection from disease.

Feed companies identified useful species and strains for animal probiotics, but mostly this research was undertaken privately and not published in peer-reviewed journals. The lack of published evidence did not discourage farmers. In their experience, these beneficial bacteria reduced the incidence of diarrhoea and other infections in animals. Thus demand for these products grew.

Feed companies and others related to farming developed a wide range of products. As many as twenty-six different species of bacteria and three fungi had been used in animal probiotic products by the 1990s [15].

Probiotics become fashionable again

In the 1990s, probiotics for human consumption started to become more popular, due to changes in attitudes among doctors and among the general public.

The complexity and resilience of bacteria

Among doctors there has been an increased respect for the complexity and resilience of bacteria. As they are so small and consist of only one cell, scientists tended to assume that they were rather simple organisms and that conquering disease caused by bacteria would be relatively straightforward. With the discovery of antibiotics, there was an assumption that bacterial disease was beaten.

Resistant strains appeared to each new antibiotic, however, and much more quickly than expected. It became clear that the ability of bacteria to share pieces of DNA with other bacteria played a role in the rapid spread of resistance genes.

Also, the appearance of multiply-resistant bacteria made treating an infected patient much more complicated. Bacteria were not only accepting resistance genes, but also linking them together and integrating them into their chromosome. Previously, microbiologists had no idea this could be done. Pathogenic bacteria were starting to be seen as more formidable adversaries.

A clincher in transforming attitudes to bacteria came with the discovery of the cause of stomach ulcers.

The cause of stomach ulcers

It used to be thought that stomach ulcers were caused by excessive stress. The prevailing theory was that a stressed individual produced more stomach acid than was necessary to digest food and that this excess acid harmed the lining of the stomach and the duodenum (first part of the small intestine).

In 1982, Australian researchers Barry Marshall and Robin Warren put forward the idea that stomach ulcers were caused by a spiral-shaped bacterium named *Helicobacter pylori*. This theory was so contrary to conventional wisdom that a major debate ensued. Criticism of the Australians was fierce. As they were so sure that their theory was correct, and in order to win over the doubters, Marshall and another colleague infected themselves with *H. pylori* and both men developed gastritis (inflammation of the stomach and duodenum).

They recovered from the gastritis once they took antibiotics, which strengthened the argument that a bacterium was the cause of gastric ulcers.

Other researchers showed that antibiotics healed ulcers and prevented recurrence in 90 per cent of cases. The U.S. Government-funded National Institutes of Health monitored the research closely and in 1994 concluded that *H. pylori* "plays a significant role in the development of ulcers."

This shift by the scientific establishment has been described as "one of the most chastening lessons in gastroenterology this century, and has heightened awareness of the role of bacteria in the gut" [16].

Pathogenic bacteria were recognised as being more adaptable than had previously imagined. Most doctors had thought that it was impossible for a microbe to live permanently in the stomach, because of the acidic environment. Bacteria were also thought to be responsible for acute disease (appearing suddenly), rather than chronic disease (lasting a long time). As stomach ulcers tend to be long-term conditions, *H. pylori* changed that view too.

As doctors' attitudes towards bacteria changed, so did their views on probiotics. Attitudes among the general public were also changing and becoming more open to the probiotic idea. Digestive disorders continued to be common and troublesome. There also was a growing public concern at the excessive use of pharmaceutical products, including antibiotics, often with associated side effects. Finally, the concept of wholistic health, in which overall body systems are improved, rather than targeting a specific disease, had grown in popularity. Promotion of health was being seen as important as treating disease.

Now, public and medical attitudes are receptive to the idea of probiotics both in aiding good health and in reducing illness. However, it is also fair to say that public understanding of what probiotics involve is poor, and is often little more than a feeling that these products are 'good for you'.

Summary of main points

- ❖ Fermented drinks and foods have been consumed for thousands of years
- ❖ The use of particular microbes to improve health is about 100 years old
- ❖ Probiotic products became popular at the beginning of the 20th century, went out of fashion, and then re-gained popularity towards the end of the century
- ❖ One of the factors in the greater interest in probiotics has been the rise of strains of pathogens that resist the effects of several different types of antibiotic.

6
Probiotic Benefits for the Intestine

This chapter reports on evidence of benefit from probiotics and *pre*biotics for specific intestinal diseases. It summarises what the evidence may mean for prevention and therapy. The next chapter covers the same topic for other parts of the body.

Illnesses that have a connection with disturbance of the microflora of the gastro-intestinal tract are:

- ❖ Infectious diarrhoea
- ❖ Antibiotic-associated diarrhoea
- ❖ Constipation
- ❖ Irritable bowel syndrome (IBS)
- ❖ Inflammatory bowel disease (IBD)
- ❖ Lactose intolerance
- ❖ Gastritis and stomach ulcers.

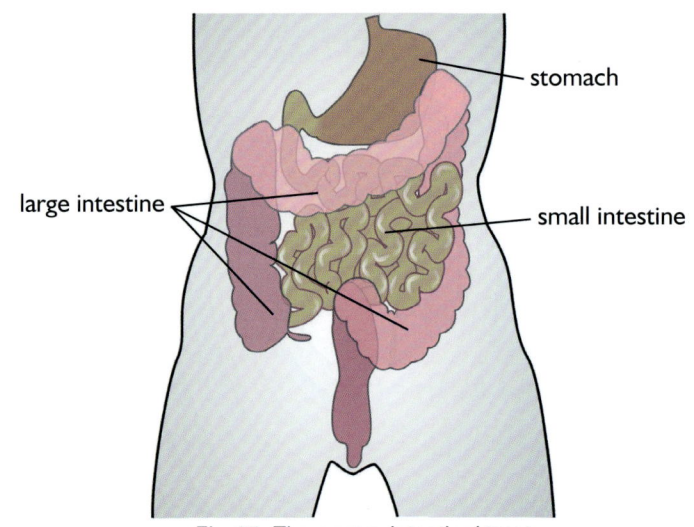

Fig 17: The gastro-intestinal tract

Infectious diarrhoea

Infectious diarrhoea is caused by pathogenic microbes. The word 'infectious' not only refers to the involvement of microbes, but also means that the pathogen can be spread to other humans, either directly between individuals or indirectly via an unhygienic environment.

Diarrhoea is a state in which the passing of loose, watery stools is frequent and urgent. It is usually a sign of an underlying health problem, and its precise form gives a clue as to the problem. It can signify a more serious condition such as inflammatory bowel disease or colo-rectal cancer, but in most cases it is caused by a microbial infection.

Pathogens that cause infectious diarrhoea can be any type of microbe, be it virus, bacterium, yeast or protozoan. Such diarrhoea is caused by the body wanting to flush away the pathogen or its toxins. This is achieved in three ways: fluid enters the intestinal space from the body [1], the amount of water absorbed into the body from the intestine is reduced, or peristalsis (intestinal muscle contractions) accelerates. If all these factors operate at the same time, diarrhoea can develop very quickly and be powerful.

The abdominal cramps that often accompany infectious diarrhoea are due to the intestinal muscle contractions straining to push the fluid contents. Pain may also be caused if the intestine becomes distended by the sheer volume of fluid contents.

Infectious diarrhoea tends to be self-limiting, meaning that the body resolves the problem by itself. In most cases of infectious diarrhoea, normal bowel movements return after about three days. For such a short period, it hardly seems worth considering the use of probiotics, but there are some situations when probiotics can be very useful, such as:

- ❖ A child with acute diarrhoea
- ❖ On vacation in an unfamiliar hot country.

Children with acute diarrhoea

Each year, at least two million children under the age of five die as a consequence of intestinal infection. That is about one death every 15 seconds [2]. Most of these deaths occur in underdeveloped parts of the world. In developed countries, the death-rate from infectious diarrhoea has fallen sharply in recent decades, but the rate of such infection still remains high [1,3].

In medicine, the term 'acute' means severe or coming sharply to a crisis. It is usually contrasted with a chronic condition, which persists for a long time. Acute diarrhoea therefore means that it is severe and has arisen quickly.

For children, acute diarrhoea can be dangerous because of the risk of dehydration. The majority of our body is made of water, and therefore the loss of a large amount of water will cause the body to malfunction, and may even prove fatal.

Of the various microbes that cause infectious diarrhoea in infants, rotavirus is the most common, occurring in about one third of cases [4].

A virus is not really a living entity in the way we normally think of life. It is inert, except when it enters a living cell and multiplies within, using the cell's biological mechanisms. Such entry and multiplication within a human cell causes the cell to be damaged, and eventually to die when the large number of viruses contained within burst out of the cell. As such, all viruses are pathogens. Most viruses are much smaller than bacteria, but they can be just as harmful as pathogenic bacteria because they multiply so rapidly.

Most children worldwide will have been infected with rotavirus by their first birthday, although many will only have had mild symptoms. Rotavirus causes vomiting, diarrhoea and mild fever. The main treatment is 'rehydration therapy', which is the provision of a solution of salts and carbohydrate in sterile water to replace the loss of water from diarrhoea. Vomiting may be a problem if the infant vomits up the rehydration solution or milk. About one-half of all infants hospitalised for infectious diarrhoea and related dehydration have rotavirus infection.

Rotaviral diarrhoea usually last three days, although it occasionally persists for up to nine days. Probiotics have been tried in a large number of clinical studies as a supplement to rehydration therapy in the treatment of infectious diarrhoea in infants. The results have been positive and remarkably consistent, with a range of different probiotic types being used [5]. On average, the duration of the diarrhoea was reduced by 30.5 hours [6].

In addition to viral infectious diarrhoea, probiotics have been shown to alleviate bacteria-caused diarrhoea. Pathogenic *E. coli* and *Shigella* species are the most common causes of bacterial diarrhoea [7].

In addition to effectively *treating* infectious diarrhoea in children, probiotics have also been shown to be effective in *preventing* the development of infectious diarrhoea in young children. The types of probiotic microbes used in these effective studies are lactobacilli and other lactic acid bacteria, bifidobacteria, a probiotic *E. coli* [8] and a probiotic yeast (*S. boulardii*).

For example, a *Lactobacillus rhamnosus* was given to 45 children hospitalised for reasons other than diarrhoea. They were aged between one and 36 months, and a lower rate of diarrhoea (7%) developed in the probiotic group compared with a non-probiotic group (33%) [9].

Traveller's diarrhoea

There are fewer studies on adults with infectious diarrhoea, but the results show that probiotics are at least as effective as they are in children [7]. Infectious diarrhoea in adults is not as dangerous as in infants, because adults have more developed bodies and immune systems. As such, many adults will take little or no action to treat such diarrhoea other than drinking plenty of fluids and resting, because the disease will usually pass in a few days.

The use of probiotics is more likely to be considered by adults in the case of traveller's diarrhoea (TD). Tourism from developed countries to developing countries, especially if the climate is hot, carries with it a risk of infectious diarrhoea. The proportion of people from the West travelling to areas of high risk of TD, who have episodes of such diarrhoea is usually in the range of 30-50% [10,11].

The diarrhoea may be caused by the water supply being contaminated with faecal matter. Local strains of pathogens may also be new to the body of the visitor, and therefore the microbes may have a greater effect than similar microbes from the home country. Food may also be contaminated, not only by microbes, but also by toxins secreted by such pathogens. The latter, which cause food poisoning, can lead to very rapidly-developing diarrhoea, as well as nausea and vomiting.

To reduce the risk of infection, it is sensible to avoid salads, unpeeled fruits, raw or poorly-cooked meats and seafood, cold sauces, reheated food, unpasteurised dairy products and tap water.

Increasing numbers of travellers are also considering the use of probiotics as a preventative. Probiotics have been used in a number of studies, with mixed results. For example, in a group of Finnish tourists visiting Alanya in Turkey, 24% of those who took a lactobacillus probiotic developed diarrhoea, compared with 40% of those who did not [12]. In some other trials, however, there were no benefits from probiotics.

Why did the trials give mixed responses? One explanation is that the cause of traveller's diarrhoea differs depending on the local situation. If travellers risk infectious diarrhoea from a variety of different pathogens, it would seem logical that a probiotic product containing a number of different strains is more likely to be protective than a single-strain product.

Can *pre*biotics help prevent TD? *Pre*biotics are foods that feed probiotic bacteria and are described in chapter 11. In a group of 244 travellers, 11% of a group that took a *pre*biotic developed diarrhoea, compared with 20% in the group that had no *pre*biotic [10]. This was not statistically significant, but a study using another type of *pre*biotic did provide statistically-significant benefits, both in prevention of diarrhoea and reduced severity of symptoms [13].

Antibiotic-associated diarrhoea

Antibiotics have revolutionised the treatment of bacterial infections, saving countless lives. Antibiotics do however have some drawbacks. One is the tendency to promote the rise of resistant-strains of bacteria and so reduce the effectiveness of the antibiotic. Another drawback is the tendency of antibiotics to disturb the microflora, making you vulnerable to subsequent pathogenic infection.

Such infection of the intestine usually leads to diarrhoea and, as such, it is described as 'antibiotic-associated diarrhoea' (AAD). The proportion of people developing AAD after taking a course of antibiotics is about 20% [14].

In a number of studies probiotics have prevented such diarrhoea, although not all studies have shown probiotics to be effective [5,15]. The average reduction, over all studies, has been by one-half [16].

An example of a successful study involved 113 elderly patients from three hospitals in London, England. Thirty-four per cent of those who did not receive a probiotic developed AAD, compared with 12% who received a probiotic product containing lactic acid bacteria [17]. There is also evidence of similar benefit from *Saccharomyces boulardii* and *Clostridium butyricum* [18,19].

Clostridum difficile

Clostridium difficile is responsible for about one-fifth of all cases of AAD [20]. This bacterium can be found living benignly in the gut of some people, probably because its numbers are kept in check by the gut microflora. When antibiotics disturb the microflora, *C. difficile* increases to infection levels, and secreted toxins cause disease and diarrhoea [2].

Infection by *C. difficile* is usually overcome by antibiotic treatments, but in a minority of cases, the *C. difficile* recurs. Each time it recurs it is more likely to recur again, probably because it can form spores, which are an inert form of the bacterium with a toughened surface that is difficult to penetrate. Later, the spores can germinate and a fresh *C. difficile* infection can start again. Persistent *C. difficile* infection may lead to the development of a serious condition known as pseudomembranous colitis, so it is important that persistent recurring *C. difficile* infection is eradicated.

In several studies, the probiotic yeast *Saccharomyces boulardii* has been shown to be helpful in reducing the rate of *C. difficile* reinfection in people who already have a pattern of recurrence [21]. *S. boulardii* is added to the antibiotics used as standard treatment [4]. There is also some evidence that probiotic lactobacilli may be helpful [22]. Furthermore, there has been one study in which the *prebiotic* FOS reduced the risk of recurrence of *C. difficile* infection [23].

Constipation

Constipation is the opposite of diarrhoea. While diarrhoea is the frequent and urgent passing of liquid stool, constipation is the infrequent and difficult passing of hardened stool. Constipation may not be quite as easy to identify as diarrhoea, however. According to doctors, some of their patients who claim to be suffering from constipation have a frequency of bowel movement that is within the normal range.

Constipation is quite a common condition. Based on surveys in North America, Europe, Australia, New Zealand, Japan and Korea, the proportion of the population suffering from constipation at any one time is about 15-17%. Among women the prevalence is greater [24].

Constipation may be a sign of an underlying disease (see below) but, if not, does it matter if you are constipated? Constipation does seem to cause a general feeling of abdominal discomfort. Furthermore, straining to pass stool may put pressure on the tissues and structures of the anal area with potential negative consequences, such as haemorrhoids (piles).

What causes constipation?

Just as there are many causes of diarrhoea, there are also a number of causes of constipation. The main one is a shortage of fibre in the diet. A high-fibre diet leads to a substantial amount of undigested food entering the large bowel. Fibre draws water to it and the content of the bowel increases in bulk. The bulkier faeces press on the wall of the intestine and this stimulates the muscles to contract and force the contents forward.

If there is insufficient fibre in the diet, the faeces will move more slowly and there will be more time for water to be absorbed into the body, leaving the faeces smaller and harder, which in turn is more difficult to move.

Other factors in the development of constipation may be lack of exercise [25], or the consumption of certain drugs, such as antidepressants. Diseases associated with constipation are irritable bowel syndrome and cancer of the large bowel.

What is standard treatment?

The main approach in relieving constipation is to increase the amount of fibre in the diet. The easiest way to do this is to eat more vegetables and fruit, plus wholemeal bread and wholegrain breakfast cereals. A cheap additional boost to dietary fibre consumption is to add wheat bran to food.

The only drawback with a high-fibre diet is that sometimes it leads to uncomfortable bloating and flatulence, which is excessive gas in the intestine produced by some of the microfloral bacteria.

In a small proportion of people, a high-fibre diet does not fully resolve the constipation problem. In such cases, there are various medicines that have a laxative effect. Laxatives should not, however, be used for long periods as they may encourage a long-term pattern of weak gut-wall muscle contractions.

Abdominal pain occasionally arises from constipation and relief of this can be problematic, because the main drugs used as painkillers (non-steroidal anti-inflammatory drugs or NSAIDs) have a constipating effect.

Do probiotics help with constipation?

There are several studies which show probiotics relieving constipation [26,27,28,29]. The improvements mostly ranged between a 20% and a 50% increase in the number of bowel movements a week. These studies used either a *Lactobacillus casei*, a *Bifidobacterium animalis* or a probiotic *E. coli*. It is not known by which mechanism the probiotics had their effects. It may be that not all probiotic strains are effective against constipation [25].

*Pre*biotics, which are described in chapter 11, also may be helpful with constipation. It is known that lactulose, FOS and GOS all have mild laxative effects, with evidence for lactulose being strongest [23]. As *pre*biotics are a type of soluble fibre, the laxative effect is probably by osmosis. Osmosis is a process of water flowing from a dilute solution to a concentrated solution. In this case it will be water flowing from the body into the intestinal tube because the carbohydrate (*pre*biotic) dissolved in water forms a more concentrated solution in the intestine than in the nearby tissues of the body.

It is likely that other *pre*biotics will act as laxatives [30], with the shorter-chain molecules (di- and oligosaccharides) possibly having a greater effect as a higher proportion of their molecules will dissolve in water compared with the longer-chained polysaccharides.

For people with constipation, *pre*biotics may have the added benefit of boosting the numbers of bifidobacteria and lactobacilli, and these extra probiotic bacteria are likely to further accelerate transit of large bowel contents.

Irritable bowel syndrome (IBS)

Irritable bowel syndrome (IBS) is a common condition (affecting 10-15% of the population) [31] and the main symptoms are:
- ❖ abdominal discomfort and pain, relieved by the passing of wind or stool

- altered bowel habit (diarrhoea or constipation or fluctuation between the two)
- bloating and flatulence.

All these symptoms appear to arise from the malfunctioning of the intestine, but there is no obvious damage to the bowels. The latest research suggests that malfunction of the nerves of the gut wall is a major factor, and that these nerves communicate with the brain, and vice versa.

Treatment of IBS is often unsuccessful. Changes to diet, including avoidance of excessive alcohol, sometimes helps. Controlling the amount of dietary fibre consumed can influence symptoms. For example, too much fibre can aggravate abdominal pain and bloating, while too little can contribute to chronic constipation. Doctors will sometimes prescribe antidiarrhoeal drugs or laxatives, depending on the type of bowel disturbance. Muscle relaxants may also be prescribed (e.g. peppermint oil), because people with IBS often seem to have hypersensitivity or spasm of the smooth muscle of the bowel wall.

Interest in trying probiotics has increased with two current hypotheses that IBS might be caused by small bowel bacterial overgrowth or 'low-grade' inflammation.

Small bowel bacterial overgrowth

This hypothesis suggests that there is a single unifying explanation for all the various symptoms associated with IBS. The proposed explanation is that bacteria from the large bowel move from the caecum into the ileum part of the small intestine, which is the opposite direction to the normal flow of intestinal contents.

On appearing in the ileum, the predominantly anaerobic bacteria increase in numbers, because there is plenty of food. The bacterial population starts to approach the numbers found in the large bowel. This bacterial increase is called an 'overgrowth', because the numbers are much greater than normally found in the ileum. Large numbers of such bacteria obstruct the absorption of digested carbohydrates, possibly because the bacteria are degrading the sugars for their own use. It may also be that the absorptive capacity of the small intestine is reduced because the bacteria stimulate the immune system and the resulting inflammation disrupts the absorptive capacity of the intestinal lining.

There are various characteristics of IBS that fit within this explanation, notably the high proportion of people who report bloating as a symptom. Bloating of the abdomen is due to excess gas in the intestine, mostly caused by bacterial metabolism. Evidence points to the bloating taking place in the small bowel. This is unusual, as normally most bacterial gas is produced in the large bowel [31].

Low-grade inflammation

The other hypothesis proposes that some people with IBS have 'low grade' inflammation of the intestine, possibly arising from a bout of microbial infection of the bowel [32]. As explained in chapter 4, inflammation is a process controlled by immune cells and molecules, as part of the defence of the body against pathogens. An intestinal infection that was overcome by an inflammatory process may have left a residual effect. The resultant mild inflammation appears to make the intestine sensitive to lots of things that it should ignore.

Supporting this explanation is the statistic that 25-30% of IBS patients have had acute infectious diarrhoea before developing their IBS [31]. Also, such patients are more likely to have a 'leaky gut', whereby it is easier for microbes to cross into the gut wall and beyond. It is not therefore surprising to find that post-infective IBS patients have more lymphocytes (immune cells) in the inner lining of the intestines, indicating an inflammatory process at work.

Difficulty in researching IBS

Clearly, both of these hypotheses imply that probiotics might play a role in reducing IBS, because probiotics can influence both the microflora and the immune system. There are several reasons, however, why testing these hypotheses is a difficult task. Firstly, there are fewer objective measures of disease than in many other conditions. The doctor has to rely on symptoms, as described by the patient, or on signs observed by the doctor when examining the patient. Both symptoms and signs are prone to human error, and therefore there can be an element of uncertainty as to whether progress has been made in the tested treatment.

Furthermore, there seems to be a psychological element to IBS. This is shown by the fact that patients with IBS show a much stronger than normal positive response when receiving inactive placebo [33].

A placebo is a blank substance that is used in clinical trials on some of the participants (often half) to check that there are no other factors, including psychological, that may influence the outcome of the study. It is not known why the placebo response occurs, or why it is so substantial in people with IBS.

Probiotic studies

One study involving 264 patients used a two-strain probiotic (an *E. coli* and an *Enterococcus faecium*). In a 'global symptom score' measurement, 73% of the probiotic group responded compared to 45% of the placebo group. Of those who responded, there was at least a 50% decrease in symptom levels [34].

In another study, 330 patients received a *Bifidobacterium* strain or a placebo, and the symptom score in the probiotic group was more than 20% better than the placebo group [34]. In other positive studies, reductions in flatulence and bloating were the most consistently-experienced benefit [32,36,37].

Inflammatory bowel disease (IBD)

Inflammatory bowel disease is often referred to by its initials IBD. This sometimes leads to confusion with IBS (irritable bowel syndrome), which is a very different condition. IBD is much less common than IBS, with less than 1% of the population affected by IBD. Also, while there is no obvious physical damage to the intestine in IBS, there is definitely damage in IBD. Such damage is caused by persistent inflammation of the intestine, and the symptoms of IBD include diarrhoea, abdominal pain, urgency to go to the toilet, and a sense of incomplete emptying of the bowels.

In IBD, the immune system of the intestinal wall appears to be behaving as if the intestine is being attacked by a pathogen and requires defending. Despite detailed investigations, such a pathogen has not been identified. In fact, the prevailing view is that IBD is not caused by a pathogen, but rather is a malfunction of the immune system. The immune system is believed to be reading the gut microflora as if it was a collection of harmful microbes rather than as a benign community of organisms.

IBD is a general term that covers a range of similar conditions, and by far the most common types of IBD are ulcerative colitis (UC) and Crohn's disease (CD). UC only affects the large bowel, and the inflammation is usually found in the rectum and the sigmoid colon, but can be found anywhere along the large bowel.

CD can affect any part of the digestive tube from the mouth to the anus, but is most often found in the area of the junction of the ileum and the caecum (where the small intestine joins the large intestine).

In a minority of cases, of very severe UC, surgery is needed to remove the whole of the large bowel to stop the debilitating symptoms and to remove the risk of the bowel wall perforating. CD may also involve surgery, in which damaged sections of the digestive tract are cut out. After surgery, CD inflammation may return to a different section of the intestine. The depth of the intestinal wall that is affected is usually greater in CD than UC.

In other words, while there can be mild versions of UC and Crohn's, both these conditions can be severe and very troublesome. Anti-inflammatory drugs are prescribed, but usually they do not cure the disease. Rather these conditions tend to fluctuate between quiescent and active phases, but rarely cease altogether.

There is evidence that people with IBD have a different mixture of microbes in the microflora of the gut lining and, as probiotics can influence both microflora and immune system, IBD has been one of the conditions for which probiotics has been an obvious target.

Evidence of probiotic benefit

The evidence of benefit from probiotics in UC is strong, while the evidence in Crohn's is weak. At the time of writing, there have been eight controlled trials involving people with UC and seven of these showed significant benefit. Of the seven successful trials, probiotics were shown to extend periods of remission or reduce active disease [38]. For example, an *E. coli* probiotic was found to be as effective as the standard drug for UC (but without the side-effects) in preventing a relapse [39].

In comparison, several controlled trials of probiotics in people with CD have shown no benefit. Only a small controlled study using the probiotic yeast, *Saccharomyces boulardii,* has shown benefit in Crohn's. It is not known why CD has not been responsive to most probiotics so far. Recently, researchers discovered that a particular bacterium, *Faecalibacterium prausnitzii*, was reduced in numbers on the intestinal lining of people with Crohn's [40]. This bacterium was also shown to have anti-inflammatory properties. It remains to be seen whether a probiotic containing this species might prove more effective in reducing Crohn's symptoms.

Prebiotics and IBD

*Pre*biotics, foods that boost bifidobacteria numbers in the gut microflora (see chapter 11), have been shown to reduce inflammation in rodents with colitis [41]. Several small studies have also used *pre*biotics with UC patients, with some encouraging improvements. More studies are however needed to confirm that *pre*biotics definitely reduce UC disease.

Pouchitis

If the large intestine of a person with severe UC is surgically removed (as explained above), the surgeon may fashion a replacement for the colon. The end of the small intestine (ileum) is sewn into the shape of a bag and is attached to the anus. This 'ileo-anal pouch' acts like a small colon in which faeces are stored until the person is ready to excrete them normally. In about a quarter of cases [42], an inflammation of the pouch occurs, know as pouchitis. The symptoms are similar to those of UC.

Probiotics have been tested to prevent pouchitis. A single-strain probiotic was ineffective, but a high-dose multi-strain probiotic used in two studies was successful [43]. Among patients at high risk of a relapse of pouchitis inflammation, after one year of trial only 15% of the probiotic group had relapsed compared with almost all of the placebo group.

The *pre*biotic inulin was also tested on a group of patients with pouchitis and, after three weeks, the symptoms were significantly reduced compared to the placebo group.

Lactose intolerance

The term 'lactose intolerance' refers to the inability of some adults to digest the sugar lactose, which is present in milk. Lactose is digested by the enzyme lact*ase*. Those with lactose intolerance produce too little lactase to digest much of the milk sugar, and the undigested lactose causes intestinal difficulties.

The majority of the population in Europe and North America are unaffected by lactose intolerance, but in many other parts of the world, a majority are affected by this condition. For them, "lactase activity is high at birth, decreases in childhood and adolescence, and remains low in adulthood" [44]. Those with low lactase levels may be able to digest small amounts of milk, and studies suggest that most people who are lactose intolerant can tolerate 12.5g-25g of milk a day without significant symptoms developing [45].

When people with lactose intolerance consume milk they may suffer from excess gas, bloating, diarrhoea cramps, abdominal rumblings and flatulence, with occasional nausea and vomiting in severe cases.

The excess gas is probably caused by the gut microflora fermenting the lactose. The diarrhoea may be caused by an osmotic response to the lactose, leading to high water content in the faeces being maintained.

Yoghurt benefits

Yoghurt is particularly helpful in reducing the symptoms of lactose intolerance. Numerous studies have shown better lactose digestion and less flatulence in lactose-intolerant people who consumed nonheated yoghurt rather than milk or pasteurised yoghurt [44]. One study reported a two-thirds improvement in lactose digestion using yoghurt rather than milk [46].

The bacteria that turn milk into yoghurt (*Lactobacillus bulgaricus* and *Streptococcus thermophilus*) produce significant quantities of their own lactase enzyme. Evidence suggests that they are able to digest lactose in the live yoghurt product, but also to continue such digestion in the small intestine once the yoghurt has been eaten [22]. Not only is less gas produced, but diarrhoea is reduced or eliminated.

Yoghurt also slows down the rate at which milk passes through the intestine, allowing more time for lactase to digest the lactose. It is likely that yoghurt takes longer than milk to travel through the intestine because of its thicker consistency.

There is a small amount of evidence that the Russian fermented milk *kefir* is also effective in reducing lactose intolerance [47]. Studies on a range of other fermented milks (containing different bacteria) showed significantly less effect in digesting lactose [48]. Thus not all fermented milks have the same characteristics.

Other probiotics

Probiotic products in capsule, tablet or powder form (e.g. *Lactobacillus* and *Bifidobacterium* species used in non-milk products) do not appear to be as effective as yoghurt in alleviating lactose intolerance.

*Pre*biotics should be able to increase the number of lactobacilli in the microflora, which in turn should increase the digestion of lactose without the development of excess gas. One small study has supported this theory. Nine people with lactose intolerance received 10g of lactulose twice daily for a three-week period. Eight had improved symptoms, including three who had improved so much they no longer met the criteria for lactose intolerance [49].

Gastritis and stomach ulcers

Helicobacter pylori is a bacterium that causes gastritis, which is an inflammation of the mucosa (lining) of the stomach. Such infection is very common, with about half of the world's human population infected. In developing countries, *H. pylori* infection may occur in up to 80% of the population. In developed countries it is present in about 20% of people under age 30, and in 40-60% of those aged 60 [50].

Once a person's stomach has been infected by *H. pylori*, the infection tends to remain unless it is treated with drugs. The good news is that the great majority of infected individuals (about 85%) have no symptoms and are unaware of any infection. The symptoms of gastritis are abdominal pain, nausea and vomiting. Such disease also occurs in the duodenum (the first part of the small intestine).

If symptomatic gastritis is left untreated, the lining of the stomach and duodenum may become so damaged that ulcers are formed, which can be very painful. Furthermore, there is a statistical association between *H. pylori* infection and cancer of the stomach. Eradication of *H. pylori* from the stomach and duodenum is therefore an important goal.

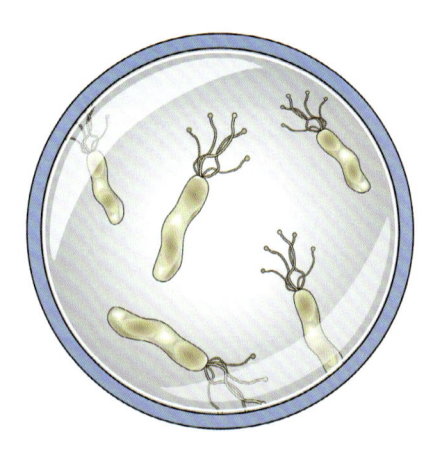

Fig 18: Helicobacter pylori

The standard treatment for eradicating *H. pylori* is the use of three drugs simultaneously. This triple therapy, consisting of two antibiotics and another type of drug (proton pump inhibitor), is usually very successful in eliminating the pathogen. But it is expensive, causes side effects, promotes antibiotic-resistant strains of *H. pylori* and fails in about 10% of cases [51].

In order to overcome the growing problem of antibiotic-resistant strains of *H. pylori*, a fourth antibiotic has been added to the standard drug cocktail, making a 'quadruple' therapy. This makes treatment even more expensive, and increases the likelihood of drug side-effects. The main side-effects are diarrhoea, vomiting, nausea, and taste disturbance. It is in the context of reduced effectiveness of expensive treatment that consideration has been given to a possible role for probiotics.

Studies using probiotics alone have not shown eradication of *H. pylori*. However, several studies have found that if probiotics are used in conjunction with the standard drugs, the rate of eradication is greater than by drug therapy alone [52]. Furthermore, the incidence of adverse side-effects from the drug therapy is halved by probiotics [50].

Most of the studies used lactobacilli, but not all strains of *Lactobacillus* were effective in reducing *H. pylori* [4,18].

	Positive RCTs*	How strong evidence?	Average benefit	Other comments
Infectious diarrhoea	> 25	Very strong, with almost all studies positive. 2,000 participants.	Duration of diarrhoea reduced by 30 hours.	Most studies with children. Reduces both viral and bacterial infection.
Lactose intolerance	> 20	Strong, with yoghurt the most effective probiotic.	Lactose and symptoms reduced by two-thirds.	Yoghurt bacteria (L. bulgaricus and S. thermophilus) very helpful.
Antibiotic-associated diarrhoea (AAD)	13	Good, but some studies failed.	AAD rate reduced by half.	Higher dosage more effective (i.e. >5 billion cells per day).
Ulcerative colitis	7	Good, but one study failed.	Prolonged remission equivalent to standard drug.	Some evidence of active disease reduction.
Irritable bowel syndrome (IBS)	7	Mixed results, but more recent studies positive.	Symptoms reduced, especially bloating and flatulence.	More large studies needed.
Gastritis and stomach ulcers	3	Similar number of positive and neutral results.	Standard drugs more effective in eliminating H. pylori.	Consistently fewer side effects from drugs.
Constipation	5	Moderate improvement.	20-50% increase in bowel movements.	*Prebiotics* may also help.

Fig 19: A summary of evidence of benefit from probiotics in seven intestinal conditions.

* Number of randomised controlled trials (RCTs) that have given positive results for probiotics.

7

Probiotic Benefits for Other Parts of the Body

The previous chapter described the benefits of probiotics for diseases of the intestine. But are there any other parts of the body that may benefit from probiotics?

The answer should be yes, for two reasons. There are microflora in different parts of the body, not just the intestine, and therefore there is potential for influencing these other areas. Furthermore, the immune system (IS) is connected to all parts of the body and so by influencing one part of the IS, probiotics may be able to influence others.

In this chapter, we will first consider the effects of probiotics on the systemic IS and then consider effects of probiotics on the non-intestinal microflora.

The systemic immune system

The mucosal IS is limited to the main surfaces of the body, such as the skin, nasal passages and intestine, while the systemic IS covers the whole of the body. The latter involves the distribution of immune cells and molecules through the blood and lymph systems. If you are unfamiliar with the IS, you may find it helpful to read Chapter 4.

Diseases of the systemic IS are mostly either allergies or autoimmune diseases. Allergies, such as asthma, hay fever, atopic eczema and allergic rhinitis, occur when harmless substances (such as food molecules) are interpreted by the IS as being harmful and reacts against them.

In autoimmune diseases, the IS misreads the body's own cells or chemicals as being foreign and attacks them. There is a range of autoimmune diseases, including multiple sclerosis, rheumatoid arthritis and type 1 diabetes [1].

Allergies

Can probiotics help prevent allergies? Almost all studies examining this question have focused on children and, so far, it is only in atopic eczema (dermatitis) that probiotics have shown effectiveness.

For example, a group of Finnish women, with a family background of allergies, consumed a probiotic and reduced the rate of chronic eczema in their infants by two-thirds [2]. In this randomised controlled trial, half of the mothers consumed the probiotic during the last two weeks of pregnancy and for the first three months of breastfeeding. The other group of mothers consumed a look-a-like placebo. At age two, 15% of the 'probiotic' infants had developed chronic eczema, compared with 47% of the 'placebo' infants.

At the time of writing, there have been 17 randomised trials of probiotics given to mothers or infants to prevent allergies, and only half of them have given positive results [3]. It is not clear why the study results are contradictory.

Assuming that a way can be found to develop probiotics that give a consistently positive effect in infants, how might such probiotics work? How is it that the addition of probiotic bacteria to the intestine of a mother can help reduce allergic skin disease in her child? The reasoning is based on the 'old friends' hypothesis (as described in Chapter 4) in which it is argued that the rise of allergic diseases is due to the absence of certain types of microbes from the intestines of people in developed countries [4].

Examination of the intestinal contents of children with atopic eczema or allergic sensitisation, has shown that the mix of microfloral species is somewhat different from that of children without allergies. There are fewer bifidobacteria (a type of probiotic microbe) in the intestines of children with these allergies than in children without allergies. Furthermore, this shortage of bifidobacteria *precedes* the development of eczema [5,6,7,8].

Probiotics influencing the IS

How do probiotic microbes improve the functioning of a person's immune system? The precise mechanisms are not yet clear, but such an effect should not be surprising, because the wall of the intestine is full of immune tissues and cells. Together, these tissues and cells are known as the gut-associated lymphoid tissue (GALT). The GALT is the largest and most complex part of the human immune system [9], and it contains about half of all lymphocytes in the body [10].

Why is the GALT so substantial? This is probably because the gut wall, especially the wall of the small intestine, has two diametrically opposite tasks. It has to be open to the absorption of digested food molecules, and it has to be closed to pathogens and toxins. Only by having a highly complex and specialised immune system in the mucosa (inner lining) of the gut wall is it able to accomplish both these tasks.

With such a concentration of immune tissues and cells in the gut wall and the known influence of the gut microflora on the GALT, there is clearly potential for probiotics to improve immune function.

Immune system actions in the intestinal mucosa can have an effect on the rest of the body, because immune cells and molecules can circulate in the body via the lymph and blood vessels.

Therefore, in the case of the Finnish mothers referred to at the beginning of this chapter, the probiotic bacteria probably worked by improving the functioning of the mother's immune system. Subsequently, immune molecules travelled in the mother's bloodstream and crossed the placenta into the unborn child. And then, on being born, the infant consumed more helpful immune molecules as part of the mother's milk. By improving the immature immune system of the baby, the tendency to allergic dermatitis is reduced [2].

Some studies in which probiotics are fed to newly-born infants have also shown positive effects in preventing eczema, although perhaps not as effectively as when mothers consumed the probiotic [11].

*Pre*biotics, which are carbohydrates that increase the numbers of bifidobacteria in the intestine (see Chapter 11), have also been shown to prevent atopic eczema. A group of 200 infants (with a parental history of allergies) were fed a *pre*biotic mixture or a placebo. At age 6 months, the *pre*biotic group had half the rate of atopic eczema compared with the placebo group [12]. Although no *pre*biotics were given after the age of five months, the benefit was maintained at least until the age of 2 years [13].

In addition to studies on the *preventive* capabilities of probiotics, there have also been studies on the use of probiotics as a *treatment* for atopic eczema. The results, so far, have been mixed, with benefits possibly associated with particular strains [14,15]. A clear picture has not yet developed as to which species or strains are best against atopic eczema.

It is also not clear whether adults with allergies might be helped by probiotics, or whether such benefits will occur solely in children. Infants have been used in most studies, because they have an immature IS which is probably easier to influence [16,17].

Can probiotics help with other allergies?

Studies of probiotics with the intention of preventing asthma or allergic rhinitis have usually not been positive [18]. This does not mean that probiotics will never be able to help other allergies. A study of adults consuming live yoghurt for a year found that the 'yoghurt group' had a significantly lower level of nasal allergy than the no-yoghurt group [19]. Perhaps, in the future, improved strains and probiotic products will be able to help reduce non-eczema allergies.

As for autoimmune diseases, there have not been sufficient studies to say whether probiotics will prove beneficial in such conditions.

Female urogenital infections

In Chapter 2, the female reproductive system was described as having a microflora. In a healthy woman, the uterus is sterile, while the vagina has a resident microbial population. These resident microbes live on the lining of the vagina wall, and most of them are lactobacilli. If the vaginal microflora is disturbed and *Lactobacillus* numbers fall, an infection of the vagina may develop.

Furthermore, the vaginal lactobacilli also appear to have a protective influence against infections of the urinary tract. This is not surprising as the urethra (tube from the bladder) has its opening close to the opening of the vagina.

Vaginal infections

Vaginitis is the term for inflammation of the vaginal lining, and such inflammation is caused by a pathogenic infection. The infection is treated by antibiotics (against bacteria) or anti-fungals (against yeasts). These drug treatments are usually effective in eliminating symptoms. There are, however, a substantial number of women in whom this type of infection recurs following standard treatment. On each recurrence, the infection becomes more difficult to treat.

The discomfort caused by a vaginal infection and the limited value of drug treatments has led women to consider other treatments, including probiotics. In fact, yoghurt has been used as a remedy for decades [20,21].

Bacterial vaginosis

If vaginitis is caused by a bacterium, it is known as bacterial vaginosis (BV). The symptoms of BV are a burning sensation during urination, itching in the vaginal area, and a greyish vaginal discharge with a fishy smell.

A wide range of bacteria can cause BV [20] and it is not clear why BV recurs in some women and not others. One possible explanation is that certain pathogens form biofilms, which are hard to eradicate. A biofilm is a community of microbes that forms on a surface and is bound together by sticky carbohydrate produced by the bacteria. In some women with recurrent BV, biofilms have been found which contain the pathogen *Gardnerella vaginalis* [22]. Biofilms with *G. vaginalis* are very resistant to antibiotic treatment.

Compared with healthy women, those with BV have, on average, 95% fewer lactobacilli in their vagina, and a substantial increase in the numbers and types of other bacteria, many of which will be pathogens [23].

Some types of lactobacilli produce hydrogen peroxide (H_2O_2), and women with such strains in their vaginal microflora are less likely to develop BV [24]. Furthermore, there is evidence that women who also have such H_2O_2-secreting lactobacilli in their intestine have an even lower-risk of acquiring BV. This suggests that beneficial bacteria in the rectum act as a reservoir to supplement the vaginal microflora when it becomes disturbed.

This information has encouraged the development of probiotics to protect the female reproductive system. Six studies undertaken on the effectiveness of probiotics in *treating* women with BV have shown mixed results. Two studies had cure rates from the probiotic at more than double the rate of the non-probiotic group. Two other studies had no effect, and a further two showed probiotics helping, but not at a statistically-significant level. The one study of BV *prevention* found probiotics effective [25].

Vaginal candidiasis

If vaginitis is caused by a fungus, in almost every case it will be a *Candida*-type of fungus. In such circumstances, the disease is known as vaginal candidiasis (VC) or colloquially as 'thrush'. Symptoms of VC are similar to BV, but the discharge is white.

Candida fungus usually exists in yeast form (individual cells), but sometimes these cells form a long chain (pseudohyphae) and some species of *Candida* are able to form a mycelium, which is a network of fine filaments. Such ability to change form makes *Candida* a particularly difficult pathogen to eradicate [26].

Candida species are found in the mouth, the intestine or the vagina in at least one-third of healthy women [27]. Although it is a pathogen, candida numbers are kept under control by the normal microflora [28], such that no symptoms are experienced. When a microflora is disturbed, an opportunity arises for *Candida* to become a dominant microbe and cause disease.

One of the main triggers for such a yeast infection is the use of antibiotics [29]. Antibiotics do not kill yeasts, and so if the antibiotics disturb the vaginal or the gut microflora, *Candida* cells are likely to increase in number. Also, the use of corticosteroids or other immunosuppressive drugs alters the functioning of the immune system and aids *Candida* infection [30].

The species of *Candida* that is the main cause of infection in humans is *Candida albicans*, but other species do cause candidiasis, including *C. glabrata*, *C. paripsilosis* and *C. tropicalis* [31].

Candidiasis of the vagina (and of the mouth and the skin) is known as 'superficial'. There is another type of candidiasis, known as 'systemic'. This involves the passage of candida cells into the bloodstream and the formation of colonies anywhere in the body. Such systemic infection can be very serious and is difficult to treat [32]. It is therefore important to control *Candida* infection while it is still superficial.

Only a small number of clinical studies have been undertaken of probiotics against *Candida*. Most of these were concerned with prevention of *Candida* infection and all but one had positive results [21,33,34]. However, a large multi-centre study was ineffective [35], possibly due to product and strain differences.

It should also be noted that there has been one study in which probiotics were taken at the same time as antifungal drugs, and the effectiveness of the antifungal was significantly improved [36].

Urinary tract infections

The urinary system maintains the proper amount of water in the body, and removes waste products in urine. It consists of two main organs: the kidneys and the bladder. Urine is produced by the kidneys and stored in the bladder. When the bladder becomes full, the urine is excreted via a tube known as the urethra.

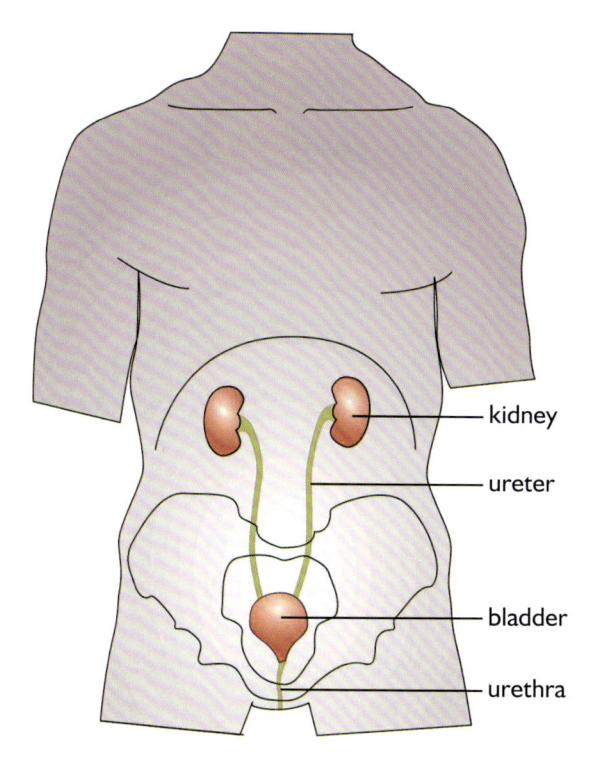

Fig 20: The urinary system

There is no microflora of the urinary system, although there may be a few microbes in the lower urethra near the exit out of the body. These microbes are transient, and are normally kept to small numbers, because the flow of urine tends to flush them away.

A urinary tract infection (UTI) is an infection of any part of the urinary system. Such infections are more common in women, and infections of the urethra are the most common form of UTI. If the infection spreads to the bladder it is known as cystitis. The infection may also spread to the kidneys, which can be a serious condition. It is therefore important to ensure that UTIs are treated effectively.

The symptoms of UTI are frequent urination associated with burning pain. The urine may be cloudy and sometimes it contains blood and pus. A range of pathogens cause the infection, but mainly they are Gram-negative bacteria, especially *E. coli*. With *E. coli* being the main causal agent of UTIs, this gives a clue as to the route of infection. *E. coli* is regularly found in the intestine and presumably it passes from the anus to the urethra.

It may be that pathogens in an infected vagina may also cause a UTI [37]. In fact, several studies have strongly suggested this is the case [38]. The opposite may also be true. If there are plenty of lactobacilli in the vaginal microflora, it may be that they will protect the urethra from pathogens, whatever their source.

Antibiotics are the normal treatment for UTIs and are usually effective. In a study of college women with acute cystitis only 6% failed to respond [39]. Unfortunately, about one quarter of women who experience an initial infection will have recurrent episodes [40].

The small number of studies of probiotics to prevent UTIs have given mixed results, but with enough encouraging responses to warrant further trials [37].

Methods of delivery

The probiotics used in positive studies for BV, VC and UTI took a number of forms. Some were taken by mouth and some were added directly to the vagina. Among the oral probiotics, some were in yoghurt or fermented-milk form, and some were freeze-dried products such as powders or capsules.

How can an oral probiotic influence the female reproductive system? The answer is not certain, but it seems likely that probiotic bacteria in the faeces may move to the nearby vaginal area. Most probiotic bacteria are not motile (do not move independently) as they do not have flagella (whip-like structures). Therefore, they may arrive at the vagina as a consequence of being dislodged by the natural movement of the body.

Another way in which oral probiotics could influence the female reproductive system is by affecting the gut immune system, which in turn may alter the immune tissues of the vaginal wall.

The vaginally-inserted probiotics were mostly in suppository (pessary) form. A suppository is a solid block that, on being inserted into the vagina, melts at body temperature, releasing the contents. In one study, a probiotic-containing tampon was used, and in another a douche was used. A douche is a procedure in which warm water is introduced into the vagina under low pressure. Normally, the water of a douche will contain a medication or a cleansing agent, but in this case it contained probiotic microbes.

It is not clear whether one method of delivery of probiotics is superior to another, although this might be clarified with further study.

Prebiotics

*Pre*biotics may also have a role in promoting urogenital health. As explained in Chapter 11, *pre*biotics are carbohydrates that increase the number of lactobacilli and bifidobacteria in the intestine. It is possible that *pre*biotics, by improving the gut microflora, may be able to improve the vaginal microflora and urethral health.

This potential was illustrated in a study involving patients in long-term hospital care. Those that received lactulose (a well-studied *pre*biotic) to relieve constipation, were found to have a much lower rate of UTI. One out of 17 patients in the lactulose group developed a UTI over a six-month period, compared with 21 out of 28 in the non-lactulose group [41].

The mouth

The mouth is highly populated with microbes, with the highest concentration on or around the teeth. Most discussions about the use of probiotics in the mouth centre on how they may be able to reduce gum disease and dental caries (tooth decay).

Dental caries

Dental caries is a process of tooth decay in which the external surface (enamel) is broken down by microbes in plaque. On breaking through the enamel, the bacteria attack the inner dentine until the tooth dies or is removed because of the associated pain. This process can be avoided by regular brushing of the teeth to remove plaque. Also, reduction in sugar consumption reduces the destructive effect of the plaque microbes.

The role of probiotics in reducing dental caries has been a matter of some debate. Although lactic acid-producing bacteria are generally considered beneficial to health, it has been uncertain whether lactic acid and other organic acids produced by probiotic bacteria might increase tooth decay [42]. Currently, it is not clear which bacteria within plaque are the primary instigator of caries.

Despite these uncertainties, a number of probiotic studies have been undertaken. In one study, 594 children attending day-care centres consumed milk either with or without lactobacilli for seven months. The group receiving the probiotic had 45% fewer cases of dental caries than the control group [43].

In another study, 74 young adults consumed a cheese either with or without lactobacilli for three weeks. It was found subsequently that the numbers of an oral pathogen, *Streptococcus mutans*, were significantly lower in the probiotic group [44]. Two studies have used bifidobacteria, and both these showed a reduction in *S. mutans* numbers.

Gum disease

Diseased gums are inflamed, and bleed easily. The disease is caused by a build-up of plaque, in which the microbes in the plaque trigger inflammation in the soft tissue surrounding the teeth. Mild gum disease is known as gingivitis and the severe form is periodontitis. The latter weakens support for the teeth and causes them to loosen and eventually fall out. It is therefore important to alter or reduce plaque so that it does not cause gum disease.

A controlled trial was undertaken on people with gum disease, and this found that the *Lactobacillus* probiotic reduced the degree of gingivitis in the study participants [45]. Two other studies also gave encouraging results, but all the studies were for relatively short periods of time, and the improvements were quite small [46].

Probiotics have also been developed for the reduction of halitosis (bad breath) or for overcoming oral thrush (a fungal infection).

Halitosis

When the microflora of the tongue of people with halitosis was compared with the microflora of people without bad breath, it was found that those with halitosis were lacking a bacterium called *Streptococcus salivarius* [47].

A lozenge containing a strain of *S. salivarius* was sucked (following the use of a mouthwash) by a group of people with halitosis. The probiotic lozenge was more effective than placebo in reducing bad breath. Another study, using a different probiotic bacterium, *Weissella cibaria*, in a gargle rinse reduced halitosis through inhibition of the production of sulphur compounds [48].

Oral thrush

An overgrowth of *Candida* yeast in the mouth (oral thrush) is a common occurrence in the elderly. A study was undertaken, in which 192 elderly people consumed a probiotic cheese or an ordinary cheese for 16 weeks. Those consuming the probiotic cheese were found to have only one-quarter the risk of developing oral thrush [49].

Methods of delivery

Not only have there been too few studies to say how effective probiotics are in oral diseases, but also it is not clear which methods of delivery are most effective.

In the various studies described, the probiotic microbes have been carried in yoghurt, ice cream, cheese, capsules, lozenges, mouthwash, chewing gum and drinking straws. In time, the most useful approaches will become clearer.

Upper respiratory tract

The upper respiratory tract (URT) consists of the nose, throat and windpipe. This is the main route through which air enters the lungs. The lungs are the organs that enable oxygen to enter the bloodstream.

The nose and throat have a microflora, and the upper part of the windpipe has a changing microbial population as cilia move mucus upwards to the throat (see Chapter 2).

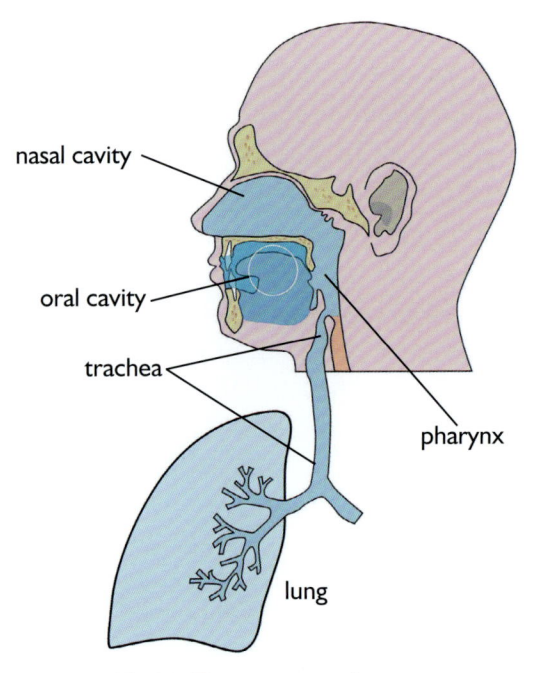

Fig 21: The upper respiratory tract

There are a number of diseases of the URT, including the common cold, sore throat, and the much more serious diphtheria. Infection of the URT may spread to the lungs, especially among the elderly, leading to such conditions as bronchitis and pneumonia.

The common cold is caused by a virus, of which there are many different types. Infection is mainly in the nose and involves sneezing, excessive mucus secretion and swelling of the nasal membranes. The throat may also be affected. Colds are particularly common among children, because they have not yet built up immunity to the wide range of viruses. Sore throat is caused by a variety of bacteria and viruses, including the bacterium *Streptococcus pyogenes*.

There have been 15 controlled studies testing the effect of probiotics in preventing respiratory tract infections (RTIs). The results suggest that probiotics do not usually reduce the risk of acquiring such an infection, but they do seem to reduce the severity and the duration of the condition. The benefit in reduced severity of RTIs by probiotics was in the range of 25-50% [50].

In one study involving 479 healthy adults over three months, the group consuming a multi-strain probiotic recovered more quickly from episodes of common cold by almost two days. The severity of the symptoms were also reduced [51].

Although a clear majority of studies showed no protection from acquiring such infections, three recent studies have all shown such benefits from probiotics. These recent studies showed a reduced risk of acquiring RTIs of between one-quarter and one-half [52,53,54]. It may be that the contradictory evidence for prevention against RTI is due to differences in the characteristics of the strains used.

Delivery and species

Most URT studies used oral probiotics, so the mechanism of action is likely to be by influencing the gut immune tissues, which in turn influences the mucosal tissues of the nose and throat.

The possibility of preventing RTIs by directly adding probiotic microbes into the nose has also been considered. In one study, adults who were nasal carriers of pathogenic strains of *Staphylococcus aureus* had nonpathogenic strains of the same species added to their noses. The nonpathogenic strains colonised the nose if added after a course of antibiotics, and pathogenic strains did not re-establish themselves. If the antibiotic was used without the addition of the non-pathogen, the original pathogen soon reappeared [55].

Although almost all of the effective probiotics against URT infection contained the usual type of microbes (lactobacilli or bifidobacteria), there has been some consideration of other types of probiotic bacteria. For example, streptococci that secrete an antibacterial substance, viridin, appear to inhibit pathogenic strains of streptococci. Furthermore, several studies have been undertaken in which patients with tonsillitis sprayed their throats with viridin-producing streptococci (following antibiotic treatment), and the rate of recurrence of tonsillitis was significantly lower in the viridin group [56,57].

Influenza vaccination

Probiotics may also improve the effectiveness of influenza vaccination in the elderly. The immune response to such a vaccination was found to be better in a group of elderly people who took a probiotic four weeks before and nine weeks after vaccination [58]. This improved immune reaction may mean an increased protection against acquiring influenza, although this is yet to be confirmed.

The skin

There is a close interrelationship between the microflora, the surface barrier and the immune system of the skin, as with other body surfaces. The difference from other surfaces is that the skin is a relatively harsh environment for microfloral species.

There is, however, still scope for the use of probiotics as a preventative and treatment for skin diseases. Oral consumption of a probiotic has provided some protection against ultraviolet radiation from the sun. Topical application of a cream containing *Vitreoscilla filiformis* (a thermal spa water bacterium) has exerted beneficial effects in patients with seborrhoeic dermatitis and atopic eczema [59]. And, as described earlier in this chapter, lactic acid bacteria have provided some protection from atopic eczema in infants.

Furthermore, a *pre*biotic skin cream has been developed with some encouraging results in controlling *Propionibacterium acnes* (an acne-associated bacterium).

These are early days, however, and much more research will be needed before probiotics become routinely used for skin conditions.

Summary of main points

- ❖ There is some evidence that probiotics can reduce the risk in infants of developing atopic eczema, by influencing the systemic immune system.
- ❖ Yoghurts, topically applied, have been used as a remedy for vaginal infections for decades.
- ❖ Formal studies of the effectiveness of probiotics in vaginal infections have given mixed results.
- ❖ There is potential for the use of probiotics in reducing bad breath, oral thrush, gum disease and dental caries.
- ❖ Probiotics can help reduce the severity and duration of upper respiratory tract infections, such as the common cold and sore throats.
- ❖ Early studies suggest that probiotics (and *pre*biotics) can protect against ultraviolet radiation, seborrhoeic dermatitis and acne.

8

Safety

The consumption of probiotics usually involves the pouring of millions of microbes down your throat. Is this safe?

Probiotic microbes have a history of safe use (see Chapter 5). There is, however, no such thing as a 100% safe microbe. So what type of risk is there and how great is it? These questions can be considered by focusing on the areas of greatest debate about probiotic safety:

❖ infection risks

❖ spread of antibiotic resistance

❖ the immunocompromised person

❖ the unborn child.

Infection risks

In very rare occasions, an infection is caused by a microbial strain from a probiotic product [1]. Such infection is usually found in the blood (bacteraemia) or in the lining of the heart (endocarditis), the latter being dangerous if not treated quickly.

Of the different types of probiotic microbes, infection does not appear to have occurred from bifidobacteria probiotics [1] or from enterococcus probiotics. There is also no evidence that any strains of probiotic *E. coli* have caused infection. The spore-forming bacterium, *Bacillus subtilis*, was thought to be an occasional infector [2,3], but more recent information has suggested that most, if not all, reported cases involved other species of *Bacillus* rather than *B. subtilis* [4].

There have been a number of cases of fungal infection from the yeast, *Saccharomyces boulardii*, but these cases appear to be limited to hospital patients in which the fungus entered into the blood via a catheter. It is thought that, on opening the packet, some yeast cells floated through the air and alighted on openings in the skin [5]. By preparing the probiotic in a separate room, the risk from *S. boulardii* is greatly reduced.

Lactobacillus bacteria from probiotic products have been responsible for some cases of infection, although these have been very rare. The rarity of such cases was reinforced by a population study in Finland, in which it was found that during a period when lactobacillus consumption increased six-fold, there was no change in the rate of *Lactobacillus* bacteraemia cases [6,7].

On the very rare occasions when lactobacilli do cause infection [8], treatment is straightforward as there are plenty of antibiotics available to which they are sensitive.

Spread of antibiotic resistance

Antibiotic drugs, first introduced in the 1940s, have dramatically improved the effectiveness of our fight against infectious diseases caused by bacterial pathogens. But these great improvements are under threat, because bacteria resistant to antibiotics have arisen as a consequence of the overuse and misuse of antibiotic drugs.

The ability of bacteria to resist antibiotics is carried by specific genes. When antibiotic drugs are taken, those pathogenic bacteria that have such genes tend to survive, while the pathogens without resistance genes tend to be killed. The more frequently antibiotic drugs are taken, the more likely that resistant strains of bacteria will become common.

A further complication is that some resistant strains have become resistant to more than one type of antibiotic, thus making them even more difficult to eradicate. These multiply-resistant bacteria, sometimes referred to as 'superbugs', are causing great concern. In response, the World Health Organisation produced a report in 2001 that stressed the seriousness of the problem and urged co-ordinated action by health authorities and doctors to counter the rise of resistant bacteria [9].

Multiple-resistance occurs when bacteria receive resistance genes from other microbes. Those genes are usually donated through physical contact between different strains and species. The question therefore arises whether probiotic bacteria have antibiotic resistance characteristics, and whether these characteristics can be passed on to pathogens in the gut to create new types of superbugs [10].

In fact, antibiotic resistance exists naturally in many different types of microbe, including probiotic bacteria [11,12]. In most cases, such resistance is not shared with other bacteria. Usually the non-shared resistance genes are found on the chromosome within the bacterial cell, while the sharable type of resistance gene tends to be carried in a circular piece of DNA known as a plasmid [13].

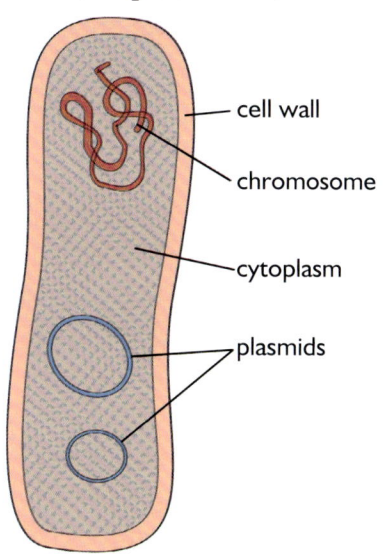

Fig 22: Chromosome and plasmids within a bacterium

In some strains of *Lactobacillus*, resistance genes have been found on both chromosomes and plasmids [14,15]. The resistance genes on the chromosome are not transferred, and it is rare for lactobacilli to transfer their plasmids [6].

The gene for resistance to the antibiotic tetracycline has been found in some strains of bifidobacteria [11,16,17], but there is no clear evidence of gene-sharing by such bifidobacteria. *Bacillus subtilis* strains also have some antibiotic-resistance genes, but they are not against any antibiotics important in medical and veterinary treatment, as listed in a report of the European Food Safety Authority [18,19].

The only probiotic bacteria in which the sharing of resistance genes is a substantial theoretical risk is *Enterococcus*. Species of *Enterococcus* are known to be 'promiscuous' with genetic material; not only in receiving such material, but also in passing it on to other bacteria [20]. Enterococci should therefore be used cautiously as probiotics, perhaps with a restriction to only those strains that have a much-reduced tendency to promiscuity. It is also important not to confuse two *Enterococcus* species with similar names: *E. faecalis* and *E. faecium*. The former is far more likely to carry antibiotic resistance genes than the latter, and is also known to carry some pathogenic genes [21].

As concern about the rise of multiply-resistant bacteria grows, it is likely that there will be a greater demand for probiotic companies to check the level of risk of their strains spreading resistance genes.

The immunocompromised person

The immune system (IS) has the sole function of defending the body from attack by harmful substances and microbes. It consists of specialist cells and molecules that are found in and are circulated between various tissues, vessels and organs. It is essential for the IS to work well, otherwise the body may be harmed and the person become disabled or even killed.

When the IS is not working well, the body is said to be 'immunocompromised'. Such a weakened IS can be caused by a range of factors, including illness and particular drug treatments. The IS also tends to be weaker in young children (when the IS has not had time to develop fully) and in the elderly (when the general ageing process also weakens the IS).

An immunocompromised person is more likely to develop an infection, and logically such a person may have an increased risk of infection from probiotic microbes. But does such an increased risk exist? A good way of looking at this question is to consider those infected with the HIV virus.

HIV/AIDS

The 'human immunodeficiency virus' (HIV) attacks the immune system by infecting various types of immune cells, especially T cells. The infection of T cells causes them to die or be killed by other immune cells. Despite new T cells being produced, the number of T cells in the body declines. When T-cell numbers fall below a certain level, the infected person starts to develop various additional infections, and sometimes cancers.

When such infections develop, the HIV infection is said to have caused 'acquired immunodeficiency syndrome' (AIDS). In AIDS, the body is vulnerable to infections that normally it would be able to resist.

People with HIV/AIDS therefore have substantially weakened immune systems, and consequently if probiotics carry a risk among the immunocompromised, then such a risk should be seen in people who are HIV-positive.

A *Lactobacillus* strain was given to eight children with congenital HIV (they acquired the HIV virus from their mother through the placenta). None of these children suffered any side effects from the probiotic or withdrew from the study [22].

In a similar study, this time involving 39 children who acquired HIV from their mothers, all but one of the children finished the three-week probiotic treatment. There were no reported adverse effects, and the children had an increase in their T-cell numbers [23].

And in a study of adults with HIV/AIDS, twelve women received a probiotic-supplemented yoghurt for two weeks without adverse effects. In fact, the T-cell count increased over time, while a group receiving a non-supplemented yoghurt had a slight decrease in T-cell numbers [24].

In another study of adults, eight HIV-infected patients with diarrhoea received a *Lactobacillus* probiotic for two weeks without side effects [25].

All four of these studies involved patients who were not hospitalised and, as such, their symptoms tended to be troublesome but not severe.

Organ transplant patients

Another group of patients who are immunocompromised, are those undergoing organ transplant. In order to help ensure that a transplanted organ is not rejected by the receiving body, drugs are given that suppress immune function.

In a group of 66 patients who had undergone surgery for liver transplant, half received a four-strain probiotic (plus a *pre*biotic) and the other group just received the *pre*biotic. Both groups also received the standard nutrition for such post-surgery patients. There were no side-effects associated with the probiotic and, furthermore, the proportion who developed bacterial infections was much lower in the probiotic group (4% against 48%) [26].

Premature infants

Could probiotics pose a risk to critically ill patients in intensive care units? The term 'critically ill' refers to a person who is extremely ill and at risk of death [27]. The fear with critically ill patients is that they can die from multiple organ failure, and that this process might be accelerated if probiotic microbes crossed over a 'leaky gut' wall and into the bloodstream.

A group that are at high risk of becoming critically ill are babies born prematurely and/or of very low birthweight (less than 1,500 grams). A condition to which these babies are particularly vulnerable is necrotising enterocolitis (NE). This condition is a severe malfunction of the intestine, which may involve bleeding into the gut, tissue death of parts of the intestinal wall, as well as a state of whole-body inflammation known as sepsis. NE occurs in 5-10% of newly-born babies of very low birthweight, and death from NE occurs in 20-40% of cases. The causes of the condition are not known.

Tiny babies are vulnerable to NE, because their immune system is not fully developed, and premature infants are without protective antibodies from their mothers. A question arises, therefore, whether probiotic microbes are dangerous to such babies.

There have been 11 randomised controlled trials using probiotics in newly-born babies that were of very low birthweight and/or of premature delivery. The risk of developing NE was reduced by between one-half and two-thirds in those given probiotics, and mortality was reduced by half [28,29,30]. Importantly, for our discussion, there were no apparent side effects or harm from the probiotics in this extremely vulnerable group of infants.

Acute pancreatitis

A recent study of probiotics in pancreatitis, however, raises some safety questions. The pancreas is a long thin organ that lies below the stomach. It plays an essential role in the digestion of food, by secreting a pancreatic juice into the duodenum. The juice consists of an alkali that neutralises stomach acid, and various enzymes to digest most types of food.

Pancreatitis is the inflammation of the pancreas and, in acute form, is a serious, potentially life-threatening illness. It is dangerous because if the enzymes leak into the local tissues rather than into the duodenum, the tissues and organs will be damaged. The most common cause of death from pancreatitis is multiple organ failure, and death can be rapid. The most common causes of pancreatitis are excessive alcohol consumption and the blockage of the pancreatic duct by gallstones.

Probiotics were considered as a possible supportive treatment in acute pancreatitis, because it is common for there to be bacterial overgrowth in the small intestine, and for gut bacteria to cross the gut wall into the body.

The probiotics study that showed the unexpected harmful consequence [31] involved participants with acute pancreatitis that were expected to develop a more severe version of the disease. In this large, controlled study, just under 300 patients participated, with one half receiving a probiotic. Thirty-three patients died, which at 11% of the total is within the normal range of deaths for acute pancreatitis [32]. There were, however, 24 deaths in the probiotic group and just 9 deaths in the control group. These deaths were 16% of the probiotic group and 6% of the control group. On discovering the statistics, the study was immediately stopped.

This study caused dismay among scientists involved in probiotic research, partly because the result was unexpected, and partly because the cause was unknown. Examination of those who died found that there were no infections by any of the probiotic bacteria. Most died from multiple organ failure, but it was unclear how probiotic microbes could have contributed to this. At the time of writing, there is still no clear explanation for the harmful effects of the probiotic on the pancreatitis patients.

Until things are clearer, doctors will have to be cautious in their use of probiotics in immunocompromised patients, and will need to examine the evidence for each condition, before using their judgement.

The unborn child

Is it safe to take probiotics during pregnancy? A recent review was undertaken of eight randomised controlled trials (RCT) of probiotics consumed by pregnant women. A total of 1,546 women were involved in the studies, and half of them were treated with probiotics that were either *Lactobacillus* species or in combination with *Bifidobacterium* species.

There were no reported adverse effects (such as increased rate of Caesarean-section or lower infant birthweight) in any of the eight studies.

In six of the studies, the probiotics were taken at 32-34 weeks of pregnancy, while two occurred during the first trimester of pregnancy. In the latter two studies, there were no reports of miscarriages or malformations, but the reviewers commented that it was not possible to conclude that probiotics have no effect on miscarriage or malformation incidence until more studies have been undertaken (Dugoua et al, 2009).

A final thought

Even though, in the great majority of situations, probiotics are extremely safe, it is important to remember that each human being is unique. Even in identical twins, who have identical genes, the action of those genes is influenced by environmental factors (e.g. food, infectious agents, climate, stress). Given that each person is unique, the risk to the health of their body is unique and cannot be completely predicted.

Summary of main points

- Probiotic strains are very safe, but there is a very small risk of infection in vulnerable individuals.
- There is a theoretical risk that genes of resistance to antibiotics can be passed from probiotic strains to pathogens in the human gut (increasing the risk of 'superbug' development).
- Most of those probiotic bacteria that carry antibiotic-resistance genes, do so in a form that is not shared with other microbes.
- The genus *Enterococcus* is prone to sharing genes, and therefore the strains of *Enterococcus* used in probiotics should be checked to ensure they are not carrying shareable resistance genes.
- Studies in people who are immunocompromised (e.g. people with HIV/AIDS, organ transplant patients, premature infants) have shown that there is almost no risk from probiotics.
- A study in patients with severe acute pancreatitis found that probiotics worsened the condition; and therefore there remains a doubt about when it is safe to use probiotics in immunocompromised people.
- A small number of studies of probiotic use in pregnant women have not shown any harm to the unborn child.

Part III

PRACTICAL QUESTIONS AND SOLUTIONS

Choosing a Good Probiotic Product

Types of Probiotic Microbes

What are *Pre*biotics?

Young and Old

Future Developments

~~~

9

Choosing a Good Probiotic Product

If you type 'probiotic products' into an internet search engine, you will find a huge range of products for sale - so many and so varied it can be bemusing and somewhat dispiriting.

How can you choose a good quality product? This is not an easy question to answer, because probiotic products contain live organisms and are therefore vastly more complicated than a drug or a health food product.

An indication of the complicated characteristics of bacteria is given by their genes. An average bacterium will contain about 4,000 genes, while a human being is made from about 25,000 genes. Bearing in mind the huge difference between a human being and a bacterium, it is somewhat surprising that bacteria have such a relatively large number of genes to control a mere microscopic single-cell entity.

Bacteria are thought to be one of the earliest forms of life, and sometimes people assume that bacteria have remained unchanged over the millennia, while other life forms have evolved. Of course, bacteria have to compete with other organisms on a daily basis and therefore they have continued to evolve as well. Bacteria can also access genes from other microbes and therefore have an effective way of increasing the genes available to them.

The purpose of this chapter is to clarify the choices of available probiotics. Key factors in making a choice are covered under five headings:

- ❖ Milk-based or freeze-dried
- ❖ Multi-strain probiotics
- ❖ Types of probiotic microbes
- ❖ Evidence of health benefits
- ❖ Total number of microbes in a product.

Milk-based or freeze-dried

Probiotic microbes are sold in a wide variety of forms. They can be found in cheese, in chocolate bars, in fruit drinks, and even in the straw of a carton drink. But the most common forms, by far, are either in a milk-based product or as freeze-dried powder in a sachet or a capsule.

Milk-based probiotic products

Milk-based probiotics can mostly be found in supermarkets and grocery stores. Although some of these products consist of probiotic microbes added to milk, as in the case of 'acidophilus milk', most milk-based probiotics are a form of yoghurt.

Yoghurt is a semi-solid food formed from milk that has been fermented by two probiotic bacteria: *Streptococcus thermophilus* and *Lactobacillus bulgaricus*.

Milk is a very complex substance, and the fermentation of milk is not yet fully understood. It is known, however, that yoghurt-bacteria produce an enzyme, lactase, which breaks down the milk sugar lactose [1]. About a quarter of the lactose in milk is converted to simpler sugars that are easily absorbed by the bacteria or by the human body. Some yoghurt-bacteria break open as they travel through the stomach and duodenum and consequently release the lactase within their cells [2]. These factors probably explain why people who are lactose intolerant find it easier to digest yoghurt than milk [3].

Furthermore, *L. bulgaricus* is known to break down some of the proteins in milk, and consequently these predigested proteins in the yoghurt can be absorbed more efficiently by the human body [3].

So, it is clear that yoghurt is a particularly nutritious form of milk. Not only does it continue to carry the important minerals of calcium and phosphorus, but also it predigests some of the more complex sugars and proteins.

Sometimes, when yoghurt is produced commercially, it is pasteurised (set) in order to extend its shelf-life. Unfortunately, pasteurisation kills yoghurt-bacteria, and while there will still be nutritional benefits from the set yoghurt, the benefits will not be as great as with yoghurt still containing live bacteria.

A weakness of yoghurt-bacteria is that they are poor at surviving stomach acid, especially *S. thermophilus* [2]. This means that it is uncertain how many of these bacteria are alive and active in the small intestine and colon. There is evidence that the yoghurt bacteria can survive transit through the whole length of the intestine, but it is unclear what proportion survive. It does appear that *L. bulgaricus* is better at surviving than *S. thermophilus* [4,5].

The uncertainty about survival of live yoghurt bacteria in the intestine has led some yoghurt-producing companies to add other types of probiotic bacteria to their yoghurt. The added strains (usually lactobacilli and bifidobacteria) are chosen because their characteristics differ from yoghurt-bacteria.

The proportion of bacteria in yoghurt that dies while on the shelf is unclear, and seems to vary with different products and their strains. Furthermore, as the yoghurt bacteria will still be slightly active even in a refrigerated environment, they will secrete lactic acid and cause the pH of the yoghurt to fall steadily. This more acidic environment may inhibit the growth of some strains of bifidobacteria and may reduce their numbers in the yoghurt [6].

When examining the label on a yoghurt pot, it will usually be clear whether it contains live yoghurt bacteria, and whether it has other added strains; and these are the key points when considering a milk-based probiotic.

Freeze-dried probiotic products

The freeze-drying process (also known as lyophilisation) is a way of safely storing living microbes for a long time. It is quite common for a capsule probiotic product to have a high proportion of its microbes viable for two years.

Products containing freeze-dried probiotic microbes are found in three main forms: capsules, tablets and sachets. Capsules are made of gelatin or a vegetable equivalent, and the product is usually swallowed with a cold drink, because heat above body temperature will kill the microbes. Alternatively, the two halves of the capsule can be pulled apart to pour the probiotic powder into a cool drink or onto cool food.

The main issue with probiotic tablets is whether the bacteria survived when the tablet was manufactured. Tablet formation requires intense pressure to compress the material so that the tablet does not easily disintegrate. Such compression will create heat and this should not be too great, otherwise the probiotic bacteria will die. Most probiotic tablets are produced by special processes that reduce the amount of heat created.

Capsules and tablets may be packaged loosely in jars or tubs, or they may be in 'blister packs'. The former is cheaper, and the latter gives more protection against the effect of water vapour.

Sachets consist of loose freeze-dried powder in paper, plastic or foil packets. They are particularly useful for infants, because the powder can easily be added to a juice drink.

These various freeze-dried products tend to be found anywhere that vitamin and mineral supplements are sold, especially in pharmacies, drug stores and health-food stores. They can also be purchased online or by telephone from specialist distributors or the original manufacturer. Healthcare professionals, including nutritionists, may also recommend particular products, and they may even sell them.

The process of freeze-drying requires special machinery. Essentially, it involves freezing the bacteria and then removing the water. The bacteria become completely inactive, but are still alive. When water is added, they return to their normal living state.

Before freeze-drying, the bacterial mixture has a cryoprotectant added to it. This is a neutral substance that coats the bacteria and helps protect them from the harshness of the freeze-drying process [7].

Freeze-drying undertaken to a high standard should mean that the bacteria remain viable at room temperature, and should not need refrigeration. The viability of such bacteria will, however, be reduced at high temperatures, especially in direct sunlight. Placing freeze-dried capsules in a refrigerator should have no detrimental effect if the container is unopened. But if the capsules are loose within a container, as soon as the sealed container is opened, some water vapour in the air of the refrigerator will start to slowly pass through the capsule wall and gradually kill the bacteria. This is because those bacteria in a capsule that are touched by water molecules will become alive again, but they will have little or no food available. This is less likely to happen if the capsules are in a blister pack, or if the container has a water-absorbing sachet in with the loose capsules.

If the freeze-dried bacteria are in a paper sachet, it is best not to keep them refrigerated, because water vapour can pass through the paper. Plastic and foil sachets will, however, protect the contents from water vapour. The situation with freeze-dried bacteria in tablets is more complicated and the recommended storage should be checked with the manufacturer.

Freeze-dried bacteria are powder-like in appearance and, when turning them into a product, neutral substances are added to bulk up the volume.

Comparing milk-based and freeze-dried products

There is no clear difference in the attractiveness of milk-based and freeze-dried probiotic products. Both have their advantages and their disadvantages.

For milk-based products their advantages are:

- convenient to purchase
- easy to use as substitutes for other foods
- the milk carrier provides some protection for the microbes from stomach acid.

The disadvantages of milk-based products are:

- label rarely states how many live bacteria in the product
- relatively short shelf-life (and potentially large loss of bacterial numbers) [8].

For freeze-dried supplements, their advantages are:

- easy to transport on journeys
- label usually states numbers of bacteria
- more often contain multiple strains
- much longer shelf-life.

The disadvantages of freeze-dried supplements are:

- some delay in full activity of bacteria, as they 'recover' from a freeze-dried state
- less easy to integrate into daily routine.

In other words, your choice between a milk-based probiotics and freeze-dried probiotics will depend on your individual circumstances. You can make good choices with either form of product.

Multi-strain probiotics

There is a lot of variation among probiotic species and strains [9]. Therefore, for a probiotic product to have, say, five different strains, each from a different species, and some of these species from different genera, the potential for a variety of behaviours is much greater than in a product containing a single strain.

Furthermore, the different strains may be synergistic. By this is meant that the effects of a combined product are greater than the sum of the effects of the individual strains. The mechanisms of such synergy is poorly understood, but one mechanism may be through a strain releasing a metabolic by-product that another strain can use [10].

The evidence favours multi-strain probiotics. In a review of six studies that compared mono-strain with multi-strain products, the multi-strain versions consistently outperformed the mono-strain products [11]. These results applied to both milk-based and freeze-dried products.

A multi-strain probiotic product is likely to be especially useful in protecting against a range of unknown pathogens. For example, traveller's diarrhoea may be caused by a number of different pathogens, and a multi-strain probiotic is more likely to carry a strain with characteristics effective against the local pathogen. Similarly, the level of risk for antibiotic-associated diarrhoea is influenced by the type of antibiotic used, as well as by the particular pathogens in the local environment. A multi-strain product is more likely to protect against the range of risks.

On the other hand, there are some single probiotic strains that have been carefully selected and have been shown to have a wide range of benefits and/or to be of benefit in specific illnesses. Examples of such widely-tested strains are *Lactobacillus rhamnosus* GG and *Lactobacillus plantarum* 299v. Secondly, it is possible that strains in a multi-strain product may inhibit each other, by releasing antimicrobial substances, and thus reducing the overall effectiveness of the product [11].

In conclusion, on the balance of evidence, it is fair to say that the more strains the better in a probiotic product, but it is worth checking with the producer what evidence they have that there are no substantial antagonisms between the strains. Mono-strain products (or those with two or three strains) can still be valuable, especially if a well-studied strain is included, or the strains have clear research evidence of benefit in particular illnesses.

Types of probiotic microbes

Better quality probiotic products will tend to list the species and strains contained in the product. If you wish to be reminded of the naming system for microbes, please see the beginning of Chapter 2.

The main types of microbe included in probiotics are described more fully in the next chapter (Ch. 10), while this section will focus on some of the key issues when selecting a product.

Most probiotic products will contain lactobacilli and/or bifidobacteria and these genera are the best studied of the probiotic microbes. If other types of microbe are included in a product, then the company should be able to give a clear reason for this.

If the product you are considering contains mostly lactobacilli and bifidobacteria, does it matter whether they are run-of-the-mill strains or specially-selected types? All lactobacilli secrete lactic acid, and consequently they tend to increase the acidity of the intestine. Most pathogens are inhibited by an acidic environment. All bifidobacteria secrete acetic acid as well as lactic acid, and are likely to have an anti-pathogenic effect similar to that of lactobacilli.

It can be argued, therefore, that for general protection against gut infection, such as traveller's diarrhoea, any non-specialised multi-strain probiotic should be helpful. Furthermore, such a product would be a lot cheaper than a specialist product.

But if you want a top-quality product and don't mind paying a higher price, how do you know you are getting value for money? There are a number of questions that you can ask the person selling you the product. Or you can search for answers on the company's website.

Such questions could include:

- ❖ What are the characteristics of the particular strains in the product (anti-pathogen effects; influencing the immune system)?

- Is there evidence of the strains resisting the effects of acid in the stomach and of bile in the duodenum, so that they survive into the lower intestine?
- Do the strains carry antibiotic-resistant genes that could be transferred to pathogens in the human intestine, making the pathogens difficult to treat?
- Do the strains attach to the lining of the gut, and so stay longer in the intestine?
- Are there any research studies which show health benefits from the strains?
- Are the numbers of microbes claimed in the product actually present?

Let us look at the last two of these questions in a little more detail.

Evidence of health benefits

Let us suppose that you are reading the label of a probiotic product and the list of contents gives the full name of the probiotic strains - genus, species and strain. How can you know whether there is any published research on the strain, and whether any of that research shows positive characteristics for the strain? There are two main ways.

You can check in Medline, which is a major medical article database available at www.ncbi.nlm.nih.gov/pubmed . The web-page is headed 'PubMed', and in the search box you should type in the full name of the strain. If there are any published papers in which the strain is mentioned, they will appear in the list. You can click on any listed articles and read an abstract (summary), which should tell you whether the strain has any recorded desirable characteristics, and whether the strain has been shown to be beneficial in particular illnesses.

Unless you are familiar with scientific language, in particular biological language, you may find some of the abstracts hard to follow, but there is usually a conclusion section, and this should be easier to comprehend.

Alternatively, you can log onto the company/product website and look for evidence of research. Sometimes this information will be found under a section entitled 'For Professionals' or something similar. In addition to published research, the company may also record unpublished research which it has undertaken for its own purposes or has commissioned from an independent laboratory.

If you can find no research, the product still may have value and it may be that the company has focused more on undertaking high-quality commercial production of the product rather than on basic research. Scanning the company website should give you an impression of the production standards being employed.

Taxonomy problems

An added complication in understanding the characteristics of a probiotic strain is that the classification (taxonomy) of bacteria has undergone (and is still undergoing) major changes.

Historically, bacteria have been grouped and named according to their shape and other physical characteristics, their behaviour and biological chemistry, and their preferred habitats. As knowledge of bacteria has increased, however, species have been reclassified and renamed. This process has accelerated since bacteria have been analysed using genetic methods. For instance, *Lactobacillus rhamnosus* GG used to be known as *Lactobacillus casei* GG.

The classification problem exists among all types of bacteria, including the *Bifidobacterium* genus. For example, *Bif. lactis* used to be known as *Bif. bifidum*, and before that *Bif. animalis*. And on some occasions *Bif. longum* [12]. It can therefore sometimes be unclear which species has been tested, particularly in early studies when classification was less precise.

Sometimes, companies deliberately confuse matters for marketing advantage. For example, there are some probiotic products that claim to contain *Lactobacillus sporogenes*. In fact, there is no such species, and the products usually contain a *Bacillus coagulans*, which is a spore-forming bacterium very different from *Lactobacillus*. Presumably, the incorrect name is used because it is better known and will sound more reassuring, even though *B. coagulans* is a respectable probiotic species.

Total number of microbes in a product

As the lower intestine contains huge numbers of bacteria, it seems logical that a large number of microbes will be needed in a probiotic product to have any influence on the microflora. This is true, but how many exactly are needed to have any effect?

This question is not easy to answer. In fact, the correct dosage of probiotics for particular purposes remains one of the big questions yet to be resolved.

But why should this be such a difficult question? The main reason is that very few human studies have included dose comparisons, in which different strengths of probiotic have been compared in the same trial [13].

Furthermore, unlike non-living substances, probiotic products can change their strength over a relatively short time due to death or incapacity of some of the cells. It is not always clear how rapid such loss of viability is, and it can vary between products.

Minimum numbers

Given our current knowledge, is there a definite minimum number of live probiotic bacterial cells required to have a reasonable chance of a positive health effect?

In a high quality human study involving more than 350 women with IBS, they consumed a strain of *Bifidobacterium* for four weeks at doses of 1 million living cells per day or 100 million per day [14,15]. The lower dose had no effect, but the higher dose had a significant effect in reducing overall symptoms of IBS, compared with a placebo.

Also, a report by the European Food Safety Authority on eligibility of yoghurt products to carry a health claim for 'improving lactose digestion', requires a minimum concentration of 100 million live cells of yoghurt-bacteria per serving [16].

Does this mean that all probiotics with a daily dose of 100 million live cells or more will definitely have a positive effect on intestinal health? The answer is, not necessarily. The reason for the uncertainty is that there are more factors in the effectiveness of a probiotic than the initial number consumed.

The particular strain used in the IBS study above had a lot of desirable qualities, having been selected from a large number of assessed strains. Those desirable qualities included survivability through the upper intestine.

All bacteria face a harsh environment in the stomach (due to hydrochloric acid) and in the duodenum (due to bile salts) [17]. Some probiotic strains will survive well through the stomach and duodenum, either because they have natural strain-specific defences or because the product as a whole protects the strains (as with enteric coatings or micro-encapsulation).

The strains in some products may lose as much as 90% of the viable cells passing through the stomach and duodenum, and therefore a dose of 100 million cells may not be sufficient to achieve a large enough number entering the small intestine.

Another influence on the minimum number of viable cells required, is whether the strain is able to reproduce within the intestine. If a strain can multiply in the gut, then it can overcome the disadvantage of having relatively few cells consumed in the first place.

Bacteria reproduce by dividing in half. Some bacteria, in suitable environments, will reproduce every 20 minutes. Not all species multiply so quickly, and it is rare for a bacterium to live in an environment completely ideal for its growth and multiplication. But the lower intestine (terminal ileum and large intestine) is an attractive environment for many types of bacteria that are comfortable at human body temperature and that thrive in an atmosphere of little or no oxygen. There is certainly plenty of food present, and the attractiveness of the gut to bacteria is reflected in the vast numbers living on the faeces. Probably, the main inhibitor to bacterial growth is competition between bacteria for particulate nutrients.

Let us assume, for argument's sake, that the probiotic bacteria that have been consumed are able to divide every two hours. As it takes, on average, just over two days for the contents of the intestine to travel from the lower small intestine to excretion from the rectum, there would be, in this theoretical case, an opportunity for about 25 divisions of the probiotic cells to take place. If one probiotic cell and its offspring divided 25 times, that single cell would turn into more than 15 million cells! There is the potential for this to happen as the probiotic microbes are just floating along on the faeces.

If some of the probiotic cells were able to attach to the lining of the gut wall, then those attached cells (and their successors) could reproduce over a longer period of time, than those being carried along by the gut contents.

The point I am making is that the initial number of probiotic cells consumed is just one factor in the effectiveness of the probiotic product. Resistance to the harsh upper intestinal environment, ability to multiply, as well as useful metabolic and immune-influencing characteristics, all increase the ability of the probiotic strain to provide health benefits.

The selection of a suitable probiotic product should not be made solely or even mainly on the number of live cells. But bearing this advice in mind, it is still sensible to use a probiotic with a daily dose of at least 100 million cells [14,16].

Is there a risk of overdose?

So far there is no evidence of health risks occurring because of overdosing of probiotic cells. There are some probiotic products whose daily recommended dose is more than 100 billion cells, and no particular side-effects have been reported.

Why should this be? Probably, because the types of microbes in most probiotic products are similar to those that live naturally in the human gut, so nothing very peculiar is entering the intestine. It is assumed that if a very large dose of probiotics is consumed, in excess of that needed to achieve the healthy goal, the excess cells will merely pass through the gut and be excreted.

The concentration of living cells in probiotic products is steadily increasing, as new products arrive in the market. If a harmful dose level is found to exist, then you can be sure that this will be reported in the media. As described in the chapter on safety (Ch. 8), probiotics are very safe. And if you wish to be ultra-cautious, please note that the daily dose of the great majority of probiotic products does not exceed 10 billion cells.

Product inaccuracies

A further complication on the question of desirable cell numbers in probiotic products, is that the claims by companies for the number of live cells in their product may not be accurate. Also, it is not always clear whether such claims refer to the number of viable cells at the time of manufacture or to a guaranteed minimum present at the 'use by' date [18,19].

In addition, some labels will give the claimed cell number for a single capsule, while another label may give numbers per gram weight. These are not the same. It is common for a probiotic capsule to have contents that weigh about one-third of a gram.

Such uncertainty means that the choice of a probiotic product should be based on a broad picture of its characteristics, as highlighted in this chapter. Having read the chapter, you will at least be able to engage in a discussion with a health professional about any suggested product, rather than being just a passive receiver of recommendations.

Summary of main points

- ❖ There is no clear difference in the attractiveness of milk-based and freeze-dried probiotic products. Both have their advantages and disadvantages.
- ❖ A multi-strain product is usually better than a mono-strain, because a wider range of characteristics are available from the range of strains.
- ❖ There are some single-strain products that contain a carefully selected and highly-researched strain, and they can also be valuable.
- ❖ Desirable characteristics of a probiotic microbe, and how to find out about such characteristics, are listed in this chapter.
- ❖ Very few studies of probiotics have included dosage comparisons, and so the optimal dose of a particular product may not be known. A minimum daily dose of viable probiotic cells is probably 100 million.

10
Types of Probiotic Microbes

There is a growing number of different microbes being described as probiotic, but how can you distinguish the good from the bad or the indifferent? This chapter looks at the characteristics of all the main types of probiotic microbe, to help you to feel confident when looking at the labels of products and reading their list of microbial content.

Of the various types of microbe, bacteria are by far the most commonly used in probiotic products. Below is an illustration of a bacterium. Certain parts will be found in all bacteria (e.g. cell membrane, chromosome/nucleoid, ribosomes) and some will be present only in some bacteria (e.g. flagella). Bacteria take various shapes, and the rod-shape pictured below is one of them.

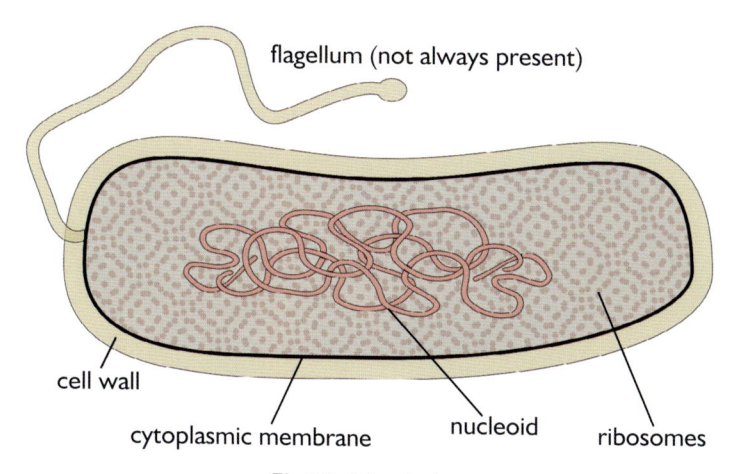

Fig 23: A bacterium

Genus *Lactobacillus*

The majority of the different species included in probiotic products are from the genus *Lactobacillus*, the bacterium favoured by Metchnikoff (see Chapter 5) in the early 20th century. The fact that lactobacilli are relatively easy to grow on a commercial scale [1] has probably helped their popularity with probiotic companies.

Another characteristic of lactobacilli is their resistance to the destructive effects of acid. As such, they tend to survive well in passage through the stomach. Lactobacilli grow in atmospheres free of oxygen (anaerobic) or containing small amounts of oxygen (microaerophilic). This means that that they are well-suited to living in the human intestine.

Lactobacilli feed almost exclusively on sugars, of which there are plenty in the intestine. They are however quite 'fussy eaters', in that they require a lot of minor nutrients in the food to enable them to live and grow. Consequently, they are a common bacterium in the small bowel, because there is a wide range of food in that part of the intestine. There are fewer lactobacilli in the large bowel because the undigested food has a smaller range of nutrients available. There are still lactobacilli in the large bowel, but they are heavily outnumbered by other types of bacteria.

Another reason why lactobacilli have been used as probiotics is the early evidence of them exerting a controlling effect on harmful *E. coli*, reducing their numbers [2]. Subsequently, many laboratory experiments have shown various *Lactobacillus* species inhibiting the growth of pathogens and also stimulating immune cells. Increasingly, animal studies and human clinical research have shown lactobacilli accelerating recovery from a range of intestinal conditions, and in preventing infection.

How do lactobacilli work probiotically?

It is not known for certain how lactobacilli work as probiotic bacteria. There are several possible explanations, all of which may contribute to the probiotic effect. Different probiotic mechanisms may operate in different species and strains, and may also depend on the local ecology (interrelationships) of the gut and bacteria.

The most likely explanations for the probiotic effect of lactobacilli are that they:

- increase the acidity of a local area of the intestine;
- produce various anti-microbial substances;

❖ attach to the intestinal lining;

❖ promote larger quantities of intestinal mucus.

Lactic acid is secreted by lactobacilli as a by-product of its living processes. The acid lowers the pH (increases acidity) of the latter part of small bowel (ileum) and the first part of the large bowel (caecum). This increased acidity discourages harmful bacteria. Some lactobacilli also produce acetic acid, and this has an even stronger anti-pathogenic effect than lactic acid [3].

Lactobacilli produce antibiotic-like proteins called bacteriocins, which may help to restrict the growth of intestinal pathogens, usually those that are of genera fairly closely-related to lactobacilli [4]. Also, some lactobacilli produce hydrogen peroxide, a chemical that has an antibacterial effect. More is produced in the small intestine than in the colon, as lactobacilli need some oxygen for the chemical process involved. Hydrogen peroxide is also produced by some types of lactobacilli in the vagina.

Effective probiotic lactobacilli tend to be good at attaching to the mucosa (mucus-covered intestinal lining) [5]. By attaching, they are able to multiply and form temporary colonies. From there they may block attachment of pathogens, and may also influence the immune cells in the gut wall.

Some probiotic lactobacilli stimulate extra production of mucus by gut wall cells, and this may be a way in which the lactobacilli inhibit the attachment of pathogenic bacteria [6]. Mucus also contains substances that are harmful to pathogens.

There are more than 150 *Lactobacillus* species [7], although not all are suitable as probiotics. The species most commonly used in probiotic products are: *L. acidophilus, L. casei, L. crispatus, L. johnsonii, L. plantarum, L. reuteri, L. rhamnosus,* and *L. salivarius*.

Other lactic acid secreting bacteria

There are other genera of bacteria that secrete lactic acid, and one of these, *Enterococcus*, has species that are used in probiotic products. The mechanisms of action of enterococci will be similar to those of lactobacilli.

Genus *Bifidobacterium*: early colonisers

Bifidobacteria are the second most commonly used type of bacteria in probiotic products. Although bifidobacteria were first identified in 1899, they were not included in a significant number of probiotic products until the final quarter of the 20th century [8]. This may have been because bifidobacteria are not as easy as lactobacilli to grow and process commercially.

Bifidobacteria have always been viewed as a valuable member of the human gut flora, ever since they were first identified. While examining the stool of a baby, Henry Tissier of the Pasteur Institute identified the unusually-shaped microbe which later became known as *Bifidobacterium*. It is their presence in very large numbers in the intestines of babies that has provided reassurance that they are not harmful, and are probably beneficial.

Research in the second half of the twentieth century has shown that bifidobacteria become the dominant bacterium in infant intestines when the baby is about one week old, increasing to as much as 90% of the microflora. From weaning onwards their numbers and proportions fall, so that the microflora moves towards the normal adult mixture of species [9].

Characteristics of bifidobacteria

The appearance of bifidobacteria varies between species, but generally they are rod-shaped, slim, and with slightly bulbous or clubbed ends. When nutrients are short, bifidobacteria tend to fork at one or both ends [8]. These split ends give the bacterium its name, from the Latin word bifidus, meaning 'split in two'.

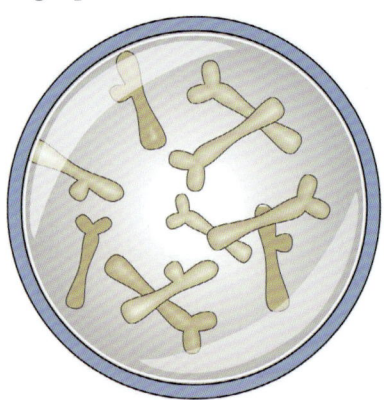

Fig 24: Bifidobacteria

Bifidobacteria are anaerobic, and within the human intestine are mostly found within the large bowel. They are, on average, about seven times more common than lactobacilli in the adult human gut, and are present in large numbers [10].

The main by-products of their metabolism are acetic acid and lactic acid, in about equal proportion. These two acids lower the pH (increase acidity) within the intestine, especially in the caecum and the ascending (right-sided) colon. It is likely that the ability of bifidobacteria to increase the acidity of intestines, together with their large numbers, are a factor in their probiotic effects, as many harmful microbes are inhibited in a low pH environment [11].

There is also some evidence that bifidobacteria produce anti-bacterial substances that inhibit harmful bacteria, such as *Yersinia* and *Shigella* species [12]. Eight *Bifidobacterium* species showed this effect in laboratory experiments [13]. The anti-bacterial substances have not yet been identified but may be similar to the bacteriocins produced by lactobacilli.

Other useful characteristics of bifidobacteria are the production of various B vitamins, and a tendency to adhere well to the intestinal wall, thus excluding pathogenic bacteria [14].

The ability of bifidobacteria to survive stomach acid varies with the strain. Some are very resistant and others are not [15]. In general, bifidobacteria are less resistant to stomach acid than are lactobacilli.

Evidence of probiotic effects

Bearing in mind that it is increasingly common for bifidobacteria to be added to fermented milk products (e.g. bio-yoghurts), it is surprising how limited is the research evidence for the beneficial health effects of this group of bacteria.

There is some human research evidence which points to bifidobacteria lessening the effects of lactose intolerance, reducing cholesterol levels, improving the gut immune system and reducing diarrhoea (both rotavirus and antibiotic-associated) [12,16]. Also, bifidobacteria appear to be helpful in preventing infections of the gut in infants [8]. However, such evidence is much less than that available for lactobacilli.

There are about 35 species of *Bifidobacterium* currently identified [12] and there is considerable potential for investigating the species and strains that have the strongest probiotic effects. Some of the species frequently used in probiotics are *Bif. adolescentis, Bif. animalis, Bif. bifidum, Bif. breve, Bif. infantis, Bif. lactis* and *Bif. longum*.

The model microbes

Model microbes are species that represent certain categories of microbe and are extremely well studied. This makes them attractive for further research, because by knowing a lot about a microbe, it becomes easier to interpret the results of the research, and apply them to other organisms.

A microbe becomes a model through a number of factors, including:

- having been identified early in the history of the scientific study of microbes
- being relatively easy to work with in the laboratory
- being fairly representative of a certain type of organism [17].

The relevance of model microbes to the subject of probiotics is that the next three probiotic organisms considered are all variants of a model microbe. The models are *Escherichia coli* (an intestinal bacterium), *Bacillus subtilis* (a spore-forming soil bacterium) and *Saccharomyces cerevisiae* (an economically-important yeast). All three have had the whole of their gene sequences recorded, being among the earliest microbes to be so analysed.

The fact that a probiotic is a strain of a well-studied model microbe, means that a product containing such strains, is less likely to produce unexpected outcomes. They can be looked upon with confidence even though they are much less well-known to the general public than lactobacilli and bifidobacteria.

Escherichia coli

The *E. coli* species was identified in 1885 by the German paediatrician Professor Theodor Escherich. He named it *Bacterium coli commune*, because he found plenty of them in the human colon. In 1930 (nineteen years after Escherich's death), the species was officially renamed *Escherichia coli*.

E. coli shares some characteristics with lactobacilli and bifidobacteria, in that it is rod-shaped and its natural habitat is the human intestine (and the intestine of other animals). Like lactobacilli, *E. coli* can live in the presence or absence of oxygen [17].

Unlike lactobacilli and bifidobacteria, *E. coli* has some pathogenic strains. Most *E. coli* are benign commensals, but there are a few types that cause disease, such as urinary tract infection and traveller's diarrhoea. Also, a strain has arisen, *E. coli* O157:H7, which causes serious food poisoning, and has received much publicity. *E. coli* is also closely related to *Shigella*, *Yersinia* and *Salmonella*, all of which are pathogenic genera. It should be stressed, however, that the great majority of *E. coli* strains are harmless, and some of them are probiotic.

The best known *E. coli* probiotic is *E. coli* Nissle 1917 (EcN). This strain was discovered in 1917, and its early history has already been described in Chapter 5. The modern-day product has an added enteric coating, so that the Nissle bacteria are protected against stomach acid. The coating does not dissolve and release the probiotics until the capsule reaches the ileum and caecum.

For many years, EcN has been used for prevention and treatment of diarrhoea, because studies had shown it was 'antagonistic' to a range of pathogens. More recently, EcN has been used successfully in other conditions, such as ulcerative colitis and long-standing constipation [18].

EcN has also been shown to reduce the level of pathogenic bacteria in the intestines of infants in the first week of their lives. EcN colonises well in infants, with almost all the infants still having EcN in their stool six months after the administration of EcN had ceased. This is a much longer period than for most other probiotics [19].

The mechanisms by which EcN has probiotic effects are not completely clear, but one appears to be the ability to strengthen the barrier function of gut epithelial cells. This makes it more difficult for microbes to enter the gut wall and pass into the body's bloodstream.

The probiotic effectiveness of EcN may be due to its closeness to pathogenic species. For example, people with ulcerative colitis (a chronic bowel disease) have a high proportion of pathogenic

E. coli living on the lining of the large bowel [20,21]. EcN reduces the inflammation of ulcerative colitis, probably by replacing those pathogenic *E. coli*. The genetic closeness of a probiotic *E. coli* with a pathogenic *E. coli* appears to aid the removal of the pathogen.

Bacillus subtilis

B. subtilis is another model bacterium. While *E. coli* is a model for Gram-negative bacteria, *B. subtilis* is a model for Gram-positive bacteria. The Gram test distinguishes bacteria on the basis of cell wall structure, which is a significant difference affecting the way that substances enter and leave the cell.

The emergence of *B. subtilis* as the model for Gram-positives may have been influenced by its early prominence as the source of an antibiotic, bacitracin, which was discovered in 1945. Another attraction of *B. subtilis* to researchers is that it forms spores, and study of spore formation throws light on how cells undergo major structural change. Also, *B. subtilis* is amenable to genetic manipulation, and this characteristic has been used for a variety of purposes, such as the production of enzymes for the brewing industry.

Although more research has been undertaken on *E. coli*, as a model bacterium, knowledge about *B. subtilis* is rapidly increasing.

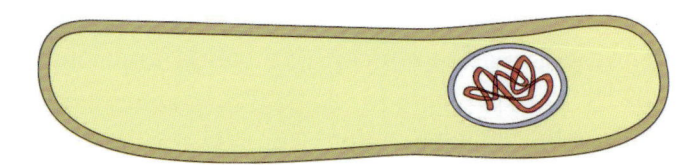

Fig 25: A Bacillus bacterium with a spore forming inside

B. subtilis as a probiotic

B. subtilis has been used as a probiotic (in spore form) for many years in parts of South-East Asia and in Eastern and Southern Europe. Only a limited range of bacterial genera are capable of forming spores, which are a dormant form of the bacterium. After being formed, a spore neither takes in nutrients nor uses any of the resources within its cell, and such inactivity explains why a bacterial spore can remain viable for a long time. An extreme example of this is a bacillus-type spore that was found in the gut of a dead bee that had been trapped within amber for an estimated 25-40 million years. Amazingly, some of these spores were germinated into active cells from a sample of tissue taken from the bee.

A spore is formed to protect the bacterium from an adverse environment, such as shortage of food, absence of water or severe temperature. The spore-form of the bacterium is considerably different from its normal (vegetative) state. The spore has much less water in the cell and has a hard shell for protection. The hard coating means that a spore is unaffected by hydrochloric acid in the stomach, and by the various secretions in the duodenum. The bacillus spore is therefore likely to arrive in the jejunum unaffected by its initial journey along the digestive tract.

But there is a question as to how a spore, in which no biochemical processes take place, can influence the intestine in any way. One possibility is that molecules on the surface of the spore influence the gut immune system, and there is some evidence to support this [22].

The other possibility is that the spores germinate within the human gut and have their influence in the normal vegetative form. Recent studies have shown that after passing safely through the stomach, some of the spores (perhaps about 10%) germinate in the jejunum, replicate for a few rounds, possibly form attached colonies, and then re-sporulate in the large intestine. In this way, the vegetative cells have an opportunity to influence the small intestine and possibly parts of the large intestine.

Although *B. subtilis* is mainly a soil bacterium, evidence is also pointing to *Bacillus* bacteria being a constituent of the normal gut microflora of humans, albeit in small numbers of about 10,000 per gram of content [23]. Despite being a minor member of the microflora, bacilli may play a significant role in the development of the gut immune tissues [24].

A majority of researchers specialising in this field now believe that the life-cycle of *B. subtilis* consists of two parts, soil-based, and animal-gut-based [23,25], and that the use of *Bacillus* spore probiotics has theoretical potential.

Despite *B. subtilis* being a well-studied model microbe, there have been very few controlled human studies on its probiotic characteristics. Animal studies do, however, suggest that *B. subtilis* has probiotic effects, by influencing the gut immune system and by stimulating the growth of lactobacilli.

Although *B. subtilis* is the most frequently used *Bacillus* species in probiotic products, there are products that contain other probiotic *Bacillus* species. Such species include *B. coagulans*, *B. licheniformis*, *B. pumilus* and *B. clausii*.

Saccharomyces cerevisiae

Saccharomyces cerevisiae is a yeast, and is responsible for the production of alcohol in wine and beer. It also makes bread rise. These popular uses have made *S. cerevisiae* a well-studied model microbe.

Although bacteria and yeasts are both single-celled organisms, yeast cells have an internal structure that is different from bacteria, in that they have membrane-enclosed areas, including a nucleus. This makes the yeasts closer to human cells than to bacterial cells. Yeast cells are therefore an obvious choice as a model for human cells, and this makes *S. cerevisiae* even more frequently studied.

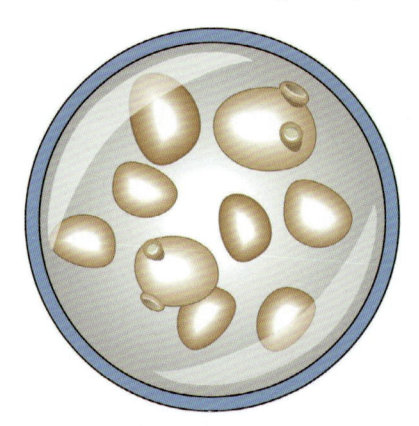

Fig 26: Saccharomyces boulardii

There is a sub-species of *S. cerevisiae* that is probiotic. It is known as *Saccharomyces boulardii*. A sub-species is an organism that is not different enough to be classified as a separate species, but has greater differences than a strain of a species. In other words, *S. boulardii* has many of the known characteristics of *S. cerevisiae*, but has some probiotic characteristics in addition.

The discovery of *S. boulardii* in Indochina has already been described in Chapter 5. It was first produced as a freeze-dried product in the 1960s. Like other yeasts, *S. boulardii* can live aerobically or anaerobically, and therefore can live in the intestine. Unlike most probiotic microbes, however, *S. boulardii* is not a resident of the human intestine and it does not colonise the gut under normal circumstances [26]. This does not stop it from being effective, and in fact the quality of research showing probiotic benefit from *S. boulardii* is high.

In a review of 12 randomised controlled trials using *S. boulardii*, the reviewers reported that, "The efficacy of this yeast has been demonstrated on a total of 2,581 patients for various indications." These indications included the prevention of traveller's diarrhoea and antibiotic-associated diarrhoea; treatment of acute or chronic diarrhoea in adults, children or AIDS patients; and treatment of the recurrence of *C. difficile* colitis [27].

Major microfloral genera

As explained in Chapter 3, most of the bacteria living in the large intestine are from a small range of genera, including *Bacteroides*, *Clostridium*, *Eubacterium*, *Lachnospira*, *Roseburia*, *Ruminococcus* and *Faecalibacterium* [28]. You will notice that none of the probiotic microbes described so far are from any of these common genera. As each genus has a large number of species, and each species has an even larger number of strains, one should expect some probiotic bacteria within these genera. Furthermore, it could be argued that such a probiotic species might be especially useful, as it would be part of a major group within the gut microflora.

To date, there is just one probiotic that falls within this category, and it is a strain of *Clostridum butyricum*. This bacterium has two distinct characteristics. Like *Bacillus subtilis* it can form spores, but unlike *B. subtilis*, it is an anaerobe and therefore should thrive in the large bowel. Also, it produces a range of by-products including butyrate.

Butyrate is a short-chain fatty acid, and is valuable because it is taken up by enterocytes (gut-lining cells), which are likely to be strengthened as a consequence. Healthy enterocytes act as an important barrier to pathogens passing through the lining of the intestine and into the gut wall and the associated blood vessels. Butyrate produced by *C. butyricum* may therefore repair a 'leaky gut' and reduce the risk of infection [29].

C. butyricum Miyairi 588 is a probiotic strain that has been incorporated into a probiotic product in Japan for the past 70 years. There is evidence of this strain being antagonistic to various pathogens, reducing the amount of harmful chemicals from putrefactive bacteria, and increasing the numbers of lactobacilli. There is also some evidence that *C. butyricum* Miyairi increases absorption of vitamins E and A.

Summary of main points

- *Lactobacillus* species tend to be resistant to the effects of stomach acid, and are more prominent in the small bowel than the large bowel.
- Lactobacilli increase acidity in their local environment, produce anti-microbial molecules, promote production of mucus lining the intestine, and fill attachment places on the gut lining. All these actions probably discourage pathogens.
- Bifidobacteria are the second most popular group of bacteria used as probiotics. They were first identified at the end of the nineteenth century as a type of microbe dominant in the intestines of breast-fed infants.
- Bifidobacteria are anaerobic (live and grow without oxygen) and are found almost exclusively in the large intestine.
- Like lactobacilli, bifidobacteria produce lactic acid, but they also produce acetic acid.
- Three model microbes that have probiotic versions are:
  - *Escherichia coli* (*E. coli*)
  - *Bacillus subtilis*
  - *Saccharomyces cerevisiae*
- Like lactobacilli and bifidobacteria, *E. coli* is a member of the intestinal microflora of vertebrate animals. The great majority of strains of *E. coli* are benign commensals, but a few are pathogens. *E. coli* Nissle 1917 (EcN) is a probiotic bacterium.
- For a majority of the twentieth century, EcN has been used as an anti-diarrhoeal, and more recently is being used to treat constipation and ulcerative colitis.

- *Bacillus subtilis* is a spore-forming bacterium. The spore protects the cell from stomach acid and, once in the small intestine, some of the spores germinate and have an influence on the gut. There are other species of *Bacillus* that are used in probiotic products.
- *Saccharomyces cerevisiae* is a yeast used in wine, beer and bread production. The probiotic yeast *Saccharomyces boulardii* is a sub-species of *S. cerevisiae*.
- *S. boulardii* is not a resident of the human intestine, but it is able to live there temporarily. There is very good evidence of the anti-diarrhoeal effects of *S. boulardii*.
- The major genera of bacteria in the large intestine are likely to include some probiotic species. The only species of such genera that is currently used as a probiotic is *Clostridium butyricum*.

11
What are *Prebiotics*?

The background to *prebiotics*

Probiotic microbes face a number of challenges within the digestive tract to overcome in order to have a chance of improving the health of their human host. Such challenges include the acidic environment of the stomach, secretions into the duodenum, low levels of oxygen, and competition from the resident microflora.

Because of these challenges, some scientists have wondered whether improvement of the microflora could be tackled from a different direction. Instead of adding beneficial microbes to the gut (or to other parts of the body where there is a microflora), could the existing beneficial bacteria within the microflora be increased by non-living substances? In the case of the gut flora, this would mean the consumption of food that favours the growth of beneficial bacteria.

This idea was supported by the fact that mother's milk, among its many benefits to the infant, has substances that act to boost bifidobacteria numbers dramatically.

As awareness rose of the beneficial potential of bifidobacteria, formula milk companies investigated the components of human breast milk. They wanted to identify which parts of the milk boosted bifidobacterial numbers, so that these could be added to formula milks for the benefit of human infants. Any food or part of food that increased the numbers of bifidobacteria was described as being 'bifidogenic'.

In 1995, two European scientists broadened the bifidogenic concept and introduced the term '*prebiotic*' [1]. A revised version of their definition was proposed by a committee of the United Nations: "A *pre*biotic is a non-viable food component that confers a health benefit on the host associated with the modulation of the microbiota" [2].

The term 'non-viable' means that it is not living, and the word 'microbiota' has the same meaning as microflora. In other words, a *pre*biotic is a non-living substance that acts as a food for the more desirable members of our microflora. The definition of *pre*biotic covers improved health through changes in any members of the microflora and not just an increase in bifidobacteria.

Initially, the identification of substances that act as *pre*biotics was a daunting task. Studies on influencing the gut microflora by a change of diet produced few significant results. The genera of bacteria within the gut flora remained remarkably unchanged by changes in the diet. Partly, this is because the established microflora is usually very stable and resistant to change.

More recently, it has become clear that the microflora can be changed by substances other than mother's milk. Such changes appear to occur most easily by alterations in biochemical activities undertaken by the microflora, rather than changes in the predominant species. Changes to the types and numbers of species and strains may occur through diet, but usually either by a long-term severe change of diet or by the use of specific food extracts.

Non-digestible food

Most *pre*biotics are types of food-extract that are non-digestible. In this context, 'non-digestible' means that the substance is not digested by enzymes secreted by the small intestine of the person taking the *pre*biotic. In a normal diet, there is always a substantial amount of non-digestible food. This is why we excrete stool. There is a difference, however, between the amount of food left undigested at the end of the small intestine and the amount excreted in stool. This difference is accounted for by the action of bacteria in the large intestine.

Bacteria are able to break down undigested food (chyme/faeces), because the microbes produce enzymes that are not produced by the human body. They are so effective at 'feeding' on undigested food that, when solid waste is excreted, about half of the weight of stool is bacterial cells [3].

The parts of food that are non-digestible by human enzymes are known as dietary fibre. Dietary fibre is a collection of complex molecules from edible plants. Dietary fibre can be divided into two categories, insoluble and soluble. Insoluble fibre is mostly comprised of plant cell walls. In addition to not being digested in the small intestine, most insoluble fibre is not digested by bacteria in the gut either. In contrast, soluble fibre is easily digested by gut bacteria.

Systematic examination of the molecules that make up dietary fibre has shown that certain types consistently increase the numbers of bifidobacteria and lactobacilli. Most of these *pre*biotic molecules are known a 'non-digestible oligosaccharides' (NDOs).

Non-digestible oligosaccharides (NDOs)

A carbohydrate is an energy food, a molecule of which is made up of sugars linked together to form a chain. If a large number of sugars are linked together, the carbohydrate is known as a polysaccharide ('poly' means many, and 'saccharide' means sugar). If the carbohydrate molecule is relatively small, consisting of just one sugar, it is known as a monosaccharide; and if consisting of two sugars, a disaccharide.

An oligosaccharide is also a carbohydrate, consisting of three to ten sugars linked together [4]. 'Oligo' means few. Bifidobacteria, and to a lesser extent lactobacilli, produce enzymes that are very efficient at breaking the links between the sugars of oligosaccharides. Breaking those links releases energy, and also makes the sugars available for absorption into and fermentation within the bacterial cell.

NDOs are types of soluble fibre that are found in the main body of some plants, where they act as a store of potential energy. The fact that NDOs can dissolve in water means that bacteria find them much easier to digest than longer-chain carbohydrates.

Boosting numbers of beneficial bacteria

The majority of bacterial species in the colon are saccharolytic (ferment carbohydrates), including the probiotic bifidobacteria and lactobacilli [4]. In comparison, many harmful bacteria are proteolytic (ferment protein).

This might suggest that all that is needed to achieve a healthier bacterial balance is to increase the amount of carbohydrate in the colon, which in turn would boost numbers of the saccharolytic bacteria. However, some saccharolytic bacteria are more beneficial than others, and it is desirable to target the best, by selecting particular carbohydrates for the *pre*biotic purpose.

There are other carbohydrates that are not digested in the small intestine, for example, resistant starch, but it is the NDOs that seem to be the most effective at stimulating the growth of probiotic bacteria.

NDOs as food

Some NDOs are found naturally in plants. The vegetables and fruits in Fig 30 contain the *pre*biotics inulin and oligofructose (FOS).

Fig 27: Prebiotic foods
1. Jerusalem artichoke, 2. Onions, 3. Garlic, 4. Asparagus, 5. Chicory, 6. Leek, 7. Banana

In general terms, increasing the amount of these foods in your diet will help to increase the numbers of beneficial bacteria in your lower intestines.

But how much *pre*biotic is needed to have an effect in increasing the numbers of bifidobacteria? Most effective studies have used quantities in the range of 8-15 grams a day [5,6].

A normal diet contains 5-10 grams per day of NDOs [7,8]. Therefore, consuming at least an extra 8 grams a day of NDO to have a *pre*biotic effect involves an approximate doubling of the amount of NDOs consumed in a normal diet.

It does not seem very practical for most people to double the amount of food containing NDOs, such as wheat and onions, in their daily diet for a sustainable period. An alternative is to look at NDO products, developed from plants and sugars, which might be used as *pre*biotic supplements.

The NDOs that have best evidence of *pre*biotic effect are:
- galacto-oligosaccharides (GOS)
- fructo-oligosaccharides (FOS).

Galacto-oligosaccharides (GOS)

Galacto-oligosaccharides (GOS) are made up of chains of lactose. Lactose is a sugar found in all types of milk, including human breast milk. Seven per cent of human milk is carbohydrate, of which 90% is lactose or oligosaccharides based on lactose [9]. There are more than 130 different oligosaccharides in human milk and galacto-oligosaccharide is a generic term covering many of them.

GOS is very stable under hot and acidic conditions, and therefore can survive the high temperatures of baking and resist being broken down by stomach acid.

In Japan, GOS is included in a range of products, including bread, 'sports' drinks, jams and marmalades, fermented milk products, confectionary products and desserts. In Europe, GOS is incorporated into infant formula foods [10].

Laboratory studies have consistently shown that GOS increases the numbers of bifidobacteria and lactobacilli, but human studies in adults have given inconsistent results, for reasons that are not yet known. Studies with infants have been more clear-cut. Four studies tested the effect of GOS-supplemented infant formula milk and found that bifidobacteria numbers increased to levels similar to those found in breast-fed infants. Two of the studies also found increased numbers of lactobacilli [10].

Fructo-oligosaccharides (FOS)

FOS (also known as oligofructose) is a carbohydrate consisting of a chain of several fructose molecules. Fructose is a sugar found in fruits and honey. The molecules of FOS are between two and eight fructoses long, with an average of four [11].

As a *prebiotic*, the characteristics of FOS are:
- low calorific value
- survives intact to reach the large bowel (about 90%)
- boosts the number of bifidobacteria.

FOS has a higher purity than GOS, with fewer digestible sugars, and consequently it has the potential to be a low-calorie sweetener.

In a review of four human studies, in which volunteers were fed a diet supplemented with between four and 12 grams a day of FOS, it was reported that all studies "showed a significant increase in bifidobacteria" [12].

The recorded effects on other bacteria have varied in different studies, possibly because of the variability in content of different FOS products (i.e. different mixtures of chain lengths) [13].

There are two other *prebiotics* which have good research evidence of bifidogenic effect. Both are carbohydrates, but neither are oligosaccharides. One is a polysaccharide (inulin) and the other a disaccharide (lactulose).

Inulin

As a polysaccharide, inulin has many more sugar chains per molecule than most *prebiotics*. It is usually obtained from the roots of the chicory plant, and is produced commercially in Europe as an industrial food ingredient [14]. More than 70% of the dried root of chicory is inulin.

The inulin is removed by soaking chicory in hot water. The resulting product is approximately 90% inulin, so there is a high level of purity. The remaining 10% is comprised mostly of short-chain sugars.

Several studies have shown that inulin boosts the numbers of beneficial bacteria, mainly bifidobacteria, and does not increase genera such as *Clostridium* and *E. coli*, which include pathogenic strains. In a study of eight subjects, it was found that the addition of 15 grams of inulin to the diet led to bifidobacteria becoming the largest bacterial group in the faeces [15]. In a further study, initiated to test the effects of lactose (milk sugar) or inulin on bowel habits of constipated elderly patients, inulin significantly increased the numbers of bifidobacteria [16].

Lactulose

Like GOS, lactulose is produced from lactose, but unlike GOS, it is a disaccharide (a two-sugar chain carbohydrate). Lactulose has the same number of carbon, hydrogen and oxygen atoms as lactose (milk sugar), but it differs from lactose as it is not humanly digestible. Its purity is about 80%, with the remaining 20% being digestible sugars.

Since 1957, lactulose has been recognised as being bifidogenic [17]. For example, a well-designed controlled human study showed that 20 grams per day of lactulose over a four-week period led to a substantial increase in bifidobacteria and lactobacilli numbers (approximately 1000-fold and 100-fold respectively). The study also showed a decrease in potentially harmful bacteria. For example, clostridia were reduced to less than one per cent of their original number [18]. Three other studies also showed a bifidogenic effect from lactulose, and they used less than 20 grams per day [17].

In some countries, including the U.K., lactulose is classified as a drug rather than as a food. This is because, since the 1950s, it has been used for medical purposes, notably hepatic encephalopathy (coma caused by liver disease) and chronic constipation.

In Italy, the Netherlands and Japan, however, lactulose is classified as a food. In fact, in Japan lactulose is added to some manufactured baby foods. In countries where lactulose is only available as a drug, a pharmacist or physician has to authorise its issue.

Lactitol is similar to lactulose. It is a disaccharide produced from lactose, and is used as a medicine for the same purposes as lactulose. It acts as a *pre*biotic, but the evidence suggests that it is less bifidogenic than lactulose.

Other *prebiotics*

In addition to the 'big four' *pre*biotics, there are other substances that are potential *pre*biotics, emanating from Japan. These are:

- Isomalto-oligosaccharides (IMO) – from starch
- Soyo-oligosaccharides (SOS) – from soya beans
- Xylo-oligosaccharides (XOS) – from corn cobs
- Lactosucrose (LS) – a synthesis of sucrose and lactose.

All the above are used in foods in Japan, particularly in soft drinks and as dining table sweeteners. There are very few studies on how they may alter the bacterial flora in humans, although the limited evidence points to bifidobacteria numbers being increased [17].

An additional difficulty in assessing research findings, is that the purity of some products used in these studies is poor. One study found that the XOS came with large quantities of starch and some simple sugars. The proportion of xylo-oligosaccharide by weight was only 34% [5].

Other *pre*biotics for which there is even less evidence are: gluco-oligosaccharides, including polydextrose (synthesised from glucose); palatinose (synthesised from sucrose); and pyrodextrin (from maize or potato starch).

Other carbohydrates are being considered as *pre*biotics, such as resistant starch, and acacia gum (gum arabic), but again information is very limited [19].

The appearance and taste of prebiotics

Most *pre*biotics are available in the form of syrups or white powder. The degree of sweetness is influenced by the chain-length of the molecules. The shorter the chain length, the sweeter the taste. Thus lactulose, a disaccharide, is almost as sweet as sucrose (table sugar); galacto-ologosaccharides are about one-third as sweet as sucrose; and inulin, a polysaccharide, has no sweet taste at all.

Advantages of *pre*biotics

The main advantage of a *pre*biotic is that it can increase the numbers of beneficial bacteria already present in the microflora, rather than trying to introduce new strains, as with probiotics.

*Pre*biotics can also be used in probiotic products to strengthen the probiotic bacteria by providing them with readily available food that they are able to ferment.

Unlike some probiotics, which have to be stored carefully (e.g. refrigerated) and have a shelf life of only a few months, *pre*biotics do not have any significant storage problems. This is because they do not have live contents.

Another advantage is that some *pre*biotics occur naturally in plants and therefore may be part of a normal diet. Increasingly, food companies are using NDOs in their products. They are used to replace sugar and fat, to add bulk, and to improve the texture of the food, without adding substantially to its calorific value.

Food companies are also attracted to the idea that NDOs have the potential to turn their products into 'functional foods', which are foods that have health benefits in addition to usual nutritional benefits. Manufacturers are therefore becoming increasingly likely to identify *pre*biotic NDOs in product contents.

The cost of producing NDOs is relatively low compared with probiotics, because of large-scale demand from food companies, and because NDOs are much easier to manufacture than probiotics. The potential for greater profits for food companies through the promotion of 'functional foods' (also known as nutraceuticals) may mean more funding for research into NDO *pre*biotics.

Disadvantages of *pre*biotics

Gas production

The main side effect reported by people participating in NDO *pre*biotic trials is an increase in intestinal gas, resulting in more flatulence and sometimes uncomfortable bloating.

For example, there were noticeable increases in flatulence among 64 healthy young women, who were taking part in a study consuming 14 grams daily of inulin (as part of a low-fat spread). The increase in gas production was usually described as mild, but 12% of the participants described the discomfort as 'severe' [20].

As bifidobacteria produce no gas in their fermentation of carbohydrates, why should increased gas production be a problem with NDOs? It is almost certainly because other bacteria in the microflora are fermenting some of the NDO and consequently producing gas.

In theory, it should be possible to control the excess gas. As bifidobacteria are the most efficient type of intestinal bacteria in fermenting NDOs, the more bifidobacteria there are, the less *pre*biotic will be left for gas-producing bacteria to ferment. Therefore, if less NDO is taken when there are fewer bifidobacteria present and then steadily increased as the bifidobacteria increase in numbers, there should be very little spare NDO for other bacteria to use.

One study of six healthy volunteers taking 20 grams per day of oligofructose for 11 days, found no gas problems. The oligofructose had been introduced gradually, starting with a quarter of the dose and steadily increasing it [21].

Another way of controlling gas may be in the choice of *pre*biotic. There is some indication that different prebiotics lead to different levels of gas production. For example, inulin may produce above-average amounts of gas, compared with other NDOs, while GOS may produce less than average. Current evidence as to which NDOs lead to the least gas is, however, too limited to be a reliable guide.

Unclear picture of the gut microflora

One significant weakness in research on the effects of *pre*biotics is that studies have usually only measured the changes in the gut flora at the genus level, rather than at the species level.

It is known that the behaviour of bacteria varies considerably according to species, and may even vary between strains of the same species. Such uncertainty applies to both probiotic bacteria and to commensal bacteria in the microflora.

McBain and Macfarlane have stated that, "it is simplistic to assume that all species or strains of bifidobacteria and lactobacilli have probiotic properties and, in any case, these will be highly variable" [22].

Furthermore, the species of the gut flora are not yet fully mapped. It is not known what many of the different species do, or how they interact with each other and with the human host. Therefore, a *pre*biotic has the potential of influencing some species of the microflora, the consequences of which are uncertain.

Until changes caused by *pre*biotics are measured in greater detail, it is difficult to know precisely the effect of specific *pre*biotics on the gut microflora.

An example of the unclear picture of the gut microflora, is that it is widely recognised that *pre*biotics do not seem to increase the numbers of bifidobacteria very much if those numbers are already at a high level. But they are very effective if the person taking the NDO starts with low numbers of bifidobacteria [5]. Why this should be, and what role the other microfloral bacteria play is not known.

Effect on very disturbed microflora

If bifidobacteria and lactobacilli are missing from the gut flora, due to any number of factors (such as disease, ageing, antibiotic or drug therapy), a *pre*biotic is unlikely to be effective [9]. If there are very few probiotic bacteria in the gut, much of the *pre*biotic will be fermented by other microbes, some of which may be undesirable.

Under these circumstances, it may be preferable to mix *pre*biotics with probiotics. The term for such a combination is a synbiotic. The term 'synbiotic', meaning a mixture of probiotics and *pre*biotics should not be confused with 'symbiotic', which means a relationship between two living organisms.

Synbiotics

A synbiotic is a combination of a probiotic and a *pre*biotic to maximise the health benefits of both components. The prefix 'syn' suggests that a synergy is involved, in that the combined effect is greater than the sum of the effects of the two independent parts. But it is unclear whether this is a requirement for a product to claim to be a synbiotic. It may be enough for a *pre*biotic to improve the effect of a probiotic for the synbiotic term to be used [1,23].

The synbiotic combination has three potential benefits. The *pre*biotic may physically protect bacteria from stomach acid and other harsh intestinal chemicals. Secondly, the *pre*biotic may act as food to the probiotics, while they pass down the gut and while they live in the slow-moving lower gut. Thirdly, the *pre*biotic may also stimulate health-promoting bifidobacteria and lactobacilli that are already part of the gut flora.

The idea of combining probiotics and *pre*biotics is therefore attractive. But at the moment, there have been very few studies in animals or humans that compare synbiotics with *pre*biotics or probiotics alone, to confirm the concept [24,25].

Clinical studies using *pre*biotics

There have been very few controlled clinical studies using *pre*biotics alone (as opposed to mixing them with probiotics). Therefore, it is too soon to say that their effect of increasing bifidobacteria numbers translates into human health benefits [26]. Two IBS studies have, however, given encouraging results. In one study, patients taking 3.5 grams of GOS per day had a significant reduction in combined symptoms, while the placebo group was unchanged [27]. In the other study, patients taking 5 grams of FOS per day had an average reduction in intensity of digestive disorders of 44%, while the placebo group had a 14% increase in symptom intensity ($p=0.026$) [28].

Summary of main points

- A *pre*biotic is a food component that provides a health benefit by altering the the mixture of bacteria in a microflora [2].
- So far, only carbohydrates have been found to be *pre*biotic, especially non-digestible oligosaccharides (NDOs).
- Unlike most carbohydrates (sugars and starch), NDOs are not digested in the small intestine. They work by being fermented in the terminal ileum and the large bowel by certain resident probiotic bacteria.
- The NDOs boost the numbers of bifidobacteria if those numbers are low, but not if the numbers are already high.
- Some NDOs are found naturally in some food plants, and consumption of such foods are likely to improve the numbers of beneficial bacteria in the gut.
- Consuming enough *pre*biotic by diet change alone may involve a major change in the types of food eaten. *Pre*biotic supplements are therefore worth considering.
- There are two main NDOs that have confirmed *pre*biotic effects: galacto-oligosaccharides (GOS) and fructo-oligosaccharides (FOS).
- Inulin is another *pre*biotic, which is a polysaccharide, rather than an oligosaccharide.
- Lactulose is a disaccharide *pre*biotic, which in some countries is classified as a medicine rather than as a food additive.
- There are other types of *pre*biotic, but very little research has been undertaken in humans on their potential *pre*biotic effects.

- ❖ The main advantage of a *pre*biotic is that it can increase the numbers of beneficial bacteria already present in the microflora rather than trying to introduce new strains, as with probiotics.
- ❖ Compared with probiotics, *pre*biotics are easier to store and cheaper to produce.
- ❖ A drawback with prebiotics is the tendency to increase intestinal gas (flatulence and bloating). The amount of gas produced by the gut flora may vary between different types of *pre*biotic, and the gas may be reduced if the *pre*biotic is introduced gradually.
- ❖ A synbiotic is the combining of a probiotic and a *pre*biotic to maximise the effects of both.
- ❖ The small number to date of controlled clinical trials of *pre*biotics, means that it is not yet possible to say definitely that their bifidogenic effects lead to improved human health.

12
Young and Old

In the early stages of life, the body is growing and changing. In the latter stages of life, the body is deteriorating. What are the special factors for children and the elderly that one should bear in mind for probiotics?

In this section, reference will be made to the gut microflora, but not to the microflora of other parts of the body. This is because very little, if anything is known about any variations to those other microflora in the young or the old.

Children

In adults, each individual's microfloral mix is relatively stable. If it is disturbed by, say, an infection, the original microflora will usually restore itself fairly quickly. The microflora in children is less stable. This is not surprising, because children are continually developing physically from birth through to the teen years.

How do children acquire and develop their microflora? Before birth, the foetus in the uterus (womb) is sterile. It has no microflora. This is because the uterus is microbe-free, and the placenta that connects the mother's body with the foetus carries blood that is usually free of microbes.

The process of birth and the early days of nurturing involve the acquisition of bacteria from a variety of sources. These microbes come mainly from the mother's vagina, intestine and skin, especially from the vaginal microflora [1]. To a lesser extent, the newly-born baby acquires bacteria from the hospital staff and environment.

During the first week of life, there are often wild changes to the species present in the gut. From the second week onwards, the microflora becomes a little more stable and, until the time of weaning, the predominant microbe is the *Bifidobacterium* [2,3].

The number of different species in the early microflora is much smaller than in the established microflora of adults [3]. In the first few months of life, while the bifidobacteria usually remain dominant, the rest of the bacterial species in the intestine commonly change quite radically. These changes are probably because the baby's microflora is not well-established and it is relatively easily influenced by newly-arrived bacteria.

Gradually, as the child reaches six months of age, the range of resident bacteria becomes broader. From about six months of age, the baby undergoes weaning, in which solid foods are gradually introduced. It is at this point that the microflora starts to change towards a more adult-like state, including a much more diverse collection of microbes [4].

At the point where breastfeeding ends, the microfloral changes include a major fall in the number of bifidobacteria [3], closer to the proportion (about 3%) in adult gut microflora.

It is not yet clear when, in a child's life, the full adult microflora will have developed.

It can be seen, however, that in the important first year of life, when the baby is particularly vulnerable (being small and with an immature immune system), the natural processes are providing the baby with a healthy microflora. Childbirth gives the baby lactobacilli (from the mother's vagina), and mother's milk stimulates the growth of bifidobacteria. Nature is providing probiotic bacteria for protection.

Birth by caesarean section

Caesarean section (C-section) is a surgical procedure that involves the removal of the baby from the abdominal cavity. Unlike the natural vaginal birth process, in C-section the baby leaves the mother's body with the amniotic membrane still intact [4]. This membrane covers the whole of the baby's body.

It is not surprising, therefore, to discover that babies born by C-section acquire a higher proportion of their initial bacteria from the environment rather than from their mother [4]. In particular, caesarean-born babies tend to have fewer bifidobacteria [5], and their gut microflora tends to resemble the human skin microflora with an abundance of *Staphylococcus* species [1]. Furthermore, during the first week of life, C-section infants have smaller total numbers of bacteria than vaginally-delivered babies.

It is not clear whether there are any health consequences for having an abnormal gut microflora in the first few days of life; one review [6] calculated that C-section was only associated with between 1% and 4% of future cases of allergy. And although in a study of two US hospitals, 16 out of 22 cases of infection by 'superbug' MRSA were in C-section newborn babies, it was not clear whether the microflora were a factor, or just the longer hospital-stay involved in recovering from C-section [7].

Antibiotics in the early months

The administration of antibiotics to infants has consistently been shown to reduce the microfloral numbers, including reduced numbers of bifidobacteria [5].

There is also some evidence that antibiotic use in the first year of life is a risk factor for the development of asthma later in childhood. It must be said, however, that a careful analysis of the studies to date suggests that the association between antibiotics and asthma may be coincidental [8].

If there is a true causal relationship, it may be specific to particular types of antibiotic, and may have a more profound effect on pre-term and low birthweight infants [9].

Of course, antibiotics may also be given to mothers, and notably this occurs prior to C-section. Administration of antibiotics to women in late pregnancy has been shown to alter the microflora on the vaginal-side of the cervix, sometimes leading to an overgrowth of potential pathogens [9], which in turn may alter the health of the mother or the baby.

It should be borne in mind, however, that although antibiotics may affect the microflora, the infections they are fighting against are sometimes very dangerous. The use of some antibiotics as a preventative or a treatment may be unavoidable during the pre-and post-natal period.

Formula feeding

Those babies raised on formula milk have fewer bifidobacteria in their microflora, although if the formula milk also contains *pre*biotics, then the numbers of bifidobacteria and lactobacilli will be greater than in infants fed on unsupplemented formula [5,10].

It is not clear whether such differences in early microflora have any long-term consequences.

More recently, probiotic strains have been added to some formula milk products. A review of the studies of such products was unable to reach a conclusion as to their value and safety, because the studies were not of a sufficiently high standard [11].

Pre-term infants

As well as usually being below normal weight, babies born prematurely are usually lacking some or all of the maternal antibodies passed across the placenta in the last two weeks of a full-term pregnancy. The absence of these antibodies is particularly important because a newborn has an immature immune system, and consequently has a weak defence against pathogens. The pre-term infant may not receive maternal milk and therefore will also miss out on antibodies present in the milk [12].

Such a vulnerable child could do with the defences provided by a normal gut microflora, but frequently preterm infants have abnormal microflora. The establishment of lactobacilli and bifidobacteria is often delayed [13,14], the range of bacterial species is lower, and numbers of the pathogen *Clostridium difficile* are greater, compared with full-term babies [5]. Presumably, the pathogens are acquired from the 'intensive-care' hospital environment, as pre-term infants will be hospitalised for a longer period. Pre-term infants are also usually given antibiotics, and this may play a role in the microfloral abnormality.

Giving probiotics to children

As described in Chapter 6 (Probiotic Benefits for the Intestine), probiotics have consistently been found to be effective in treating children with infectious diarrhoea. On average, they reduce the duration of diarrhoea by 30 hours [15]. Furthermore, probiotics reduce the risk in children by half of developing antibiotic-associated diarrhoea [16]. There were no signs of side-effects from the probiotics in these studies, and this is perhaps slightly surprising, because young children have an immature immune system as well as a simple microflora.

The degree to which probiotics have proven to be very safe in children is illustrated in prematurely-born infants and the serious disease necrotising enterocolitis (NE). As described in Chapter 8 (Safety), the risk of developing NE is reduced by at least one-half in premature infants given probiotics, and there are no apparent side-effects for the infants.

It should not be that surprising that probiotics can help protect premature infants, because their microflora has very low levels of bifidobacteria [14]. Therefore, any added probiotic microbes are likely to be especially valuable, and also influential due to the relatively unstable mixture of microbes present.

Probiotics have also been shown to reduce the risk of developing allergic disease in children delivered by C-section. Pregnant mothers with a family history of allergy took a four-strain probiotic for the last month of pregnancy, and the infant took the probiotic for the first six months of its life. At age 5, of those children that had been caesarean-born, 24% of the probiotic group had experienced allergic disease compared with 41% in the placebo group [17].

Cow's milk allergy

While probiotic products are very safe, they are not completely free of risk. The probiotic bacteria are produced in fermentation tanks and are fed on a range of foods, often based on cow's milk. When the bacteria are turned into freeze-dried powder form, there may be tiny amounts of milk remaining. In children with a cow's milk allergy, the residual milk proteins have the potential of worsening atopic dermatitis.

Different probiotic products have different quantities of residual milk proteins, and these have different degrees of sensitising effect [18]. Alternatively, there are probiotic products that contain bacteria grown on carbohydrate, and therefore the milk allergy risk is removed.

Dosage for children

What dose of probiotic is appropriate for children? One team of medical doctors has claimed that 'practitioners' have used one-quarter the adult dose in infants and one-half the adult dose in children [19]. By 'infants' is meant babies up to 24 months of age, and a 'child' is in the age range of two years to puberty.

How do these proportions translate into actual doses (numbers of live microbes per day)? As explained in Chapter 9 (Choosing a Good Probiotic Product), there is no agreed dose for adults, because of the wide range of characteristics of probiotic products. There are different strains and different delivery systems (i.e. milk-based, capsules, powders, tablets). Furthermore, different illnesses may require different doses.

There have been very few dose-comparison studies in adults, and even fewer in children.

The elderly

Do the intestines change as an adult gets older? In most parts of the body, such as bones, brain, blood vessels, immune system, skin, and the senses (e.g. vision, hearing), there is deterioration with age. But the digestive system is essentially unchanged [20,21]. The ability to digest food is usually unaffected by age, and of course that is the main function of the intestinal tract.

There are, however, a few changes, and those that may have relevance to probiotics are:

- ❖ altered bacterial mixture in the microflora
- ❖ reduced stomach acid secretion
- ❖ constipation associated with physical inactivity and other factors
- ❖ diarrhoea caused by medications
- ❖ development of diverticula in the large intestine.

Altered microflora

People over the age of 65 years have fewer bifidobacteria in their gut microflora compared with young adults [22]. There is usually also an increase in the diversity of species [23].

It is not known why the microflora change in this way, but change of diet might be a factor. Some elderly people have a reduced ability to taste and smell, and consequently find food bland and uninteresting. Some have reduced ability to chew food due to loss of teeth and muscle bulk, and others have swallowing difficulties. Consequently, some elderly people choose a narrow and nutritionally imbalanced diet, and this may influence the microfloral changes [24].

Another possible explanation for the change in the microfloral mix, is that the mucus layer lining the gut wall is different in older people. Furthermore, strains of bifidobacteria that adhere less well to mucus are more common in the elderly [25].

What is the consequence of an altered microflora in people over the age of 65? It is not clear, but as bifidobacteria are usually acknowledged as being beneficial microbes, their loss seems undesirable.

It may therefore be that the consumption of a probiotic product containing bifidobacteria will provide general intestinal benefit. A milk-based probiotic would have the added benefit of providing nourishment to those consuming an imbalanced diet.

Reduced stomach acid secretion

The amount of hydrochloric acid secreted into the stomach tends to fall as people age [26]. It is not clear whether this is due to wasting of the stomach tissues, the presence of *Helicobacter pylori* infection, the drugs used to eradicate *H. pylori*, or some other cause [27].

Whether or not *H. pylori* infection is a factor in reduced acid production, it is likely that less acid in the stomach makes it easier for *H. pylori* to thrive. And it is the case that *H. pylori* infection is more common in the elderly [28]. As described in Chapter 6 (Probiotic Benefits for the Intestine), probiotics have been shown to support standard anti-*H. pylori* drug treatment, both in improving cure rates as well as reducing drug side-effects.

The reduced level of acid production also increases the risk of bacterial overgrowth in the small intestine (SIBO). Symptoms that are sometimes experienced with SIBO are abdominal discomfort, nausea and diarrhoea [29]. Furthermore, SIBO may interfere with the absorption of nutrients [30]. The usual way to treat SIBO is by antibiotics, but there is potential for a probiotic containing lactobacilli to help.

Constipation in the elderly

Constipation is a common complaint of the elderly, and possible contributing factors are: physical inactivity, various medications, and unsuitable diet [26,28].

One small study found that constipation in a group of people over the age of 60 was associated with a diet of low calorie-value, high protein and low fluid intake. There was also an association with various psychological problems, including depression [31].

Lactobacilli have been shown to alleviate constipation, with intestinal transit-time for faeces being reduced by between 20% and 50%. Animal studies have suggested that bifidobacteria may also reduce constipation, and may be more influential than lactobacilli. There is some evidence to suggest that the production of acetic acid by bifidobacteria (as a metabolic by-product) is a factor in accelerating gut transit [32,33].

Prebiotics may also help relieve constipation. Inulin was given to 10 constipated elderly hospital patients, and the constipation was reduced in nine of them. A dose of 20 grams per day led to an increase of bowel movements per week from one or two to eight or nine, without any diarrhoea. While there was an increase in numbers of bifidobacteria there was also a substantial increase in water in the stool. This suggests that the *prebiotic* was alleviating constipation partly through increased bifidobacteria and partly through osmosis of water from the body into the intestinal space [34,35].

Diarrhoea caused by medications

Although constipation is common among the elderly, diarrhoea is also relatively common. If the diarrhoea is caused by a microbial infection, the causal agent may be *Clostridium difficile*, which often arises following administration of antibiotics. Reduction in the effectiveness of immune cells in some elderly people may also be a factor in infectious diarrhoea [35,36].

Bacterial overgrowth of the small intestine, as mentioned under the section on stomach acid secretion, may involve pathogens that can cause infectious diarrhoea.

Clearly, probiotics are best known for preventing and treating infectious diarrhoea, and therefore here is another good reason to consider the use of probiotics as a daily preventative for older people.

Non-infectious diarrhoea may be provoked by various medicines, including those prescribed for diseases of the cardiovascular system and the central nervous system [21,28]. Diarrhoea is also more common in people with diabetes mellitus, perhaps due to abnormal activity of nerves to the stomach and intestine [37].

It is not known, however, whether probiotics can be of assistance with non-infectious types of diarrhoea.

Development of diverticula

Diverticular disease is essentially a disease of the elderly. It occurs in the large intestine and consists of small amounts of the inner lining of the gut wall squeezing through the muscle layers of the gut wall, and protruding out the other side. The protrusion is a sac or balloon, about the size of a small grape.

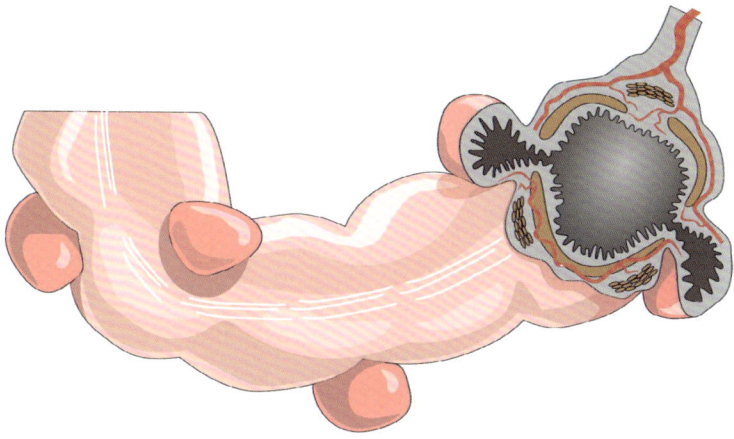

Fig 28: Diverticula in a section of the colon

The protrusions are known as diverticula, and they develop because of a lack of fibre in the diet. Although diverticula are quite common in people over the age of 60, they usually give no symptoms. Sometimes, however, an infection occurs in or near a diverticulum, and the resultant inflammation is called diverticulitis.

Diverticulitis can be very painful, and there is a small but serious risk of perforation of the diverticulum. If perforation occurs, this allows pathogens to enter the abdominal cavity and cause peritonitis, which is a dangerous condition, requiring surgery [28].

Treatment for diverticulitis is usually antibiotics. More recently, probiotics have shown some encouraging results, when combined with antibiotics or with anti-inflammatory drugs. But these studies did not have placebo treatments and so their value is hard to judge [38].

Summary of main points

- In infants, the predominant microbe in the intestine is *Bifidobacterium*, until weaning when a more adult-like microflora starts to develop.
- Birth by Caesarean section, antibiotic treatment of mother or infant, and formula milk feeding, all have the potential to influence the gut flora in babies. It is not clear, however, whether such changes to the microflora have any significant long-term effects.
- People over the age of 65, have fewer bifidobacteria in their gut microflora compared to young adults.
- Older people tend to have less hydrochloric acid in their stomach, and a higher incidence of *Helicobacter pylori* infection.
- The elderly are prone to developing diverticula protrusions through the outer wall of the large intestine. This may lead to an infection known as a diverticulitis, and in addition to antibiotics, probiotics may help with the treatment.

13

Future Developments

The amount of research produced each year on probiotics is accelerating. What might be discovered and developed in the future?

An ideal microflora?

While it is clear that probiotics can help remedy and prevent disease associated with a disturbed microflora, this has been achieved by only a few types of probiotic microbe. Could probiotic products be more effective if they included a wider range of microbes? Each person carries about 250 different species in their gut. Are any more of these probiotic?

Another way of looking at this question is to ask whether there is an 'ideal' mixture of species in a microflora, which can give us maximum protection from illness? Is there an ideal microflora for each part of our body surfaces, and should it be the ultimate goal of a probiotic product to promote such a microflora? And are there particular lifestyles that could aid the achievement of an ideal microflora?

For example, are the ten most common microbial species found living on the skin the best for protecting our skin? If they are the best species, what proportions of the different species are best?

By examining the skin microflora of healthy people in different parts of the world, and comparing them with diseased skin, it should be possible to obtain a clear picture of a healthy skin microflora. This information could be used to develop probiotic skin creams. And health professionals could develop advice on what to do to keep your skin microflora healthy. For example, is it better to bare one's skin to the sun or cover it up with clothing?

This approach could be used for all of the body's microflora. But it would be much more complicated with the gut flora, because there is such a large number of species involved. Analysis is made more complicated because there appears to be quite a lot of variation between individuals. It may even be that the concept of an ideal microflora in the gut is fulfilled by the combined metabolic processes of the microflora, rather than a fixed proportion of genera and species [1]. When the gut microflora is better understood, perhaps there will be a diet identified that is able to promote an ideal gut microflora.

The pursuit of the identification of ideal microflora is likely to continue, and clearer pictures are likely to appear. This knowledge should facilitate the development of more effective probiotic and *pre*biotics products that are specific to different parts of the body.

The effects of stress

There are many aspects of the microflora that remain a puzzle, and among these is the relationship between stress in humans and the resident microbes. Stress can initiate or worsen disease, and this occurs through an interaction between the body's nervous system and immune system [2].

Intestinal diseases are among those influenced by stress, and this involves the nervous and immune tissues of the gut wall and the bacteria living in the intestine. Stress has been recorded as reducing the number of lactobacilli and bifidobacteria in the gut, and increasing the number of Gram-negative pathogens. Furthermore, members of the microflora are able to sense when their host is stressed and change their behaviour into a disease-causing form.

There is some evidence of probiotics relieving the intestinal effects of stress, particularly in reducing 'leaky gut' [3,4]. A clear picture of how probiotics influence the nervous system has not yet been achieved, but it is known that lactobacilli convert nitrate to nitric oxide, which has substantial influence on the nervous system. There is also some evidence that the gut microflora influence the production of hormones that affect the brain [5], and there is potential for the use of probiotics here.

The selection of strains of bacteria to reliably influence stress may not develop rapidly until a better understanding is gained of how the nerves in the brain and the gut interrelate, and how they relate with the immune and hormonal systems.

The choice of antibiotics

Antibiotics are powerfully-effective drugs against bacterial pathogens, but they also damage our microflora [6]. How can the damage to the microflora be minimised? One way is to take probiotics at the same time as antibiotics. We know, from the reduction in risk of developing antibiotic-associated diarrhoea, that probiotics can limit the anti-microfloral effects of antibiotics, but probiotics do not stop the damage completely.

Different antibiotics have different effects on the microflora, and the question arises of whether the selection of antibiotic drugs to treat a disease should involve consideration of the drug's degree of harm to the microflora.

The reason why different antibiotics have different effects on the microflora is that they are administered in different ways, work in different ways, and are eliminated in different ways. Most antibiotics are taken orally, but they may be administered by injection into veins or muscles. Generally, oral antibiotics are more harmful to the gut microflora, especially if they are poorly absorbed into the body, leaving substantial amounts in the intestine. Antibiotics administered by other routes can still harm the gut microflora. Some of the surplus drug may be removed from the body by secretion into the intestine (via the gut lining or in bile), rather than excreted safely in urine via the bladder [7].

Some oral antibiotics have a much-reduced harmful effect on the gut microflora, because they are in 'prodrug' form. This involves producing the antibiotic in an inactive form so that it has no antibacterial effect in the gut, but when it is absorbed into the tissues it is chemically converted into an active drug. Of course, such prodrugs may still harm the microflora if they are subsequently secreted in an active form into the gut.

Another factor in the complicated question of whether a particular antibiotic drug will seriously harm the microflora, is whether it is broad-spectrum or narrow-spectrum. A narrow-spectrum antibiotic works against a characteristic of a particular type of bacterium, while a broad-spectrum antibiotic works against characteristics that are widely shared among microbes. Thus, standard penicillin is narrow-spectrum, because it works better against Gram-positive bacteria than against Gram-negative bacteria (a division based on differences in cell wall structure). In comparison, tetracycline is broad-spectrum, because it works against both Gram-positives and Gram-negatives.

In medicine, broad-spectrum antibiotics are more commonly prescribed, because the species causing the disease may not be known. The use of a wide-acting drug is more likely to achieve eradication of the infecting bacterium, but the negative consequence for the microflora is naturally greater.

In order to select antibiotics that cause least damage to the gut microflora, it is necessary to develop a clear record of the microfloral effects of different antibiotics. Unfortunately, such a record has not yet been produced. Recent technological advances have enabled an accurate map of all the species in the gut microflora. This makes it possible to check the effect of a specific antibiotic by comparing the microfloral species before and after consumption of the drug.

For example, a recent study using ciprofloxacin, a broad-spectrum antibiotic thought to have relatively few intestinal side effects, was analysed in detail for its effects on gut microflora. It was found that 30% of species were substantially reduced, but within four weeks of completion of the antibiotic course, the microfloral mix had returned to near normal. There were, however, a few species that had not returned even after six months [8].

I expect that in the coming years all commonly-used antibiotic drugs will be tested for their microfloral effects and this information will be provided to doctors. In future, therefore, when prescribing antibiotics, doctors may select a particular drug not only to target the infection, but also to limit damage to the microflora.

Additional conditions to benefit from probiotics

With microflora being present on all surfaces of the human body, and the ability of these resident microbes to influence the immune system, there is potential for a wide range of health benefits from probiotics. This section lists a few illnesses which may, in the future, be found to be improvable through the use of probiotics.

Colo-rectal cancer

One of the areas of the body more commonly affected by cancer is the large intestine, especially the latter part of the colon and the rectum. This is often referred to as colo-rectal cancer, and probiotics have been considered for its prevention.

The cause of colo-rectal cancer is not clear, although diet is believed to be a factor. The gut microflora may also be involved. The mixture of microfloral species in the stool of people at high risk of colorectal cancer were found to differ from those at low risk [9].

Some types of bacteria in the gut microflora convert substances into cancer-causing molecules. They do this through the use of certain enzymes. In laboratory experiments, probiotics have been used with a view to reducing the production of such harmful enzymes. These experiments have given encouraging results [10].

Animals at high risk of developing colon cancer were given probiotics and the researchers looked for the appearance of tumours, or early signs of damage to the intestinal surface (aberrant crypt foci - ACF). Ten animal studies were undertaken and all demonstrated a protective effect from the probiotics, with a reduction in the appearance of ACF by almost 50% [11].

*Pre*biotics have also been used in animal studies; and inulin, a long-chain carbohydrate, was particularly effective in reducing colonic cancer [12]. *Pre*biotics also increased the effectiveness of anti-cancer drugs in one study [13].

It is difficult to do human trials on the prevention of cancer, because it usually takes 10-30 years for cancer to develop, and such a lengthy study is very difficult to organise and fund [14].

An alternative is to measure bio-markers (indicators) for high risk of developing colo-rectal cancer. Although some markers are being investigated for their predictive reliability, they are not yet fully validated. Some of these markers are found in 'faecal water', which is the liquid that is separated from the solids in human faeces. Faecal water is analysed for its chemical contents, with certain compounds identified as likely to cause cancerous mutations.

A human study was undertaken on 34 patients with colon cancer and on 40 patients who had had malignant polyps removed. The latter group is at high risk of developing further malignancies. A probiotic and *pre*biotic mixture (synbiotic) was consumed for 12 weeks by both groups. The study analysed cancer-related biomarkers in biopsies (small tissue samples), in blood, and in stool.

The study found that the synbiotic "exerted marked effects on several of the studied markers and no effects on other markers" [15]. This gives some support to the role of probiotics and *pre*biotics in reducing the risk of developing colo-rectal cancer. There is, however, much that needs to be discovered, not least which species and strains are most useful in producing anti-cancer effects.

Radiation-induced diarrhoea

Irradiation of malignant tumours (radiotherapy) is one of the mainstream treatments for cancer. Radiotherapy of the abdomen and the pelvic region is undertaken for a variety of cancers, and has the potential to disturb the intestine.

In the UK, 12,000 individuals are treated with radiotherapy for pelvic cancer annually, and for the rest of the Western world, figures probably total about 150,000 [16]. About 80% of abdominally-irradiated patients develop diarrhoea, and less commonly constipation, faecal incontinence, nausea and vomiting [17]. These effects are sometimes mild, but in other cases are more serious, and may lead to suspension of treatment.

There have been four randomised-controlled trials of probiotics to prevent or treat radiation-induced diarrhoea. The results of the probiotic studies suggest that the proportion of people who develop such diarrhoea may be reduced by about one-third [18]; and probiotics may also aid recovery from such diarrhoea. To prevent diarrhoea it may be better to use a probiotic from a few days before the start of radiotherapy to a week or two after completion of therapy. Probiotics have not yet been accepted as a standard supportive therapy.

Obesity

Various studies have suggested that obese people have a different mixture of bacteria in their gut microflora than lean people. The connection between obesity and bacteria is probably because gut bacteria differ in their ability to break down undigested food in the large intestine. These differences mean that different amounts of energy molecules are released by the bacteria, which are then taken up by the human body and stored as fat.

The differences in the microflora of obese people have only been identified in a broad manner - at the phylum level of classification, which is broader than the genus level, covering a much wider range of species. Obese people appear to have more Firmicutes and fewer Bacteroidetes [1,19]. This broad picture will need to be made much more specific through more research, if 'slimming bacteria' (if there are such things) are to be identified.

Despite the early stage of research, some people are wondering whether probiotic products might be devised that could aid weight loss. It is too early to say whether this is possible, or whether any weight loss due to probiotics would be substantial enough. It is worth noting, however, that evidence suggests that the microfloral mixture acquired in young children is a major determinant of adult microflora. If so, then diet and probiotics may well be especially important in the early years [1].

Whatever the outcome of future research and probiotic product development, it is safe to say that the quantity of food calories consumed is always likely to be the main factor governing obesity.

Various other conditions

There is some evidence that changes in diet and changes in gut microflora have an influence on rheumatoid arthritis (RA) [20]. People with RA seem to carry a higher level of *Clostridium perfringens*. Perhaps, there is potential for probiotics to improve RA.

A group of people with multiple sclerosis (MS), who also had infections of gut parasitic worms, were found to have improved health. Over a four-year period, the group had fewer exacerbations of their MS symptoms and a generally more stable condition, than a comparable group of MS patients without parasites [21]. The improvements were described as being "dramatic" by editors of the journal of the American Neurological Association [22].

Coeliac disease is an intestinal condition caused by an inability to digest certain proteins from cereal grains. People with coeliac disease have a different mixture of species in their gut microflora compared with healthy people. There are higher numbers of Gram-negative bacteria and lower numbers of beneficial Gram-positive bacteria.

Even though there were higher numbers of Gram-negative bacteria, the diversity of species within this category was substantially reduced [23]. Among the Gram-positives, the diversity of *Bifidobacterium* species was reduced [24]. This abnormal microflora suggests that probiotics might play a role in influencing coeliac disease.

The probiotic yeast *Saccharomyces boulardii* has been used in three studies in people with amoebiasis. This is an intestinal disease with a range of symptoms, including bloody diarrhoea, that is caused by the protozoan parasite *Entamoeba hystolytica*. The yeast was given as an addition to the standard antimicrobial drugs. In two of the studies, the yeast substantially accelerated recovery, but in the third there was no benefit [25,26,27]. A protozoan is a single-celled organism whose internal structures are more complicated than bacteria. Protozoan infections tend to occur in unsanitary and tropical environments. There has been very little research on the effects of probiotics on disease-causing protozoa, and this may change in the future.

Surgery

Infections that develop after surgery are usually caused by the patient's own microflora. The reasons for this are not fully understood, but several factors are likely to be involved. Some infection may be due to intestinal tissue damage during abdominal surgery. Another factor may be a 'leaky' gut wall. This may occur through disturbance to normal gut muscle contractions, leading to bacterial overgrowth in the small intestine, which in turn weakens the barrier of the gut lining, allowing bacteria to cross over into body tissues [28]. The use of drugs to suppress immune function may also play a role in post-surgery infections, as may patient stress.

Whatever the causes, the standard procedure to protect against such infection has been to provide antibiotics before and after surgery. But due to the rise of antibiotic resistance the risk of infection remains a serious problem, and some thought has therefore been given to the use of probiotics.

Out of 14 clinical studies, probiotics reduced the rate of post-surgery infection in nine studies [28]. The probiotics also tended to reduce the duration of stay in hospital and the length of antibiotic therapy [29]. It is not clear, however, why probiotics were not effective in all the studies. One factor may be the type of species and strains used. For example, seven strains of *Staphylococcus aureus* have been shown to accelerate wound healing, while other species of *Staphylococcus* had no such effect [30].

It seems unlikely that probiotics will be used routinely in surgery patients until it has been shown that the benefits can be consistently delivered.

Unusual approaches to probiotics

There are several types of probiotic therapy with which people are unfamiliar, and may consider strange, which may become important in the future. They are:
- bacteriophages
- faecal enemas
- worm therapy.

Bacteriophages

Bacteriopages, also known as phages, are viruses that kill bacteria. Viruses are microbes, but unlike other microbes they are not true living entities. They consist of genetic material surrounded by protein, and are completely inactive except when they enter (infect) a living cell. On entry into the cell, the virus will multiply using the cell's apparatus.

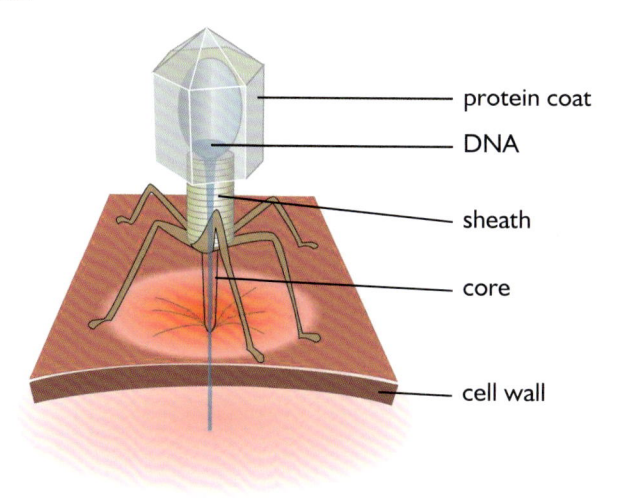

Fig 29: A bacteriophage

Different viruses infect different hosts. There are viruses of animals and viruses of plants. Phages are the viruses of bacteria and they are very specific in their target. Each type of phage will only infect one species of bacterium. As phages cannot invade human cells, the idea of using them to tackle hard-to-treat infections of known pathogens is attractive. In fact, this idea has been pursued in Eastern Europe and the former Soviet Union since 1919 [31], with phages routinely used in some hospitals as treatment for bacterial infections. Only recently has this approach been taken seriously in the West.

The potential advantage of phages is that they only target the pathogen of interest, and the gut microflora is not affected. Also, as viruses multiply within cells, only a small phage dose may be needed, as the phage numbers are increased hugely inside a target pathogen and then released to infect other cells of the same pathogen. There also appear to be very few cases of side effects. The obvious drawback is that they can only be used if the specific pathogen causing the disease has been identified.

There are many questions that still need to be addressed, such as effects on the human immune system, and the development of phage-resistant bacteria, before phage therapy becomes standard treatment throughout the world. But the experience in Eastern Europe is encouraging.

Faecal enemas

Infection with *Clostridium difficile* is a risk arising from the use of broad-spectrum antibiotics (as described in Chapter 6). This is a particular problem when the infection recurs repeatedly. Infection by *C. difficile* is treated by antibiotics, and so there is a real danger of a continuous cycle of permanently-damaged gut microflora, with recurring diarrhoea or the more severe pseudomembranous colitis.

In order to break that cycle, more than 100 patients with *C. difficile* infection have been treated with faecal enemas (or similar), with a success rate of 89% in permanently eliminating the infection. The treatment consists of liquefied stool from a healthy person introduced into the intestine of the patient, usually by a gravity-fed enema system through the anus. Sometimes, the stool is introduced by a tube through the nose, along the oesophagus, through the stomach and into the upper small intestine. The person supplying the stool is usually a family member or a close friend, and the stool is checked to make sure there are no pathogens present [32].

Prior to the faecal installation, patients are usually treated with the antibiotic vancomycin (to eliminate as many of the *C. difficile* cells as possible). The patients are then treated with a bowel-cleansing substance that cleans out most of the faeces (and the microflora).

The nasal-tube route usually only requires one installation, while the enema route requires several doses. There is also usually some leakage from the anus in the enema system. It may, therefore, be that the nasal route will prove more popular in time, as the 'faecal bacteriotherapy' approach becomes more widely accepted by the medical profession.

Faecal enemas have been tried in patients with ulcerative colitis, also to good effect [33].

Worm therapy

There is growing evidence that parasitic worms influence the immune systems of humans in ways that may help reduce allergic, autoimmune and inflammatory diseases. This was referred to in Chapter 4, when describing the rise in allergies in developed countries. One explanation for the increase in allergies is the absence in the gut of microbial 'old friends', such as parasitic worms (helminths).

This idea is supported by evidence, such as the reduction in multiple sclerosis symptoms in a small number of people who also had worm infections, as mentioned earlier in this chapter. A study of more than 12,000 Ethiopians found an association between hookworm infection and reduced risk of developing asthma [34]. And in Uganda, it was found that pregnant women with intestinal worm infection were much less likely to give birth to infants who developed atopic eczema [35].

The worms appear to stimulate the activity of a particular type of immune cell, the T-helper 2 cell. In contrast, many allergies and autoimmune diseases involve activity by the 'opposite' immune cell, T-helper 1.

Fig 30: Helminthic worms

There is a great deal to discover about the potential role of helminthic worms in conditions of immune-malfunction. It is, however, fairly clear that not all species will be suitable, not least because they may cause intestinal disease themselves [36]. Furthermore, the dose used may affect whether there is an improvement or a worsening of the condition being treated.

Despite these uncertainties, there have been some positive human treatments. Pig whipworm eggs were swallowed by people with inflammatory bowel disease [37,38], and hookworm larvae were added to the skin of people with asthma [39]. The former were more effective than the latter.

These studies involve small numbers of participants, and it is too early to say whether worm therapy will really be shown to provide reliable and substantial benefits.

Summary of main points

- It may be possible to define an ideal mixture of species for each of the body's microflora, although in the case of the gut microflora it may be an ideal set of metabolic processes.
- Human stress can influence the gut microflora, and the gut microflora may be able to influence long-term stress. In future, it may be possible to develop probiotics to relieve such stress. But much more needs to be learnt about the relationship between nerve cells in the brain and nerve cells in the intestine before the development of stress-reducing probiotics can be seriously considered.
- Different antibiotic drugs have different effects on the microflora. As these effects become better understood, it may be possible to select antibiotics so that harm to the microflora is minimised.
- Conditions currently not treatable by probiotics, but that may be influenced in the future are: colorectal cancer, obesity, rheumatoid arthritis, multiple sclerosis, coeliac disease and amoebiosis.
- Infections developing after surgery are often caused by bacteria from the gut microflora. The use of probiotics to reduce the risk of developing such infections has had mixed results. It may be necessary to understand better the causes of post-surgery infection before reliable probiotics can be developed.
- Three unusual probiotic-type therapies that may become more important in the future are: bacteriophages, faecal enemas, and worm therapy.

References

Preface
(1) AlFaleh, K.M. & Bassler, D. (2009) Probiotics for the prevention of necrotizing enterocolitis in preterm infants (Review). *Cochrane Database of Systematic Reviews*, Issue 1. Art. No.: CD005496.
(2) Whorwell, P.J., Altringer, L., Morel, J., *et al*. (2006) Efficacy of an Encapsulated Probiotic Bifidobacterium infantis 35624 in Women with Irritable Bowel Syndrome. *American Journal of Gastroenterology* 101: 1581-1590.
(3) Hatakka, K., Ahola, A.J., Yli-Knuuttila, H., *et al*. (2007) Probiotics Reduce the Prevalence of Oral Candida in the Elderly - a Randomized Controlled Trial. *Journal of Dental Research* 86: 125-130.

Chapter 1 – The Creatures With Whom We Live
(1) Line, M.A. (2002) The enigma of the origin of life and its timing. *Microbiology* 148: 21-27.
(2) Douzery, E.J.P., Snell, E.A., Bapteste, E., *et al*. (2004) The timing of eukaryotic evolution: Does a relaxed molecular clock reconcile proteins and fossils. *PNAS* 101: 15386-15391.

Chapter 2 – Our Microflora
(1) Dethlefsen, L., McFall-Ngai, M. & Relman, D.A. (2007) An ecological and evolutionary perspective on human-microbe mutualism and disease. *Nature*, October 449: 811-818.
(2) Gordon, H.A., Bruckner-Kardoss, E. & Wostmann, B.S. (1966) Aging in Germ-Free Mice: Life Tables and Lesions Observed at Natural Death. *Journal of Gerontology* 21: 380-387.
(3) Luckey, T.D. (1972) Introduction to intestinal microecology. *American Journal of Clinical Nutrition* 25: 1292-1294.
(4) Selwyn, S. (1980) Microbiology and ecology of human skin. *The Practitioner* 224: 1059-1062.
(5) Tannock, G.W. (1999) The normal microflora: an introduction. In *Medical Importance of the Normal Microflora* (Tannock, G.W., ed.). Kluwer Academic Publishers, Dordrecht, Netherlands. 1-23.
(6) Dekio, I., Hayashi, H., Sakamoto, M., *et al*. (2005) Detection of potentially novel bacterial components of the human skin microbiota using culture-independent molecular profiling. *Journal of Medical Microbiology* 54: 1231-1238.
(7) Grice, E.A., Kong, H.H., Conlan, S., *et al*. (2009) Topographical and Temporal Diversity of the Human Skin Microbiome. *Science* 324 (5931): 1190-1192.
(8) Selwyn, S. (1975) Natural antibiosis among skin bacteria as a primary defence against infection. *British Journal of Dermatology* 93: 487-493.
(9) Cogen, A.L., Nizet, V. & Gallo, R.L. (2008) Skin microbiota: a source of disease or defence? *British Journal of Dermatology* 158: 442-455.
(10) Brook, I. (2005) The Role of Bacterial Interference in Otitis, Sinusitis and Tonsillitis. *Otolaryngology – Head and Neck Surgery* 133: 139-146.
(11) Hull, M.W. & Chow, A.W. (2007) Indigenous Microflora and Innate Immunity of the Head and Neck. *Infectious Disease Clinics of North America* 21: 265-282.
(12) Rosenberg, M. (2002) The Science of Bad Breath. *Scientific American* 286(4): 58-65.

(13) Kazor, C.E., Mitchell, P.M., Lee, A.M., et al. (2003) Diversity of Bacterial Populations on the Tongue Dorsa of Patients with Halitosis and Healthy Patients. *Journal of Clinical Microbiology* 41: 558-563.

(14) Berg, R.D. (1996) The indigenous gastrointestinal microflora. *Trends in Microbiology* 4: 430-435.

(15) Kleessen, B., Bezirtzoglou, E. & Matto, J. (2000) Culture-Based Knowledge on Biodiversity, Development and Stability of Human Gastrointestinal Microflora. *Microbial Ecology in Health and Disease* Suppl 2: 53-63.

(16) Jenkinson, H.F. & Lamont, R.J. (2005) Oral microbial communities in sickness and in health. *Trends in Microbiology* 13: 589-595.

(17) Gordon, H.A. & Pesti, L. (1971) The Gnotobiotic Animal as a Tool in the Study of Host Microbial Relationships. *Bacteriological Reviews* 35: 390-429.

(18) Tamrakar, R., Yamada, T., Furuta, I., et al. (2007) Association between Lactobacillus species and bacterial vaginosis-related bacteria, and bacterial vaginosis scores in pregnant Japanese women. *BMC Infectious Diseases* 7: 128. http//:www.biomedcentral.com/1471-2334/7/128. Accessed 16 May 2008.

(19) Vitali, B., Pugliese, C., Biagi, E., et al. (2007) Dynamics of Vaginal Bacterial Communities in Women Developing Bacterial Vaginosis, Candidiasis, or No Infection, Analyzed by PCR-Denaturing Gradient Gel Electrophoresis and Real-Time PCR. *Applied and Environmental Microbiology* 73: 5731-5741.

Chapter 3 – The Gut Microflora

(1) Cash, R.A., Music, S.I., Libonati, J.P., et al. (1974) Response of Man to Infection with Vibrio cholerae. I. Clinical, Serologic, and Bacteriologic Responses to a Known Inoculum. *The Journal of Infectious Diseases* 129: 45-52.

(2) Moore, W.E.C., Cato, E.P. & Holdeman, L.V. (1969) Anaerobic Bacteria of the Gastrointestinal Flora and Their Occurrence in Clinical Infections. *Journal of Infectious Diseases* 119: 641-649.

(3) Franklin, M.A. & Skoryna, S.C. (1971) Studies on natural gastric flora: Survival of bacteria in fasting human subjects. *Canadian Medical Association Journal* 105: 1349-1355.

(4) Savage, D.C. (1977) Microbial Ecology of the Gastrointestinal Tract. *Annual Review of Microbiology* 31: 107-133.

(5) Uphill, P.F., Wilde, J.K.H. & Berger, J. (1974) Repeated Examinations, Using the Laparotomy Sampling Technique, of the Gastro-intestinal Microflora of Baboons Fed a Natural or a Synthetic Diet. *Journal of Applied Bacteriology* 37: 309-317.

(6) Cregan, J. & Hayward, N.J. (1953) The Bacterial Content of the Healthy Small Intestine. *British Medical Journal* 1: 1356-1359.

(7) Simon, G.L. & Gorbach, S.L. (1984) Intestinal Flora in Health and Disease. *Gastroenterology* 86: 174-193.

(8) Dickman, M.D., Chappelka, A.R. & Schaedler, R.W. (1976) The Microbial Ecology of the Upper Small Bowel. *American Journal of Gastroenterology* 65: 57-62.

(9) Read, N.W. & Brown, N.J. (1991) The Small Intestine and the Ileal Brake. In *Gastrointestinal Transit: Pathophysiology and Pharmacology* (Kamm, M.A. & Lennard-Jones, J.E., eds.) Wrightson Biomedical Publishing, Petersfield, England 55-64.

(10) Berg, R.D. (1996) The indigenous gastrointestinal microflora. *Trends in Microbiology* 4: 430-435.

(11) Tannock, G.W. (2003) The Intestinal Microflora. In *Gut Flora, Nutrition, Immunity and Health* (Fuller, R. & Perdigon, G., eds.). Blackwell Publishing, Oxford, U.K. 1-23.

(12) Suau, A, Bonnet, R., Sutren, M., et al. (1999) Direct Analysis of Genes Encoding 16S rRNA from Complex Communities Reveals Many Novel Molecular Species within the Human Gut. *Applied and Environmental Microbiology* 65: 4799-4807.

(13) Macfarlane, S. & Macfarlane, G.T. (2006) Composition and Metabolic Activities of Bacterial Biofilms Colonizing Food Residues in the Human Gut. *Applied and Environmental Microbiology* 72: 6204-6211.

(14) Probert, H.M. & Gibson, G.R. (2002) Bacterial Biofilms in the Human Gastrointestinal Tract. *Current Issues in Intestinal Microbiology* 3: 23-27.

(15) Luckey, T.D. (1972) Introduction to intestinal microecology. *American Journal of Clinical Nutrition* 25: 1292-1294.

(16) Luckey, T.D. (1977) Bicentennial overview of intestinal microecology. *American Journal of Clinical Nutrition* 30: 1753-1761.

(17) Finegold, S.M., Attebery, H.R. & Sutter, V.L. (1974) Effect of diet on human fecal flora: comparison of Japanese and American diets. *American Journal of Clinical Nutrition* 27: 1456-1469.

(18) Rajilic-Stanovic, M., Smidt, H. & de Vos, W.M. (2007) Diversity of the human gastrointestinal tract microbiotia revisited. *Environmental Microbiology* 9: 2125-2136.

(19) Tannock, G.W. (2007) What immunologists should know about the human bowel. *Seminars in Immunology* 19: 94-105.

(20) Qin, J., Li, R., Raes, J., *et al.* (2010) A human gut microbial catalogue established by metagenomic sequencing. *Nature* Mar 4; 464 (7285): 59-65.

(21) Tap, J., Mondot, S., Levenez, F., *et al.* (2009) Towards the human intestinal microbiota phylogenetic core. *Environmental Microbiology* 11: 2574-2584.

(22) Flint, H-J., Duncan, S.H., Scott, K.P., *et al.* (2007) Interactions and competition with the microbial community of the human colon: links between diet and health. *Environmental Microbiology* 9: 1101-1111.

(23) Kleessen, B., Bezirtzoglou, E. & Matto, J. (2000) Culture-Based Knowledge on Biodiversity, Development and Stability of Human Gastrointestinal Microflora. *Microbial Ecology in Health and Disease* Suppl 2: 53-63.

(24) Macfarlane, S. & Macfarlane, G.T. (2003) Food and the Large Intestine. In *Gut Flora, Nutrition, Immunity and Health* (Fuller, R. & Perdigon, G., eds.). Blackwell Publishing, Oxford, U.K.: 24-51.

(25) Wostmann, B.S., Larkin, C., Moriarty, A., *et al.* (1983) Dietary Intake, Energy Metabolism, and Excretory Losses of Adult Male Germfree Wistar Rats. *Laboartory Animal Science* 33:46-50.

(26) Jukes, T.H. (1977) The history of the "antibiotic growth effect". *Federation Proceedings* 37: 2514-2518.

(27) Visek, W.J. (1978) The Mode of Growth Promotion by Antibiotics. *Journal of Animal Science* 46: 1447-1469.

(28) Czuprynski, C.J. & Balish, E. (1981) Pathogenesis of Listeria monocytogenes for Gnotobiotic Rats. *Infection and Immunity* 32: 323-331.

(29) Moberg, L.J. & Sugiyama, H. (1979) Microbial Ecological Basis of Infant Botulism as Studied with Germ-Free Mice. *Infection and Immunity* 25: 653-657.

(30) Harp, J.A., Wannemuehler, M.W., Woodmansee, D.B., *et al.* (1988) Susceptibility of Germfree or Antibiotic-Treated Adult Mice to Clostridium parvum. *Infection and Immunity* 56: 2006-2010.

(31) Zachar, Z. & Savage, D.C. (1979) Microbial Interference and Colonization of the Murine Gastrointestinal Tract by Listeria monocytogenes. *Infection and Immunity* 23: 168-174.

(32) Nurmi, R. & Rantala, M. (1973) New Aspects of Salmonella Infection in Broiler Production. *Nature* 241: 210-211.

(33) Collins, F.M. & Carter, P.B. (1978) Growth of Salmonella in Orally Infected Germfree Mice. *Infection and Immunity* 21: 41-47.

(34) Miller, C.P., Bohnhoff, M. & Rifkind, D. (1956-7) The Effect of an Antibiotic on the Susceptibility of the Mouse's Intestinal Tract to Salmonella Infection. *Transactions of the American Clinical and Climatological Association* 68: 51-58.

(35) Gordon, H.A. & Pesti, L. (1971) The Gnotobiotic Animal as a Tool in the Study of Host Microbial Relationships. *Bacteriological Reviews* 35: 390-429.
(36) O'Hara, A.M. & Shanahan, F. (2006) The gut flora as a forgotten organ. *EMBO reports* 7: 688-693.
(37) Hill, M.J. (1981) Diet and the Human Intestinal Bacterial Flora. *Cancer Research* 41: 3778-3780.
(38) Finegold, S.M., Sutter, V.L., Sugihara, P.T., *et al.* (1977) Fecal microbial flora in Seventh Day Adventist populations and control subjects. *American Journal of Clinical Nutrition* 30: 1781-1792.
(39) Peltonen, R., Ling, W-H, Hanninen, O., *et al.* (1992) An Uncooked Vegan Diet Shifts the Profile of Human Fecal Microflora. *Applied and Environmental Microbiology* 58: 3660-3666.
(40) Moore, W.E.C., Peltonen, R. & Eerola, E. (1993) Effect of Substrate Composition on Intestinal Flora. *Applied and Environmental Microbiology* 59: 2763-2764.
(41) Wynne, A.G., McCartney, A.L., Brostoff, J., *et al.* (2004) An in vitro assessment of the effects of broad-spectrum antibiotics on the human gut microflora and concomitant isolation of a Lactobacillus plantarum with anti-Candida activities. *Anaerobe* 10: 165-169.
(42) Bodey, G.P., Fainstein, V., Garcia, I., *et al.* (1983) Effect of Broad-Spectrum Cephalosporins on the Microbial Flora of Recipients. *Journal of Infectious Diseases* 148: 892-897.
(43) Bartosch, S., Fite, A., Macfarlane, G.T., *et al.* (2004) Characterization of Bacterial Communities in Feces from Healthy Elderly Volunteers and Hospitalized Elderly Patients by Using Real-Time PCR and Effects of Antibiotic Treatment on the Fecal Microbiota. *Applied and Environmental Microbiology* 70: 3575-3581.
(44) Sullivan, A., Edlund, C. & Nord, C.E. (2001) Effect of antimicrobial agents on the ecological balance of human microflora. *The Lancet Infectious Diseases* 1: 101-114.
(45) Giuliano, M., Barza, M., Jacobus, N.V., *et al.* (1987) Effect of Broad-Spectrum Parenteral Antibiotics on Composition of Intestinal Microflora of Humans. *Antimicrobial Agents and Chemotherapy* 31: 202-206.

Chapter 4. – The Immune System and the Microflora

(1) Honjo, T. & Melchers, F. (2006) Preface. In *Gut-Associated Lymphoid Tissues* (Honjo, T. & Melchers, F., eds). Springer, Heidelberg, Germany. :i-iii.
(2) Rakoff-Nahoum, S. & Medzhitov, R. (2006) Role of the Innate Immune System and Host-Commensal Mutualism. *Current Topics in Microbiology and Immunology* 308: 1-18.
(3) Forchielli, M.L. & Walker, W.A. (2005) The role of gut-associated lymphoid tissues and mucosal defence. *British Journal of Nutrition* 93, Suppl. 1: S41-S48.
(4) O'Hara, A.M. & Shanahan, F. (2006) The gut flora as a forgotten organ. *EMBO reports* 7: 688-693.
(5) Cebra, J.J. (1999) Influences of microbiota on intestinal immune system development. *American Journal of Clinical Nutrition* 69 (suppl): 1046S-1051S.
(6) Tannock, G.W. (2007) What immunologists should know about the human bowel. *Seminars in Immunology* 19: 94-105.
(7) Moreau, M-C. (2006) Influence of the Intestinal Microflora on Host Immunity: Normal Physiological Conditions. In *Gut Microflora: Digestive Physiology and Pathology* (Rambaud, J.-C., Buts, J-P., Corthier, G. & Flourie, B., eds). John Libbey Eurotext, Montrouge, France.: 131-149.
(8) Penders, J., Stobberingh, E.E., van den Brandt, P.A. & Thijs, C. (2007) The role of the intestinal microbiota in the development of atopic disorders. *Allergy* 62: 1223-1236.
(9) Riedler, J. Braun-Fahrlander, C., Eder, W. *et al.* (2001) Exposure to farming in early life and development of asthma and allergy: a cross-sectional survey. *The Lancet* 358, October 6: 1129-1133.
(10) Strachan, D.P. (2000) Family size, infection and atopy: the first decade of the "hygiene hypothesis". *Thorax* 55(Suppl 1): S2-S10.

(11) Rook, G.A.W. & Brunet, L.R. (2005) Microbes, immunoregulation, and the gut. *Gut* 54: 317-320.

(12) Kelly, D., Conway, S. & Aminov, R. (2005) Commensal gut bacteria: mechanisms of immune modulation. *Trends in Immunology* 26: 326-333.

(13) Simhon, A., Douglas, J.R., Drasar, B.S. *et al.* (1982) Effect of feeding on infants' faecal flora. *Archives of Disease in Childhood* 57: 54-58.

(14) Pordeus,V., Szyper-Kravitz, M., Levy, R.A., *et al.*(2008) Infections and Autoimmunity: A Panorama. *Clinical Reviews in Allergy and Immunology* 34:283-299.

(15) Shoenfeld, Y., Gilburd, B., Abu- Shakra, M., *et al.* (2008) The Mosaic of Autoimmunity: Genetic Factors Involved in Autoimmune Diseases – 2008. *IMAJ* 10: 3-9.

(16) Bach, J-F. (2005) Infections and autoimmune diseases. *Journal of Autoimmunity* 25: 74–80.

(17) Ouwehand, A., Isolauri, E. & Salminen, S. (2002). The role of the intestinal microflora for the development of the immune system in early childhood. *European Journal of Nutrition* 41 (Suppl 1): 1/32-1/37.

Chapter 5 – A History of Probiotics

(1) Newman, J. (2000) Wine. In *The Cambridge World History of Food* (Kiple, K. & Ornelas, K.C., eds.) Cambridge University Press, Cambridge, U.K.: 730-737.

(2) Cantrell, P. (2000) Beer and Ale. In *The Cambridge World History of Food* (Kiple, K. & Ornelas, K.C., eds.) Cambridge University Press, Cambridge, U.K.: 619-625.

(3) Bengmark, S, (1998) Ecological control of the gastrointestinal tract. The role of probiotic flora. *Gut* 42: 2-7.

(4) Cambell-Platt, G. (1994) Fermented Foods – a world perspective. *Food Research International* 27: 253-257.

(5) Postgate, J. (2000) *Microbes and Man*. Cambridge University Press, Cambridge, U.K.: 18.

(6) Gordon, H.A. & Pesti, L. (1971) The Gnotobiotic Animal as a Tool in the Study of Host Microbial Relationships. *Bacteriological Reviews* 35: 390-429.

(7) Medical Press and Circular (1916) Metchnikoff and Buttermilk. *Journal of the American Medical Association* 67: 939.

(8) de Kruif, P. (1926) *Microbe Hunters*. Harcourt Brace, SanDiego, USA.: 201-227.

(9) Kulp, W. L. & Rettger, L.F. (1924) Comparative Study of Lactobacillus Acidophilus and Lactobacillus Bulgaricus. *Journal of Bacteriology* 9: 357-394.

(10) Cheplin, H. A. & Rettger, L.F. (1922) The Therapeutic Application of Lactobacillus Acidophilus. *Abstracts of Bacteriology* 6: 24.

(11) Shortt, C. (1999) The probiotic century: historical and current perspectives. *Trends in Food Science and Technology* 10: 411-417.

(12) Schulze, J., Schiemann, M. & Sonnenborn, U. (2006) *120 Years of E. coli*. Alfred-Nissle-Gesellschaft, Hagen, Germany.: 25-28.

(13) Mazza, P. (1994) The use of Bacillus subtilis as an anti-diarrhoeal microorganism. *Bollettino Chimico Farmaceutico* 133: 3-18.

(14) Nurmi, E., and Rantala, M. (1973) New Aspects of Salmonella Infection in Broiler Production. *Nature* 241: 210-211.

(15) Fuller, R. (1999) Probiotics for Farm Animals. In *Probiotics: A Critical Review* (Tannock, G., ed.) Horizon Scientific Press, Wymondham, U.K.: 15-22.

(16) Cummings, J. H. & Macfarlane, G.T. (2001) Is there a role for microorganisms? In *Challenges in Inflammatory Bowel Disease* (Jewell, D. P., Warren, B.F. & Mortensen, N.J., eds.). Blackwell Science, Oxford, U.K.: 42-51.

Chapter 6 – Probiotic Benefits for the Intestine

(1) Casburn-Jones, A.C. & Farthing, M.J. (2004) Management of Infectious Diarrhoea. *Gut* 53: 296-305.

(2) Reid, G., Jass,J., Sebulsky, M.T., et al. (2003) Potential Uses of Probiotics in Clinical Practice. *Clinical Microbiology Reviews* 16: 658-672.

(3) Colbere-Garapin, F., Martin-Latil, S., Blondel,B., et al (2007) Prevention and treatment of enteric viral infections: possible benefits of probiotic bacteria. *Microbes and Infection* 9:1623-1631.

(4) Sullivan, A. & Nord, C.E. (2005) Probiotics and gastrointestinal diseases. *Journal of Internal Medicine* 257: 78-92.

(5) Floch, M.H. & Montrose, D.C. (2005) Use of Probiotics in Humans: An Analysis of Literature. *Gastroenterology Clinics of North America* 34: 547-570.

(6) Lemberg, D.A., Ooi, C.E. & Day, A.S. (2007) Probiotics in paediatric gastrointestinal diseases. *Journal of Paediatrics and Child Health* 43: 331-336.

(7) Allen, S.J., Okoko, B., Martinez, E., et al. (2003) Probiotics for treating infectious diarrhoea. *Cochrane Database of Systemic Review* Issue 4. Art. No.: CD003048. pub2.

(8) Henker, J., Laass, M., Blokhin, B.M., et al. (2007) The probiotic Eschericjia coli strain Nissle 1917 (EcN) stops acute diarrhoea in infants and toddlers. *European Journal of Pediatrics*: 166: 311-318.

(9) Szajewska, H., Kotowska, M., Mrukowicz, J.Z., et al. (2001) Efficacy of Lactobacillus GG in prevention of nosocomial diarrhea in infants. *Journal of Pediatrics* 138: 361-365.

(10) Cummings, J.H., Christie, S. & Cole, T.J. (2001) A study of fructo-oligosaccharides in the prevention of travellers' diarrhoea. *Alimentary Pharmacology & Therapeutics* 15: 1139-1145.

(11) Yates, J. (2005) Traveler's Diarrhea. *American Family Physician* 71: 2095-2100.

(12) McFarland, L.V. (2007) Meta-analysis of probiotics for the prevention of traveler's diarrhea. *Travel Medicine and Infectious Disease* 5: 97-105.

(13) Drakoularakou, A., Tzortzis, G., Rastall, R.A., et al. (2010) A double-blind, placebo-controlled, randomized human study assessing the capacity of a novel galacto-oligosaccharide mixture in reducing travellers' diarrhoea. *European Journal of Clinical Nutrition* 64: 146-152.

(14) Rolfe, R.D. (2000) The Role of Probiotic Cultures in the Control of Gastrointestinal Health. *Journal of Nutrition* 130: 396-402.

(15) Szajewska, H., Setty, M., Mrukowicz, J., et al. (2006) Probiotics in Gastrointestinal Diseases in Children: Hard and Not-So-Hard Evidence of Efficacy. *Journal of Pediatric Gastroenterology and Nutrition* 42: 454-475.

(16) Johnston, B.C., Supina, A.L., Ospina, M. et al. (2007) Probiotics for the prevention of pediatric antibiotic-associated diarrhea (Review) *Cochrane Database of Systematic Reviews* 2: CD004827.pub2

(17) Hickson, M., D'Souza, A.L., Muthu, N., et al. (2007) Use of probiotic Lactobacillus preparation to prevent diarrhoea associated with antibiotics: randomised double blind placebo controlled trial. *BMJ* July 14; 335 (7610): 80-84.

(18) Fedorak, R.N. & Madsen, K.L. (2004) Probiotics and prebiotics in gastrointestinal diseases. *Current Opinion in Gastroenterology* 20: 146-155.

(19) Kotowska, M., Albrecht, P. & Szajewska, H. (2005) Saccharomyces boulardii in the prevention of antibiotic-associated diarrhoea in children: a randomized double-blind placebo-controlled trial. *Alimentary Pharmacology & Therapeutics* 21: 583-590.

(20) Bartlett, J.G. & Gerding, D.N. (2008) Clinical Recognition and Diagnosis of Clostridium difficile Infection. *Clinical Infectious Diseases* 46: S12-S18.

(21) Surawicz, C.M., McFarland, L.V., Greenberg, R.N., et al. (2000) The Search for a Better Treatment for Recurrent Clostridium difficile Disease: Use of a High-Dose Vancomycin Combined with Saccharomyces boulardii. *Clinical Infectious Diseases* 31: 1012-1017.

(22) Doron, S. & Gorbach, S. (2006) Probiotics: their role in the treatment and prevention of disease. *Expert Review of Anti-Infective Therapy* 4: 261-275.

(23) Macfarlane, G.T., Steed, H. & Macfarlane, S. (2008) Bacterial metabolism and health-related effects of galacto-oligosaccharides and other prebiotics. *Journal of Applied Microbiology* 104: 305-344.

(24) Peppas, G., Alexiou, V.G., Mourtzoukou, E., et al. (2008) Epidemiology of constipation in Europe and Oceania: a systemic review. *BMS Gastroenterology* 8: 5.

(25) Fernandez-Banares, F. (2006) Nutritional care of the patient with constipation. *Best Practice & Research Clinical Gastroenterology* 20: 575-587.

(26) Marteau, P., Cuillerier, E., Meance, S., et al. (2002) Bifidobacterium animalis strain DN-173 010 shortens the colonic transit time in healthy women: a double-blind, randomized, controlled study. *Alimentary Pharmacology & Therapeutics* 16: 587-593.

(27) Mollenbrink M. & Bruckschen, E. (1994) Behandlung der chronischen Obstipation mit physiologischen Escherichia-coli-Bakterien. *Medizinische Klinik* 89: 587-593.

(28) Koebnick, C., Wagner, I., Leitzmann, P., et al. (2003) Probiotic beverage containing Lactobacillus casei Shirota improves gastrointestinal symptoms in patients with chronic constipation. *Canadian Journal of Microbiology* 17: 655-659.

(29) Matsumoto, K., Takada, T., Shimizu, K., et al. (2006) The Effects of a Probiotic Milk Product Containing Lactobacillus Strain Shirota on the Defecation Frequency and the Intestinal Microflora of Sub-optimal Health State Volunteers. *Bioscience Microflora* 25: 39-48.

(30) Den Hond, E., Geypens, B. & Ghoos, Y. (2000) Effect of High Performance Chicory Inulin on Constipation. *Nutrition Research* 20: 731-736.

(31) Lin, H.C. (2004) Small Intestinal Bacterial Overgrowth. A Framework for Understanding Irritable Bowel Syndrome. *JAMA* 292: 852-858.

(32) Spiller, R. (2008) Review article: probiotics and prebiotics in irritable bowel syndrome. *Alimentary Pharmacology & Therapeutics* 28: 385-396.

(33) Patel, S.M., Stason, W.E., Legedza, A., et al. (2005) The placebo effect in irritable bowel syndrome trials: a meta-analysis. *Neurogastroenterology and Motility* 17: 332-340.

(34) Enck, P., Zimmermann, K., Menke, C. et al. (2008) A mixture of Escherichia coli (DSM 17252) and Enterococcus faecalis (DSM 16440) for treatment of the irritable bowel syndrome - A randomised controlled trial with primary care physicians. *Neurogastroenterology and Motility* 20: 1103-1109.

(35) Whorwell, P.J., Altringer, L., Morel, J., et al. (2006) Efficacy of an encapsulated probiotic Bifidobacteria infantis 35624 in women with irritable bowel syndrome. *American Journal of Gastroenterology* 101: 1581-1590.

(36) Kajander, K., Myllyluoma, E., Rajilic-Stojanovics, M., et al. (2008) Clinical trial: multi-species probiotic supplementation alleviates the symptoms of irritable bowel syndrome and stabilises intestinal microbiota. *Alimentary Pharmacology & Therapeutics* 27: 48-57.

(37) O'Mahony, L., McCarthy, J., Kelly, P., et al. (2005) Lactobacillus and Bifidobacterium in Irritable Bowel syndrome: Symptom Responses and Relationship to Cytokine Profiles. *Gastroenterology* 128: 541-551.

(38) Rioux, K.P. & Fedorak, R.N. (2006) Probiotics in the Treatment of Inflammatory Bowel Disease. *Journal of Clinical Gastroenterology* 40:260-263.

(39) Kruis, W., Fric, P. Pokrotnieks, J. et al. (2004) Maintaining remission of ulcerative colitis with the probiotic Escherichia coli Nissle 1917 is effective as with standard mesalazine. *Gut* 53: 1617-1623.

(40) Sokol, H., Pigneur, B., Watterlot, L., et al. (2008) Faecalibacterium prausnitzii is an anti-inflammatory commensal bacterium identified by microbiota analysis of Crohn's disease patients. *PNAS* 105 (43): 16731-16736.

(41) Ewaschuk, J.B. & Dieleman, L.A. (2006) Probiotics and prebiotics in chronic IBD. *World Journal of Gastroenterology* 12: 5941-5950.

(42) Mahadevan, U. & Sandborn, W.J. (2003) Diagnosis and Management of Pouchitis. *Gastroenterology* 124: 1626-1650.

(43) Gionchetti, P., Rizzello, F., Venturi, A. et al. (2000) Oral Bacteriotherapy as Maintenance Treatment in Patients with Chronic Pouchitis: A Double-Blind, Placebo-Controlled Trial. *Gastroenterology* 119: 305-309.

(44) de Vrese, M., Stegelmann, A., Richter, B., et al. (2001) Probiotics – compensation for lactase insufficiency. *American Journal of Clinical Nutrition* 73: 421S-429S.

(45) Szilagyi, A. (2002) Review article: lactose – a potential prebiotic. *Alimentary Pharmacology and Therapeutics* 16: 1591-1602.

(46) Newcomer, A. D. & McGill, D.B. (1984) Clinical Importance of Lactose Deficiency. *The New England Journal Of Medicine* 310: 42-43.

(47) de Vrese, M., Keller, B. & Barth, C.A. (1992) Enhancement of intestinal hydrolysis of lactose by microbial b-galactosidase of kefir. *British Journal of Nutrition* 67: 67-75.

(48) Martini, M. C., Lerebours, E.C., Lin, W-J., et al. (1991) Strains and species of lactic acid bacteria in fermented milks (yogurts): effect on in vivo lactose digestion. *American Journal of Clinical Nutrition* 54: 1041-1046.

(49) Szilagyi, A., Rivard, J. & Fokeeff, K. (2001) Improved Parameters of Lactose Maldigestion Using Lactulose. *Digestive Diseases and Sciences* 46: 1509-1519.

(50) Brooks, G.F., Butel, J.S. & Morse, S.A. (2004) Vibrios, Campylobacters, Helicobacter, & Associated Bacteria (Ch 18). *Jawetz, Melnick, & Adelberg's Medical Microbiology* (Brooks, G.F., et al., eds.) Lange Medical Books/McGraw-Hill, New York, U.S.A.: 269-278.

(51) Lesbros-Pantoflickova, D., Corthesy-Theulaz, I. & Blum, A.L. (2007) Helicobacter pylori and Probiotics. *The Journal of Nutrition 137: 812S-818S.*

(52) Kamiya, S., Takahashi, M., Manzoku, T. et al. (2006) Probiotics and Helicobacter pylori infection. *Microbial Ecology in Health and Disease* 18: 177-180.

Chapter 7 – Probiotic Benefits for Other Parts of the Body

(1) Rook, G.A. & Brunet, L.R. (2005) Microbes, immunoregulation, and the gut. *Gut* 54: 317-320.

(2) Rautava, S., Kalliomaki, M & Isolauri, E. (2002) Probiotics during pregnancy and breastfeeding might confer immunomodulatory protection against atopic disease in the infant. *Journal of Allergy and Clinical Immunology* 109: 119-121.

(3) Johannsen, H. & Prescott, S.L. (2009) Practical prebiotics, probiotics and synbiotics for allergists: how useful are they? *Clinical and Experimental Allergy* 39: 1801-1814.

(4) Ouwehand, A., Isolauri, E. & Salminen, S. (2002). The role of the intestinal microflora for the development of the immune system in early childhood. *European Journal of Nutrition* 41 (Suppl 1):

(5) Boyle, R.J. & Tang, M.L. (2006) The Role of Probiotics in the Management of Allergic Disease. *Clinical and Experimental Allergy* 36: 568-576.

(6) Kalliomaki, M., Kirjavainen, P., Eerola, E., et al. (2001a) Distinct patterns of neonatal gut microflora in infants in whom atopy was and was not developing. *Journal of Allergy and Clinical Immunology* 107: 129-134.

(7) Bjorksten, B., Sepp, E., Julge, K., et al. (2001) Allergy development and the intestinal microflora during the first year of life. *Journal of Allergy and Clinical Immunology* 108: 516-520.

(8) Watanabe, S., Narisawa, Y., Arase, S., et al. (2003) Differences in fecal microflora between patients with atopic dermatitis and healthy control subjects. *Journal of Allergy and Clinical Immunology* 111: 587-591.

(9) Mowat, A.M. (2003) Anatomical basis of tolerance and immunity to intestinal antigens. *Nature Reviews Immunology* 3: 331-341.

(10) Honjo, T. & Melchers, F. (2006) Preface. In *Gut-Associated Lymphoid Tissues* (Honjo, T. & Melchers, F., eds). Springer, Heidelberg, Germany. : i-iii.

(11) Kalliomaki, M., Salminen, S., Arvilommi, H., et al. (2001b) Probiotics in primary prevention of atopic disease: a randomised placebo-controlled trial. *Lancet* 357: 1076-1079.

(12) Moro, G., Arslanoglu, S., Stahl, B., *et al*. (2006) A mixture of prebiotic oligosaccharides reduces the incidence of atopic dermatitis during the first six months of age. *Archives of Disease in Childhood* 91: 814-819.

(13) Arslanoglu, S, Moro, G.E., Schmitt, J., *et al*. (2008) Early dietary intervention with a mixture of prebiotic oligosaccharides reduces the incidence of allergic manifestations and infections during the first two years of life. *Journal of Nutrition* 138: 1091-1095.

(14) Boyle, R.J., Bath-Hextall, F.J., Leonardi-Bee, J., *et al*. (2009) Probiotics for the treatment of eczema: a systematic review. *Clinical & Experimental Allergy* 39: 1117-1127.

(15) Wickens, K., Black, P.N., Stanley, T.V., *et al*. (2008) A differential effect of 2 probiotics in the prevention of eczema and atopy: a double-blind, randomized, placebo-controlled trial. *Journal of Allergy and Clinical Immunology* 122: 788-794.

(16) Penders, J., Stobberingh, E.E., van den Brandt, P.A., *et al*. (2007) The role of the intestinal microbiota in the development of atopic disorders. *Allergy* 62: 1223-1236.

(17) Sudo, N., Sawamura, S., Tanaka, K., *et al*. (1997) The requirement of intestinal bacterial flora for the development of an IgE production system fully susceptible to oral tolerance induction. *Journal of Immunology* 159: 1739-1945.

(18) Rook, G.A. & Witt, N. (2008) Probiotics and Other Organisms in Allergy and Autoimmune Diseases. In *Therapeutic Microbiology: Probiotics and Related Strategies* (Versalovic, J. & Wilson, M., eds.). ASM Press, Washington, U.S.A.: 231-247.

(19) Van de Water, J., Keen, C.L. & Gershwin, M.E. (1999) The Influence of Chronic Yoghurt Consumption on Immunity. *Journal of Nutrition* 129: 1492S-1495S.

(20) Sieber, R. & Dietz, U-T. (1998) Lactobacillus acidophilus and Yoghurt in the Prevention and Therapy of Bacterial Vaginosis. *International Dairy Journal* 8: 599-607.

(21) Hilton, E., Isenberg, H.D., Alperstein, P., *et al*. (1992) Ingestion of Yogurt Containing Lactobacillus acidophilus as Prophylaxis for Candidal Vaginitis. *Annals of Internal Medicine* 116: 353-420.

(22) Hay, P. (2009) Recurrent Bacterial Vaginosis. *Current Opinion in Infectious Diseases* 22: 82-86.

(23) Aleshkin, V.A., Voropaeva, E.A. & Shenderov, B.A. (2006) Vaginal microbiota in healthy women and patients with bacterial vaginosis and non-specific vaginitis. *Microbial Ecology in Health and Disease* 18:71-74.

(24) Antonio, M.A., Rabe, L.K. & Hillier, S.L. (2005) Colonisation of Rectum by Lactobacillus Species and Decreased Risk of Bacterial Vaginosis. *JID* 192 (1st August): 394-398.

(25) Barrons, R. & Tassone, D. (2008) Use of Lactobacillus Probiotics for Bacterial Genitourinary Infections in Women: A Review. *Clinical Therapeutics* 30: 453-468.

(26) Gow, N.A., Brown, A.J. & Odds, F.C. (2002) Fungal morphogenesis and host invasion. *Current Opinion in Microbiology* 5: 366-371.

(27) Ruhnke, M. (2002) Skin and Mucous Membrane Infections. In *Candida and Candidiasis* (Calderone, R.A., ed.) ASM Press, Washington, D.C., U.S.A.: 307-325.

(28) Matthews, H.L. & Witek-Janusek, L. (2002) Host Defense against Oral, Esophageal, and Gastrointestinal Candidiasis. In *Candida and Candidiasis* (Calderone, R.A., ed.). ASM Press, Washington, D.C., U.S.A.: 179-192.

(29) Mavromanolakis, E., Maraki, S., Cranidis, A., *et al*. (2001) The Impact of Norfloxacin, Ciprofloxacin and Ofloxacin on Human Gut Colonisation by Candida albicans. *Scandinavian Journal of Infectious Diseases* 33: 477-478.

(30) Mitchell, T.G. (2004) Medical Mycology. In *Jawetz, Melnick & Adelberg's Medical Microbiology* (Brooks, G.F., Butel, J.S. & Morse, S.A., eds.). Lange Medical Books/McGraw-Hill, New York, U.S.A.: 623-659.

(31) Pfaller, M.A. & Diekema, D.J. (2007) Epidemiology of invasive candidiasis: a persistent public health problem. *Clinical Microbiology Reviews* 20: 133-163.

(32) MacCallum, D. (2007) Candida albicans: New Insights in Infection, Disease and Treatment. In *New Insights in Medical Mycology* (Kavanagh, K., ed.). Springer, Dordrecht, The Netherlands.: 99-129.

(33) Falagas, M.E., Betsi, G.I., & Athanasiou, S. (2006) Probiotics for prevention of recurrent vulvovaginal candidiasis: a review. *Journal of Antimocrobial Chemotherapy* 58: 266-272.

(34) Manzoni, P., Mastert, M., Leonessa, M.L., et al. (2006) Oral supplementation with Lactobacillus casei Subspecies rhamnosus Prevents Enteric Colonisation by Candida Species in Pre-term Neonates: A Randomised Study. *Clinical Infectious Diseases* 42: 1735-1742.

(35) Pirotta, M, Gunn, J., Chondros, P., et al. (2004) Effect of lactobacillus in preventing post-antibiotic vulvovaginal candidiasis: a randomised controlled trial. *BMJ*: 329 (7465): 548.

(36) Martinez, R., Franceschini, S., Patta, M. et al. (2009) Improved treatment of vulvovaginal candidiasis with fluconazole plus probiotic Lactobacillus rhamnosus GR-1 and Lactobacillus reuteri RC-14. *Letters in Applied Microbiology* 48: 269-274.

(37) Reid, G. (2008) Probiotics and Diseases of the Genitourinary Tract. In *Therapeutic Microbiology: Probiotics and Related Strategies* (Versalovic, J. & Wilson, M., eds.). ASM Press, Washington, DC, U.S.A.: 271-284.

(38) Kirjavainen, P.V., Pautler, S., Baroja, M.L., et al. (2009) Abnormal Immunological Profile and Vaginal Microbiota in Women Prone to Urinary Tract Infections. *Clinical and Vaccine Immunology* 16: 29-36.

(39) Hooton, T.M. (2001) Recurrent urinary tract infection in women. *International Journal of Antimicrobial Agents* 17: 259-268.

(40) Satkunaratnam, A. & Drutz, H.P. (2003) Urinary Tract Infections in the Non-pregnant Woman. In *Female Pelvic Medicine and Reconstructive Pelvic Surgery* (Drutz H.P., et al., eds.). Springer, London, U.K.

(41) McCutcheon, J. & Fulton, J.D. (1989) Lowered prevalence of infections with lactulose therapy in patients in long-term hospital care. *Journal of Hospital Care* 13: 81-86.

(42) Meurman, J.H. (2005) Probiotics: do they have a role in oral medicine and dentistry? *European Journal of Oral Sciences* 113: 188-196.

(43) Nase, L., Hatakka, K. Savilahti, E., et al. (2001) Effect of long-term consumption of a probiotic bacterium, Lactobacillus rhamnosus GG, in milk on dental caries and caries risk in children. *Caries Research* 35: 412-420.

(44) Ahola, A.J., Yli-Knuuttila, H., Suomalainen, T., et al. (2002) Short term consumption of probiotic-containing cheese and its effect on dental caries risk factors. *Archives of Oral Biology* 47: 799-804.

(45) Krasse, P., Carisson, B., Dahl, C., et al. (2006) Decreased gum bleeding and reduced gingivitis by the probiotic Lactobacillus reuteri. *Swedish Dental Journal* 30: 55-60.

(46) Haukioja, A. (2010) Probiotics for Oral Health. *European Journal of Dentistry* 4: 348-355.

(47) Kazor, C.E., Mitchell, P.M., Lee, A.M., et al. (2003) Diversity of Bacterial Populations on the Tongue Dorsa of Patients with Halitosis and Healthy Patients. *Journal of Clinical Microbiology* 41: 558-563.

(48) Meurman, J.H. & Stamotova, I. (2007) Probiotics: contribution to oral health. *Oral Diseases* 13: 443-451.

(49) Hatakka, K., Ahola, A.J., Yli-Knuuttila, H., et al. (2007) Probiotics Reduce the Prevalence of Oral Candida in the Elderly - a Randomized Controlled Trial. *Journal of Dental Research* 86: 125-130.

(50) Vouloumanou, E.K., Makris, G.C., Karageorgopoulos, D.E., et al. (2009) Probiotics for the prevention of respiratory tract infections: a systematic review. *International Journal of Antimicrobial Agents* 34: 197.e1-197.e10.

(51) De Vrese, M., Winkler, P., Rautenberg, P., et al. (2005) Effect of Lactobacillus gasseri PA 16/8, Bifidobacteriu longum SP 07/3, B. bifidum MF 20/5 on common cold episodes: a double-blind, randomized, controlled trial. *Clinical Nutrition* 24: 481-491.

(52) Leyer, G.J., Li, S., Mubasher, M.E., et al. (2009) Probiotic effects on cold and influenza-like symptom incidence and duration in children. *Pediatrics* 124: e172-e179.

(53) Cox, A.J., Pyne, D.B., Saunders, P.U., et al. (2010) Oral administration of the probiotic Lactobacillus fermentum VRI-003 and mucosal immunity in endurance athletes. *British Journal of Sports Medicine* 44: 222-226.

(54) Berggren, A., Lazou Ahren, I., Larsson, N., et al. (2010) Randomised, double-blind and placebo-controlled study using new probiotic lactobacilli for strengthening the body immune defence against viral infections. *European Journal of Nutrition* Aug 28 [Epub ahead of print]

(55) Boris, M., Sellers, T.F., Eichenweld, H.F., et al. (1964) Bacterial Interference. *American Journal of Diseases of Children* 108: 252-261.

(56) Brook, I. (2005) The Role of Bacterial Interference in Otitis, Sinusitis and Tonsillitis. *Otolaryngology – Head and Neck Surgery* 133: 139-146.

(57) Roos, K., Holm, S.E., Grahn-Hakansson, E., et al. (1996) Re-colonisation with selected alpha-streptococci for prophylaxis of recurrent streptococcal pharyngotonsillitis - a randomised placebo-controlled multicentre study. *Scandinavian Journal of Infectious Diseases* 28: 459-462.

(58) Boge, T., Remigy, M., Vaudaine, S., et al. (2009) A probiotic fermented dairy drink improves antibody response to influenza vaccination in the elderly in two randomised controlled trials. *Vaccine* 27: 5677-5684.

(59) Krutmann, J. (2009) Pre- and probiotics for human skin. *Journal of Dermatological Science* 54: 1-5.

Chapter 8 – Safety

(1) Mack, D.R. (2009) Safety Issues of Probiotic Ingestion. In *Probiotics in Pediatric Medicine* (Michael, S. & Sherman, P.M., eds.). Humana Press, Totowa, NJ, U.S.A.: 69-80.

(2) Joint FAO/WHO Working Group on Evaluation of Probiotics (2002) Guidelines for the Evaluation of Probiotics in Food (London Ontario, Canada). *Food and Agriculture Oganization of the UN/World Health Organization*. ftp://ftp.fao.org/es/esn/food/wgreport2.pdf [Accessed 13 September 2010]

(3) Oggioni, M.R., Pozzi, G., Valensin, P.E., et al. (1998) Recurrent Septicaemia in an Immunocompromised Patient Due to Probiotic Strains of Bacillus subtilis. *Journal of Clinical Microbiology* 36: 325-326.

(4) Sanders, M.E., Morelli, L. & Tompkins, T.A. (2003) Sporeformers as Human Probiotics: Bacillus, Sporolactobacillus, and Brevibacillus. *Comprehensive Reviews in Food Science and Food Safety* 2: 101-110.

(5) Hennequin, C., Kauffmann-Lacroix, C., Jobert, A., et al. (2000). Possible role of catheters in *Saccharomyces boulardii* fungemia. *European Journal of Clinical Microbiology and Infectious Diseases* 19: 16-20.

(6) Snydman, D.R. (2008) The Safety of Probiotics. *Clinical Infectious Diseases* 46: S104-S111.

(7) Salminen, M.K., Tynkkynen, S., Rautelin, H., et al. (2002) Lctobacillus bacteraemia during a rapid increase in probiotic use of Lactobacillus rhamnosus GG in Finland. *Clinical Infectious Diseases* 35: 1155-1160.

(8) Salminen, S., von Wright, A., Morelli, L., et al. (1998). Demonstration of safety of probiotics – a review. *International Journal of Food Microbiology* 44: 93-106.

(9) W.H.O. (2001) Global Strategy for Containment of Antimicrobial Resistance WHO/CDS/CSR/DRS/2001.2. *World Health Organisation*, Geneva, Switzerland.

(10) Courvalin, P. (2006) Antibiotic resistance: the pros and cons of probiotics. *Digestive and Liver Disease* 38 Suppl. 2: S261-S265.

(11) Charteris, W.P., Kelly, P.M., Morelli, L., et al. (1998a) Antibiotic susceptibility of potentially probiotic Bifidobacteria isolates from the human gastrointestinal tract. *Letters in Applied Microbiology* 26: 333-337.

(12) Charteris, W.P., Kelly, P.M., Morelli, L., et al. (1998b) Antibiotic susceptibility of potentially probiotic Lactobacillus species. *Journal of Food Protection* 61: 1636-1643.

(13) Mathur, S. & Singh, R. (2005) Antibiotic resistance in food lactic acid bacteria – a review. *International Journal of Food Microbiology* 105: 281-295.

(14) Klare, I., Konstabel, C., Werner, G, *et al.* (2007) Antimicrobial susceptibilities of Lactobacillus, Pediococcus and Lactococcus human isolates and cultures intended for probiotic or nutritional use. *Journal of Antimicrobial Chemotherapy* 59: 900-912.

(15) Bernardeau, M., Vernoux, J.P., Henri-Dubernet, S., *et al.* (2008) Safety assessment of dairy microorganisms: the Lactobacillus genus. *International Journal of Food Microbiology* 126: 278-285.

(16) Masco, L., Van Hoorde, K., De Brandt, E., *et al.* (2006) Antimicrobial susceptibility of Bifidobacterium strains from humans, animals and probiotic products. *Journal of Antimicrobial Chemotherapy* 58 85-94.

(17) Meile, L., Le Blay, G. & Thierry, A. (2008) Safety assessment of dairy microorganisms Propionibacterium and Bifidobacterium. *International Journal of Food Microbiology* 126: 316-320.

(18) EFSA (2005) Opinion of the Scientific Committee on a request from EFSA related to a generic approach to the safety assessment by EFSA of microorganisms used in food/feed and the production of food/feed additives. *EFSA Journal* 226: 1-12.

(19) Logan, N.A. (2004) Safety of Aerobic Endospore-Forming Bacteria. In *Bacterial Spore Formers: Probiotics and Emerging Applications* (Ricca E. *et al.*, eds.). Horizon Bioscience, Wymondham, Norfolk, UK.: 93-105.

(20) Gilmore, M.S. & Ferretti, J.J. (2003) The Thin Line Between Gut Commensal and Pathogen. *Science* 299: 1999-2002.

(21) Eaton, T.J. & Gasson, M.J. (2001) Molecular Screening of Enterococcus Virulence Determinants and Potential for Genetic Exchange between Food and Medical Isolates. *Applied and Environmental Microbiology* 67: 1628-1635.

(22) Cunningham-Rundles, S., Ahrne, S., Bengmark, S., *et al.* (2000) Probiotics and Immune Response. An *American Journal of Gastroenterology* 95 (1 Suppl.): S22-S25.

(23) Trois, L., Cardoso, E. M., & Miura, E. (2008) Use of Probiotics in HIV-infected Children: A Randomised Double-blind Controlled Study. *Journal of Tropical Pediatrics* 54: 19-24.

(24) Anukam, K.C., Osazuwa, E.O., Osadolor, H.B., *et al.* (2008) Yoghurt Containing Probiotic *Lactobacillus rhamnosus* GR-1 and *L. Reuteri* RC-14 Helps Resolve Moderate Diarrhoea and Increases CD4 Count in HIV/AIDS Patients. *Journal of Clinical Gastroenterology* 42:239-243.

(25) Salminen, M.K., Tynkkynen, S., Rautelin, H., *et al.* (2004) The Efficacy and Safety of Probiotic Lactobacillus rhamnosus GG on the Prolonged, Noninfectious Diarrhea in HIV Patients on Antiretroviral Therapy: A Randomized Placebo-Controlled Crossover Study. *HIV Clinical Trials* 54: 183-191.

(26) Rayes, N., Seehofer, D., Theruvath, T., *et al.* (2005) Supply of Pre- and Probiotics Reduces Bacterial Infection Rates After Liver Transplantation. *American Journal of Transplantation* 5: 125-130.

(27) Morrow, L.E. (2009) Probiotics in the intensive care unit. *Current Opinion in Critical Care* 15: 144-148.

(28) Deshpande, G., Rao, S. & Patole, S. (2007) Probiotics for prevention of necrotising enterocolitis in preterm neonates with very low birthweight: a systematic review of randomised controlled trials. *The Lancet* 369, May 12: 1614-1620.

(29) Deshpande, G., Rao, S., Patole, S., *et al.* (2010) Updated meta-analysis of probiotics for preventing necrotising enterocolitis in preterm neonates. *Pediatrics* 125: 921-930.

(30) Alfaleh, K., Anabrees, J. & Bassler, D. (2010) Probiotics reduce the risk of necrotizing enterocolitis in premature infants: a meta-analysis. *Neonatology* 97: 93-99.

(31) Besselink, M.G., van Santvoort, H.C., Buskens, E., *et al.* (2008) Probiotic prophylaxis in predicted severe acute pancreatitis: a randomised double-blind, placebo-controlled trial. *The Lancet* 371; February 23: 651-659.

(32) Hirota, M., Inoue, K., Mimura, Y., et al. (2003) Non-Occlusive Mesenteric Ischaemia and Its Associated Intestinal Gangrene in Acute Pancreatitis. Pancreatology 3: 316-322.

(33) Dugoua, J-J, Machado, M., Zhu, X., et al. (2009) Probiotic Safety in Pregnancy: A Systematic Review and Meta-analysis of Randomized Controlled Trials of Lactobacillus, Bifidobacterium, and Saccharomyces spp. *Journal of Obstetrics and Gynaecology Canada* 31: 542-552.

Chapter 9 – Choosing a Good Probiotic Product

(1) Shah, N.P. (2000) Probiotic Bacteria: Selected Enumeration and Survival in Dairy Foods. *Journal of Dairy Science* 83: 894-907.

(2) Marteau, P., Minekus, M., Havenaar, R., et al. (1997) Survival of Lactic Acid Bacteria in a Dynamic Model of the Stomach and Small Intestine: Validation and the Effects of Bile. *Journal of Dairy Science* 80:1031-1037.

(3) Adolfsson, O., Meydani, S.N. & Russell, R.M. (2004) Yoghurt and gut function. *American Journal of Clinical Nutrition* 80: 245-256

(4) Elli, M., Callegari, M.L., Ferrari, S., et al. (2006) Survival of Yoghurt Bacteria in the Human Gut. *Applied and Environmental Microbiology* 72: 5113-5117.

(5) Mater, D.D., Bretigny, L., Firmesse, O., et al. (2005) Streptococcus thermophilus and Lactobacillus delbrueckii subsp. bulgaricus survive gastrointestinal transit of healthy volunteers consuming yoghurt. *FEMS Microbiology Letters* 250: 185-187.

(6) Shah, N.P., Lankaputhra, W.E.V., Britz, M.L., et al. (1995) Survival of Lactobacillus acidophilus and Bifidobacterium bifidum in Commercial Yoghurt During Refrigerated Storage. *International Dairy Journal* 5: 515-521.

(7) To, B.C. & Etzel, M.R. (1997) Spray Drying, Freeze Drying, or Freezing of Three Different Lactic Acid Bacteria Species. *Journal of Food Science* 62: 576-585.

(8) Nighswonger, B.D., Brashears, M.M. & Gilliland, S.E. (1996) Viability of Lactobacillus acidophilus and Lactobacillus casei in Fermented Milk Products During Refrigerated Storage. *Journal of Dairy Science* 79: 212-219.

(9) Hutt, P., Shchepetova, J., Loivukene, K., et al. (2006) Antagonistic activity of probiotic lactobacilli and bifidobacteria against entero- and uropathogens. *Journal of Applied Microbiology* 100: 1324-1332.

(10) Vinderola, C.G., Mocchiutti, P. & Reinheimer, J.A. (2002) Interactions Among Lactic Acid Starter and Probiotic Bacteria Used for Fermented Dairy Products. *Journal of Dairy Science* 85: 721-729.

(11) Timmerman, H.M., Konig, C.J., Mulder, L., et al. (2004) Monostrain, multistrain and a multispecies probiotics - A comparison of functionality and efficacy. *International Journal of Food Microbiology* 96: 219-233.

(12) Mogensen, G (2000) Bifidobacteria. In *LFRA Ingredients Handbook – Prebiotics and Probiotics* (Gibson, G. & Angus, F., eds.). LFRA, Leatherhead, UK: 85-115.

(13) Shornikova, A.V., Casas, I.A., Mykkanen, H., et al. (1997) Bacteriotherapy with Lactobacillus reuteri in rotavirus gastroenteritis. *Pediatric Infectious Disease Journal* 16: 1103-1107.

(14) Whorwell, P.J., Altringer, L., Morel, J., et al. (2006) Efficacy of an encapsulated probiotic Bifidobacteria infantis 35624 in women with irritable bowel syndrome. *American Journal of Gastroenterology* 101: 1581-1590.

(15) Ringel-Kulka, T. & Ringel, Y. (2007) Probiotics in irritable bowel syndrome: has the time arrived? *Gastroenterology* 132: 813-816.

(16) EFSA (2010) Scientific Opinion on the substantiation of health claims related to live yoghurt cultures and improved lactase digestion (ID 1143, 2976) pursuant to Article 13(1) of Regulation (EC) No 1924/2006. *EFSA Journal* 8(10): 1763.

(17) Bezkorovainy, A. (2001) Probiotics: determinants of survival and growth in the gut. *American Journal of Clinical Nutrition* 73 (suppl): 399S-405S.

(18) Coeuret, V., Gueguen, M. & Vernoux, P. (2004) Numbers and strains of lactobacilli in some probiotic products. *International Journal of Food Microbiology* 97: 147-156.

(19) ConsumerLab.com (2009) Product Review: Probiotic Supplements for Adults, Children and Pets. Update on www.consumerlab.com: 14/06/2010.

Chapter 10 – Types of Probiotic Microbes

(1) Tannock, G.W. (1999) Modification of the normal microflora. In *Medical Importance of the Normal Microflora* (Tannock, G.W., ed.) Kluwer Academic Publishers, Dordrecht, Netherlands.: 487-506.

(2) Fuller, R. (1989) Probiotics in man and animals. *Journal of Applied Bacteriology* 66: 365-378.

(3) Teixeira, P.C.M. (2000) Lactobacillus brevis. In *Encyclopedia of Food Microbiology, Vol. 2* (Robinson, R.K., Batt, C.A. & Patel, P.D., eds.). Academic Press, San Diego, U.S.A.: 1144-1151.

(4) Gilliland, S. E. (1990) Health and nutritional benefits from lactic acid bacteria. *FEMS Microbiology Reviews* 87: 175-188.

(5) Bengmark, S. (1998) Ecological control of the gastrointestinal tract. The role of probiotic flora. *Gut* 42: 2-7.

(6) Mack, D.R., Michail, S., Wei, S., *et al.* (1999) Probiotics inhibit enteropathogenic E. coli adherence in vitro by inducing intestinal mucin gene expression. *American Journal of Physiology* 276: G941-G950.

(7) Batt, C.A. (2000) Lactobacillus: Introduction. In *Encyclopedia of Food Microbiology, Vol. 2* (Robinson, R.K., Batt, C.A. & Patel, P.D., eds.). Academic Press, San Diego, U.S.A.: 1134-1136.

(8) Hoover, D.G. (2000) Bifidobacterium. In *Encyclopedia of Food Microbiology, Vol. 1* (Robinson, R.K., Batt, C.A. & Patel, P.D., eds.). Academic Press, San Diego, U.S.A.: 210-217.

(9) Ballongue, J. (1998) Bifidobacteria and Probiotic Action. In *Lactic Acid Bacteria* (Salminen, S. & von Wright, A., eds.). Marcel Dekker. New York, U.S.A.: 519-587.

(10) Macfarlane, G.T., Gibson, G.R., Drasar, B.S., *et al.* (1995) Metabolic significance of the gut microflora. In *Gastrointestinal and Oesophagal Pathology* (Whitehead, R., ed.) Churchill Livingstone, Edinburgh, Scotland.: 249-274.

(11) Rasic, J.L. & Kurmann, J.A. (1983) Bifidobacteria and their Role. *Experientia Supplementum* 39: 1-295.

(12) Biavati, B., Vescovo, M., Torriani, S., *et al.* (2000) Bifidobacteria: history, ecology, physiology and applications. *Annals of Microbiology* 50: 117-131.

(13) Gibson, G.R. & Wang, X. (1994) Regulatory effects of bifidobacteria on the growth of other colonic bacteria. *Journal of Applied Bacteriology* 77: 412-420.

(14) Bernet, M-F., Brassart, D., Neeser, J-R., *et al.* (1993) Adhesion of Human Bifidobacterial Strains to Cultured Human Intestinal Epithelial Cells and Inhibition of Enteropathogen–Cell Ineractions. *Applied and Environmental Microbiology* 59: 4121-4128.

(15) Berrada, N., Lemeland, J-F., Laroche, G., *et al.* (1991) Bifidobacterium from Fermented Milks: Survival During Gastric Transit. *Journal of Dairy Science* 74: 409-413.

(16) Leahy, S.C., Higgins, D.G., Fitzgerald, G.F., *et al.* (2005) Getting better with bifidobacteria. *Journal of Applied Microbiology* 98: 1303-1315.

(17) Neidhardt, F.C. (1996) The Enteric Bacterial Cell and the Age of Bacteria. In *Escherichia coli and Salmonella* (Neidhardt, F. C., ed.). ASM Press, Washington, DC, U.S.A.: 1-3.

(18) Krammer, H.J., Kamper, H., von Bunau, R., *et al.* (2006) Probiotic drug therapy with E. coli strain Nissle 1917 (EcN): results of a prospective study of the records of 3,807 patients. *Zeitschrift fur Gastroenterologie* 44: 651-656.

(19) Lodinova-Zadnikova, R. & Sonnenborn, U. (1997) Effect of Preventative Administration of a Nonpathogenic Escherichia coli Strain on the Colonization of the Intestine with Microbial Pathogens in Newborn Infants. *Biology of the Neonate* 71: 224-232.

(20) Cooke, E. M. (1968) Properties of strains of Escherichia Coli isolated from the faeces of patients with ulcerative colitis, patients with acute diarrhoea and normal persons. *Journal of Pathology and Bacteriology* 95: 101-113.

(21) Giaffer, M.H., Holdsworth, C.D. & Duerden, B.I. (1992) Virulence properties of Escherichia coli strains isolated from patients with inflammatory bowel disease. *Gut* 33: 646-650.

(22) Casula, G. & Cutting, S.M. (2002) Bacillus Probiotics: Spore Germination in the Gastrointestinal Tract. *Applied and Environmental Microbiology* 68: 2344-2352.

(23) Tam, N.K., Uyen, N.Q., Hong, H.A., *et al.* (2006) The Intestinal Life Cycle of Bacillus subtilis and Close Relations. *Journal of Bacteriology* 188: 2692-2700.

(24) Rhee, K-J., Sethupathi, P., Driks, A., *et al.* (2004) Role of Commensal Bacteria in Development of Gut-Associated Lymphoid Tissues and Preimmune Antibody Repertoire. *Journal of Immunology* 172: 1118-1124.

(25) Hong, H.A. & Duc, L.H. (2004) The Fate of Ingested Spores. In *Bacterial Spore Formers: Probiotics and Emerging Applications* (Ricca, E., Henriques, A.O. & Cutting, S.M., eds.). Horizon Bioscience, Wymondham, Norfolk, U.K.: 107-112.

(26) Buts, J-P. (2006) Example of a Medicinal Probiotic: Lyophilised Saccharomyces boulardii. In *Gut Microflora: Digestive Physiology and Pathology* (Rambaud, J-C., Buts, J-P., Corthier, G. & Flourie, B., eds.). John Libbey Eurotext, Montrouge, France.: 221-244.

(27) Periti, P. & Tonelli, F. (2001) Preclinical and Clinical Pharmacology of Biotherapeutic Agents: Saccharomyces boulardii. *Journal of Chemotherapy* 13: 473-493.

(28) Tap, J., Mondot, S., Levenez, F., *et al.* (2009) Towards the human intestinal microbiota phylogenetic core. *Environmental Microbiology* 11: 2574-2584.

(29) Hamer, H.M., Jonkers, D., Venema, K., *et al.* (2008) Review article: the role of butyrate on colonic function. *Alimentary Pharmacology and Therapeutics* 27: 104-119.

Chapter 11 – What are *Prebiotics*?

(1) Gibson, G. & Roberfroid, M.B. (1995) Dietary Modulation of the Human Colonic Microbiota: Introducing the Concept of Prebiotics. *Journal of Nutrition* 125: 1401-1412.

(2) FAO (Food and Agriculture Organisation of the United Nations) (2007) *FAO Technical Meeting on Prebiotics, September 15-16*. Food Quality and Standards Service, F.A.O. http://www.fao.org/ag/agn/agns/files/Prebiotics_Tech_Meeting_Report.pdf accessed on 30 July 2008.

(3) Macfarlane, G.T., & Macfarlane, S. (1997) Human Colonic Microbiota: Ecology, Physiology and Metabolic Potential of Intestinal Bacteria. *Scandinavian Journal of Gastroenterology* 32 Suppl 222: 3-9.

(4) Crittenden, R. (1999) Prebiotics. In *Probiotics: A Critical Review* (Tannock, G., ed.). Horizon Scientific Press, Wymondham, U.K.: 141-156.

(5) Van Loo, J., Cummings, J., Delzenne, N., *et al.* (1999) Functional food properties of non-digestible oligosaccharides: a consensus report from the ENDO project. *British Journal of Nutrition* 81: 121-132.

(6) Buddington, R.K., Williams, C.H., Chen, S-C., *et al.* (1996) Dietary supplement of neosugar alters the fecal flora and decreases activities of reactive enzymes in human subjects. *American Journal of Clinical Nutrition* 63: 709-716.

(7) Elia, M. & Cummings, J.H. (2007) Physiological aspects of energy metabolism and gastrointestinal effects of carbohydrates. *European Journal of Clinical Nutrition* 61 (suppl 1): S40-S74.

(8) Moshfegh, A.J., Friday, J.E., Goldman, J.P., *et al.* (1999) Presence of Inulin and Oligofructose in the Diets of Americans. *Journal of Nutrition* 129: 1407S-1411S.

(9) Macfarlane, G.T., Steed, H. & Macfarlane, S. (2008) Bacterial metabolism and health-related effects of galacto-oligosaccharides and other prebiotics. *Journal of Applied Microbiology* 104: 305-344.

(10) Rastall, R.A. (2006) Galacto-oligosaccharides as Prebiotic Food Ingredients. In *Prebiotics: Development & Application* (Gibson, G.R. & Rastall, R.A., eds.). John Wiley & Sons, Chichester, England. 101-109.

(11) Murphy, O. (2001) Non-polyol low-digestible carbohydrates: food applications and functional benefits. *British Journal of Nutrition* 85 Suppl. 1: 26-31.

(12) Roberfroid, M.B., Van Loo, J.A. & Gibson, G.R. (1998) The Bifidogenic Nature of Chicory Inulin and Its Hydrolysis Products. *Journal of Nutrition* 128: 11-19.

(13) Slavin, J. (1999) Dietary Fibre and Non-Digestible Oligosaccharides. In *Colonic Microbiota, Nutrition and Health* (Gibson, G.R. & Roberfroid, M.B., eds.). Kluwer Academic Publishers, Dordrecht, Netherlands.: 125-147.

(14) Franck, A.M. (2000) Inulin & Oligofructose. In *LFRA Ingredients Handbook: Prebiotics and Probiotics* (Gibson, G. & Angus, F., eds.). LFRA, Leatherhead, England. 1-18.

(15) Gibson, G.R., Beatty, E.R., Wang, X., *et al.* (1995) Selective Stimulation of Bifidobacteria in the Human Colon by Oligofructose and Inulin. *Gastroenterology* 108: 975-982.

(16) Kleeson, B., Sykura, B., Zunft, H-J., *et al.* (1997) Effects of inulin and lactose on fecal microflora microbial activity, and bowel habit in elderly constipated patients. *American Journal of Clinical Nutrition* 65: 1397-1402.

(17) Crittenden, R. (2006) Emerging Prebiotic Carbohydrates. In *Prebiotics: Development & Application* (Gibson, G.R. & Rastall, R.A., eds.). John Wiley & Sons, Chichester, England. 111-133.

(18) Ballongue, J., Schumann, C. & Quignon, P. (1997) Effects of Lactulose and Lactitol on Colonic Microflora and Enzymic Activity. *Scandinavian Journal of Gastroenterology* 32 Suppl 222: 41-44.

(19) Kravtchenko, T.P. (1998) Acacia Gum – A Natural Soluble Fibre. In *Functional Foods – The Consumer, the Products and the Evidence* (Sadler, M.J. & Saltmarsh, M., eds.). The Royal Society of Chemistry, Cambridge, U.K.: 38-46.

(20) Pedersen, A., Sandstrom, B. & Amelsvoort, J.M. (1997) The effect of ingestion of inulin on blood lipids and gastrointestinal symptoms in healthy females. *British Journal of Nutrition* 78: 215-222.

(21) Molis, C., Flourie, B., Ouarne, F., *et al.* (1996) Digestion, excretion and energy value of fructooligosaccharides in healthy humans. *American Journal of Clinical Nutrition* 62: 324-328.

(22) McBain, A.J. & Macfarlane, G.T. (2001) Modulation of genotoxic enzyme activities by non-digestible oligosaccharide metabolism in in-vitro human gut bacterial gut ecosystems. *Journal of Medical Microbiology* 50: 833-842.

(23) Schrezenmeir, J. & de Vrese, M. (2001) Probiotics, prebiotics, and synbiotics - approaching a definition. *American Journal of Clinical Nutrition* 73 (suppl): 361S-364S.

(24) Fujimori, S., Gudis, K., Mitsui, K., *et al.* (2009) A randomised controlled trial on the efficacy of synbiotic versus probiotic or prebiotic treatments to improve the quality of life in patients with ulcerative colitis. *Nutrition* 25: 520-525.

(25) Schouten, B., van Esch, B.C., Hofman, G.A., *et al.* (2009) Cow milk allergy symptoms are reduced in mice fed dietary synbiotics during oral sensitization with whey. *Journal of Nutrition* 139: 1398-1403.

(26) Roberfroid, M., Gibson, G.R., Hoyles, L., *et al.* (2010) Prebiotic effects: metabolic and health benefits. *British Journal of Nutrition* 104 Suppl 2: S1-S63.

(27) Silk, D.B., Davis, A., Vulevic, J., *et al.* (2009) Clinical trial: the effects of a trans-galactooligosaccharide prebiotic on faecal microbiota and symptoms in irritable bowel syndrome. *Alimentary Pharmacology & Therapeutics* 29: 508-518.

(28) Paineau, D., Payen, F., Panserieu, S., *et al.* (2008) The effects of regular consumption of short-chain fructo-oligosaccharides on digestive comfort of subjects with a minor functional bowel disorders. *British Journal of Nutrition* 99: 311-318.

Chapter 12 – Young and Old

(1) Dominguez-Bello, M.G., Costello, E.K., Contreras, M., et al. (2010) Delivery mode shapes the acquisition and structure of the initial microbiota across multiple body habitats in newborns. *PNAS* 107: 11971-11975.

(2) Ballongue, J. (1998) Bifidobacteria and Probiotic Action. In *Lactic Acid Bacteria* (Salminen, S. & von Wright, A., eds.). Marcel Dekker. New York, U.S.A.: 519-587.

(3) Favier, C.F., Vaughan, E.E., De Vos, W.M., et al. (2002) Molecular Monitoring of Succession of Bacterial Communities in Human Neonates. *Applied and Environmental Microbiology* 68: 219-226.

(4) Palmer, C., Bik, E.M., DiGiulio, D.B., et al. (2007) Development of the Human Infant Intestinal Microbiota. *PLoS Biology* 5: 1556-1573.

(5) Penders, J., Thijs, C., Vink, C., et al. (2006) Factors Influencing the Composition of the Intestinal Microbiota in Early Infancy. *Pediatrics* 118: 511-521.

(6) Bager, P., Wohlfahrt, J. & Westergaard, T. (2008) Caesarean delivery and the risk of atopy and allergic disease: meta-analyses. *Clinical and Experimental Allergy* 38: 634-642.

(7) Watson, J., Jones, R.C., Cortes, C., et al. (2006) Community-Associated Methicillin-Resistant Staphylococcus aureus Infection Among Healthy Newborns - Chicago and Los Angeles County, 2004. *JAMA* 296: 36-38.

(8) Marra, F., Lynd, L., Coombes, M., et al. (2006) Does Antibiotic Exposure During Infancy Lead to Development of Asthma? *Chest* 129:610-618.

(9) Bedford Russell, A.R. & Murch, S.H. (2006) Could peripartum antibiotics have delayed health consequences for the infant? *BJOG* 113: 758-765.

(10) Rinne, M.M., Gueimonde, M., Kalliomaki, M., et al. (2005) Similar bifidogenic effects of prebiotic-supplemented partiality hydrolysed infant formula and breastfeeding on infant gut microbiota. *FEMS Immunology and Medical Microbiology* 43: 59-65.

(11) Agostoni, C., Axelsson, I., Braegger, C., et al. (2004) Probiotic Bacteria in Dietetic Products for Infants: A Commentary by the ESPGHAN Committee on Nutrition. *Journal of Pediatric Gastroenterology and Nutrition* 38:365-374.

(12) Hanson, L.A., Korotkova, M., Lundin, S., et al. (2003) The Transfer of Immunity from Mother to Child. *Annals of the New York Academy of Sciences* 987: 199-206.

(13) Westerbeek, E.A., van den Berg, A., Lafeber, H.N., et al. (2006) The intestinal bacterial colonisation in preterm infants: A review of the literature. *Clinical Nutrition* 25: 361-368.

(14) Gewolb, I.H., Schwalbe, R.S., Taciak, V.L., et al. (1999) Stool microflora in extremely low birthweight infants. *Archives of Disease in Childhood. Fetal and Neonatal Edition* 80: F167-F173.

(15) Lemberg, D.A., Ooi, C.E. & Day, A.S. (2007) Probiotics in paediatric gastrointestinal diseases. *Journal of Paediatrics and Child Health* 43: 331-336.

(16) Johnston, B.C., Supina, A.L., Ospina, M., et al. (2007) Probiotics for the prevention of pediatric antibiotic-associated diarrhea (Review). *Cochrane Database of Systematic Reviews* 2: CD004827.pub2

(17) Kuitunen, M., Kukkonen, K., Juntunen-Backman, K., et al. (2009) Probiotics prevent IgE-associated allergy until five years in caesarean-delivered children but not in the total cohort. *Journal of Allergy and Clinical Immunology* 123: 335-341.

(18) Bruni, F.M., Piacentini, G.L., Peroni, D.G., et al. (2009) Cow's milk allergic children can present sensitisation to probiotics. *Acta Pediatrica* 98: 321-327.

(19) Cabana, M.D., Shane, A.L., Chao, C., et al. (2006) Probiotics in Primary Care Pediatrics. *Clinical Pediatrics* 45: 405-410.

(20) Magellan Health Services (2004) How Aging Affects the Body. www.magellanassist.com/mem/library

(21) Holt, P.R. (2003) Gastrointestinal diseases in the elderly. *Current Opinion in Clinical Nutrition and Metabolic Care* 6: 41-48.

(22) Woodmansey, E.J., McMurdo, M.E., Macfarlane, G.T., et al. (2004) Comparison of Compositions and Metabolic Activities of Fecal Microbiotas in Young Adults and in Antibiotic-Treated and Non-Antibiotic-Treated Elderly Subjects. *Applied and Environmental* Microbiology 70: 6113-6122.

(23) Tiihonen, K., Ouwehand, A.C., Rautonen, N. (2010) Human intestinal microbiota and healthy ageing. *Ageing Research Reviews* 9: 107-116.

(24) Woodmansey, E.J. (2007) Intestinal bacteria and ageing. *Journal of Applied Microbiology* 102: 1178-1186.

(25) He, F., Ouwehand, A.C., Isolauri, E., et al. (2001) Differences in Composition and Mucosal Adhesion of Bifidobacteria Isolated from Healthy Adults and Healthy Seniors. *Current Microbiology* 43: 351-354.

(26) Altman, D.F. (1990) Changes in Gastrointestinal, Pancreatic, Biliary, and Hepetic Function with Aging. *Gastroenterology Clinics of North America* 19: 227-234.

(27) Drozdowski, L. & Thomson, A.B. (2006) Aging and the intestine. *World Journal of Gastroenterology* 12(47): 7578-7584.

(28) D'Souza, A.L. (2007) Ageing and the gut. *Postgraduate Medical Journal* 83: 44-53.

(29) Saltzman, J.R. & Russell, R.M. (1998) The Aging Gut. *Gastroenterology Clinics of North America* 27: 309-324.

(30) Parlesak, A., Klein, B., Schecher, K., et al. (2003) Prevalence of small bowel bacterial overgrowth and its association with nutrition intake in nonhospitalised older adults. *Journal of the American Geriatrics Society* 51: 768-773.

(31) Towers, A.L., Burgio, K.L., Locher, J.L., et al. (1994) Constipation in the elderly: influence of dietary, psychological, and physiological factors. *Journal of the American Geriatrics Society* 42: 701-706.

(32) Scheppach, W. (1994) Effects of short chain fatty acids on gut morphology and function. *Gut* supplement 1: S35-S38.

(33) Husebye, E., Hellstrom, P.M., Sundler, F., et al. (2001) Influence of microbial species on small intestinal myoelectric activity and transit in germ-free rats. *American Journal of Physiology. Gastrointestinal and Liver Physiology* 280: G368-G380.

(34) Kleessen, B., Sykura, B., Zunft, H-J., et al. (1997) Effects of inulin and lactose on fecal microflora, microbial activity, and bowel habit in elderly constipated persons. *American Journal of Clinical Nutrition* 65: 1397-1402.

(35) Hamilton-Miller, J.M.T. (2004) Probiotics and prebiotics in the elderly. *Postgraduate Medical Journal* 80: 447-451.

(36) Aspinall, R. & Andrew, D. (2000) Immunosenescence: potential causes and strategies for reversal. *Biochemical Society Transactions* 28: 250-254.

(37) Rayner, C.K. & Horowitz, M. (2006) Gastrointestinal motility and glycemic control in diabetes: the chicken and the egg revisited? *Journal of Clinical Investigation* 116: 299-302.

(38) Sheth, A. & Floch, M. (2009) Probiotics and Diverticular Disease. *Nutrition in Clinical Practice* 24: 41- 44.

Chapter 13 – Future Developments

(1) Turnbaugh, P.J. & Gordon, J.I. (2009) The core gut microbiome, energy balance and obesity. *Journal of Physiology* 587.17: 4153-4158.

(2) Lutgendorff, F., Akkermans, L.M. & Soderholm, J.D. (2008) The Role of Microbiota and Probiotics in Stress-induced Gastro-intestinal Damage. *Current Molecular Medicine* 8: 282-298.

(3) Eutamene, H. & Bueno, L. (2007) Role of probiotics in correcting abnormalities of colonic flora induced by stress. *Gut* 56: 1495-1497.

(4) Zareie, M., Johnson-Henry, K., Jury, J., et al. (2006) Probiotics prevent bacterial translocation and improved intestinal barrier function in rats following chronic psychological stress. *Gut* 55: 1553-1560.

(5) Forsythe, P. & Bienenstock, J. (2008) Probiotics in Neurology and Psychiatry. In *Therapeutic Microbiology: Probiotics and Related Strategies* (Versalovic, J. & Wilson, M., eds.). ASM Press, Washington, DC, U.S.A: 285-298.

(6) Sullivan, A., Edlund, C. & Nord, C.E. (2001) Effect of antimicrobial agents on the ecological balance of human microflora. *The Lancet Infectious Diseases* 1: 101-114.

(7) Greenwood, D., Finch, R., Davey, P., et al. (2007) Pharmacokinetics (Ch. 14). In *Antimicrobial Chemotherapy, Fifth Edition* (Greenwood, D., et al., eds.). Oxford University Press, Oxford, U.K.: 195-206.

(8) Dethlefsen, L. Huse, S., Sogin, M.L., et al. (2008) The Pervasive Effects of an Antibiotic on the Human Gut Microbiota, as Revealed by Deep 16S rRNA Sequencing. *PLoS Biology* 6: 2383-2400.

(9) Moore, W.E. & Moore, L.H. (1995) Intestinal Floras That Have a High Risk of Colon Cancer. *Applied and Environmental Microbiology* 61: 3202-3207.

(10) Teitelbaum, J.E. & Walker, W.A. (2002) Nutritional Impact of Pre- and Probiotics as Protective Gastrointestinal Organisms. *Annual Review of Nutrition* 22: 107-138.

(11) Rafter, J. (2003) Probiotics and colon cancer. *Best Practice & Research Clinical Gastroenterology* 17: 849-859.

(12) Pool-Zobel, B., van Loo, J., Rowland, I., et al. (2002) Experimental evidences on the potential of prebiotic fructans to reduce the risk of colon cancer. *British Journal of Nutrition* 87: S273-S281.

(13) Taper, H.S. & Roberfroid, M.B. (2002) Inulin/oligofructose and anticancer therapy. *British Journal of Nutrition* 87: S283-S286.

(14) Rowland, I. (2004) Probiotics and colorectal cancer risk. *British Journal of Nutrition* 91: 805-807.

(15) Rafter, I., Bennett, M., Caderni, G., et al. (2007) Dietary synbiotics reduce cancer risks in polypectomised and colon cancer patients. *American Journal of Clinical Nutrition* 85: 488-496.

(16) Andreyev, J. (2005) Gastrointestinal complications of pelvic radiotherapy: are they of any importance? *Gut* 54: 1051-1054.

(17) Gami, B., Harrington, K., Blake, P., et al. (2003) How patients manage gastrointestinal symptoms after pelvic radiotherapy. *Alimentary Pharmacology & Therapeutics* 18: 987-994.

(18) Delia, P., Sansotta, G., Donato, V., et al. (2007) Use of probiotics for prevention of radiation-induced diarrhea. *World Journal of Gastroenterology* 13: 912-915.

(19) Turnbaug, P.J., Hamady, M., Yatsunenko, T., et al. (2009) A core gut microbiome in obese and lean twins. *Nature* 457 (7228): 480-484.

(20) Peltonen, R., Kjeldsen-Kragh, J., Haugen, M., et al. (1994) Changes of Faecal Flora in Rheumatoid Arthritis During Fasting and One-Year Vegetarian Diet. *British Journal of Rheumatology* 33: 638-643.

(21) Correale, J. & Farez, M. (2007) Association Between Parasite Infection and Immune Responses in Multiple Sclerosis. *Annals of Neurology* 61: 97-108.

(22) Correale, J. & Farez, M. (2007) Association Between Parasite Infection and Immune Responses in Multiple Sclerosis. *Annals of Neurology* 61: 97-108.

(23) Sanchez, E., Nadal, I., Donat, E., et al. (2008) Reduced diversity and increased virulence-gene carriage in intestinal enterobacteria of coeliac children. *BMC Gastroenterology* 8: 50.

(24) Sanz, Y., Sanchez, E., Marzotto, M., et al. (2007) Differences in faecal bacterial communities in coeliac and healthy children as detected by PCR and denaturing gradient gel electrophoresis. *FEMS Immunology and Medical Microbiology* 51: 562-568.

(25) Mansour-Ghanaei, F., Dehbashi, N, Yazdanparast, K., et al. (2003) Efficacy of Saccharomyces boulardii with antibiotics in acute amoebiasis. *World Journal of Gastroenterology* 9(8): 1832-1833.

(26) Dinleyici, E.C., Eren, M., Yargic, Z.A., et al. (2009) Clinical Efficacy of Saccharomyces boulardii and Metronidazole Compared to Metronidazole Alone in Children with Acute Bloody Diarrhea Caused by Amebiasis: A Prospective, Randomized, Open Label Study. *American Journal of Tropical Medicine and Hygiene* 80: 953-955.

(27) Savas-Erdeve, S., Gokay, S. & Dallar, Y. (2009) Efficacy and safety of Saccharomyces boulardii in amebiasis-associated diarrhoea in children. *Turkish Journal of Pediatrics* 51: 220-224.

(28) van Santvoort, H.C., Besselink, M.G., Timmerman, H.M., et al.(2008) Probiotics in surgery. *Surgery* 143: 1-7.

(29) Pitsouni, E., Alexiou, V., Saridakis, V, et al. (2009) Does the use of probiotics/synbiotics prevent postoperative infections in patients undergoing abdominal surgery? A meta-analysis of randomized controlled trials. *European Journal of Clinical Pharmacology* 65: 561-570.

(30) Levenson, S.M., Kan-Gruber, D., Gruber, C., et al. (1983) Wound healing accelerated by Staphylococcus aureus. *Archives of Surgery* 118: 310-320.

(31) Hanlon, G.W. (2007) Bacteriophages: an appraisal of their role in the treatment of bacterial infections. *International Journal of Antimicrobial Agents* 30: 118-128.

(32) Bakken, J.S. (2009) Fecal bacteriotherapy for recurrent Clostridium difficile infection. *Anaerobe* 15: 285-289.

(33) Borody, T.J., Warren, E.F., Leis, S., et al. (2003) Treatment of Ulcerative Colitis Using Fecal Bacteriotherapy. *Journal of Clinical Gastroenterology* 37: 42-47.

(34) Scrivener, S., Yemaneberhan, H., Zebenigus, M., et al. (2001) Independent effects of intestinal parasite infection and domestic allergen exposure on risk of wheeze in Ethiopia: a nested case-control study. *The Lancet* 358 (9292): 1493-1499.

(35) Elliott, A.M., Mpairwe, H., Quigley, M.A., et al. (2005) Helminth infection during pregnancy and development of infantile eczema. *JAMA* 294: 2032-2034.

(36) McKay, D.M. (2008) The therapeutic helminth? *Trends in Parasitology* 25: 109-114.

(37) Summers, R.W., Elliott, D.E., Urban, J.F., et al. (2005a) Trichuris suis therapy in Crohn's disease. *Gut* 54:87-90.

(38) Summers, R.W., Elliott, D.E., Urban, J.F., et al. (2005b) Trichuris suis therapy for active ulcerative colitis: a randomized controlled trial. *Gastroenterology* 128: 825-832.

(39) Feary, J.R., Venn, A.J., Mortimer, K., et al. (2009) Experimental hookworm infection: a randomized placebo-controlled trial in asthma. *Clinical and Experimental Allergy* 40: 289-306.

Bibliography

Anderson, D.M. (2002) *Mosby's Medical, Nursing & Allied Health Dictionary, Sixth Edition*. Mosby, St Louis, U.S.A.

Andrews, M. (1976) *The Life That Lives on Man*. Faber & Faber, London, U.K.

Böttcher, H.M. (1963) *Miracle Drugs*. Heinemann, London, U.K.

Gibson, G.R. & Rastall, R.A., eds. (2006) *Prebiotics: Development & Application*. John Wiley & Sons, Chichester, England.

de Kruif, P. (1926) *Microbe Hunters*. Harcourt Brace, SanDiego, USA.

Dixon, B. (1994) *Power Unseen: How Microbes Rule the World*. W.H. Freeman, New York, U.S.A.

Drasar, B.S. & Barrow, P.A. (1985) *Intestinal Microbiology*. Van Noorstrand Reinhold, Wokingham, England.

Elmer, G.W., McRarland, L.V. & McFarland, M. (2007) *The Power of Probiotics*. Haworth Press, New York, U.S.A.

Fuller, R. & Perdigon, G., eds. (2003) *Gut Flora, Nutrition, Immunity and Health*. Blackwell Publishing, Oxford, U.K.

Hart, A.L., Stagg, A.J., et al. (eds.) (2002) *Gut Ecology*. Martin Dunitz, London, U.K.

Heasman, M. & Mellentin, J. (2001) *The Functional Food Revolution*. Earthscan Publications, London, UK.

Huffnagle, G. & Wernick, S. (2007) *The Probiotics Revolution*. Vermilion, London, U.K.

Johnson, L.R. (ed.) (2007) *Gastrointestinal Physiology, 7th edition*. Mosby Elsevier, Philadelphia, U.S.A.

Karpa, K.D. (2003) *Bacteria for Breakfast*. Trafford Publishing, Victoria, Canada.

Keshav, S. (2004) *The Gastrointestinal System at a Glance*. Blackwell Science, Oxford, U.K.

Levy, S.B. (2002) *The Antibiotic Paradox*. Perseus Publishing, Cambridge, MA, U.S.A.

Madigan, M.T., Martinko, J.M., et al. (2009) *Brock Biology of Microorganisms, Twelfth Edition*. Pearson Benjamin Cummings, San Francisco, U.S.A.

Marieb, E.N. (2004) *Human Anatomy & Physiology (6th Edition)*. Pearson Benjamin Cummings, San Francisco, U.S.A.

Metchnikoff, E. (2003) *The Prolongation of Life*. University Press of the Pacific, Honolulu, Hawaii.

Nairn, R. & Helbert, H. (2002) *Immunology for Medical Students*. Mosby International, Edinburgh, U.K.

Postgate, J. (2000) *Microbes and Man*. Cambridge University Press, Cambridge, U.K.

Rambaud, J-C., Buts, J-P., et al. (eds.) (2006) *Gut Microflora: Digestive Physiology and Pathology*. John Libbey Eurotext, Esher, U.K.

Salminen, S., von Wright, A. & Ouwehand, A., eds. (2004) *Lactic Acid Bacteria: Microbiological and Functional Aspects, Third Edition*. Marcel Dekker, Inc., New York, U.S.A.

Schulze, J., Schiemann, M. & Sonnenborn, U. (2006) *120 Years of E. coli*. Alfred-Nissle-Gesellschaft, Hagen, Germany.

Singleton, P. & Sainsbury, D. (2001) *Dictionary of Microbiology and Molecular Biology, 3rd Edition*. John Wiley & Sons, Chichester, U.K.

Smith, M.E. & Morton, D.G. (2002) *The Digestive System*. Churchill Livinstone, Edinburgh, Scotland.

Spiller, R.C. & Farthing, M.J.G. (1994) *Diarrhoea and Constipation*. Science Press, London, U.K.

Tannock, G.W. (ed.) (1999) *Medical Importance of the Normal Microflora*. Kluwer Academic Publishers, Dordrecht, Netherlands.

Tortora, G.J., Funke, B.R. & Case, C.L. (2002) *Microbiology: An Introduction*. Benjamin Cummings, San Francisco, U.S.A.

Townsend, C.R., Begon, M. & Harper, J.L. (2003) *Essentials of Ecology*. Blackwell Publishing, Oxford, U.K.

Wilson, M. (2005) *Microbial Inhabitants of Humans*. Cambridge University Press, Cambridge, U.K.

Index

A

abdominal discomfort 149
absorption of nutrients 149
acidophilus milk 105
acne 5, 14
actinomycetes 19
adaptive immune system 43
advantage of a prebiotic 137
allergic rhinitis 79
allergies 47, 80
altered microflora 148
amoebiasis 160
ampicillin 38
anaerobic cocci 38
anaerobic metabolism 34
anti-bacterial substances 36
antibiotic-associated diarrhoea 62, 66, 78
antibiotic resistance 94
antibiotics 2, 7, 56
antibiotics and allergic disease 48
antibiotics to infants 145
antibodies 44, 47
appearance and taste of prebiotics 137
asthma 47, 164
atopic eczema 79, 163
autoimmune diseases 49, 79

B

Bacillus clausii 126
Bacillus coagulans 112, 126
Bacillus licheniformis 126
Bacillus pumilus 126
Bacillus subtilis 93, 95, 122, 124, 127, 128
bacteraemia 93
bacterial vaginosis 83
bacteriocins 36
bacteriophages 161
bacteriotherapy 58
Bacteroides 22, 33, 34, 38, 127
B cell 44
Bif. adolescentis 122
Bif. animalis 69, 122
Bif. bifidum 112, 122
Bif. breve 122
Bif. infantis 122
Bif. lactis 112, 122
Bif. longum 112, 122
bifidobacteria vii, 34, 38, 48, 106, 120, 132, 139
bifidobacteria probiotics 93
Bifidobacterium 9, 33, 72, 76, 100, 112, 120, 122, 143, 152
bifidogenic 136
birth by caesarean section 144
body's immune system 41
Brevibacterium 14
bronchitis 90
B vitamins 35, 121
by-products of metabolism 36

C

caecum 30, 31, 119
calcium 105
Campylobacter jejuni 5
Candida 29, 84
Candida albicans 23, 38, 84
children 143
Chlamydia trachomatis 5
choice of antibiotics 155
cilia 16
clinical studies using prebiotics 140
Clostridium 33, 34, 127, 135
Clostridium botulinum 35
Clostridium butyricum 127
Clostridium difficile 36, 38, 67, 146, 150, 162
Clostridium difficile colitis 127
Clostridium glabrata 84
Clostridium paripsilosis 84
Clostridium perfringens 159
Clostridium tetani 5
Clostridium tropicalis 84
cocci 10
coeliac disease 159
colo-rectal cancer 157
common cold 90
comparing milk-based and freeze-dried products 108
constipation 62, 67, 78, 150
contraceptive methods 22
Corynebacterium 13, 16
cow's milk allergy 147
Crohn's disease 49, 73
Cryptosporidium parvum 35
cystitis 5
cytomegalovirus 49

D

dental caries 5, 20, 87
diabetes mellitus 150
diarrhoea caused by medications 150
dietary fibre 131
digestive enzymes 29
disadvantages of prebiotics 138
diverticular disease 151
diverticulitis 151
dosage for children 147
duodenum 27

E

E. coli 57, 86, 93, 118, 135
eczema 47
effects of stress 154
elderly people 148
endocarditis 93
Entamoeba hystolytica 160
Enterococcus 33, 34, 95, 119
Enterococcus faecalis 96
Enterococcus faecium 96
enterococcus probiotics 93
Enterococcus species 22
environmental factors 49
epidermis 12
epithelial cells 36
Eppstein-Barr virus 49
Escherich, Professor Theodor 122
Escherichia 33
Escherichia coli (E. coli) 5, 9, 22, 33, 36, 122, 128
Eubacterium 33, 34, 127
European Food Safety Authority 95, 113
Evidence of probiotic effects 121

F

'friendly' bacteria (probiotics) 3
faecal enemas 161-2
Faecalibacterium 33, 127
Faecalibacterium prausnitzii 74
female reproductive system 21
female urogenital infections 82
fermentation 53
fermented food and drink 52
flatulence 138
formula milk 145
freeze-dried probiotic products 106
fructo-oligosaccharides (FOS) 134
Fusobacterium 22

G

galacto-oligosaccharides (GOS) 134
gall bladder 28
Gardnerella vaginalis 22, 83
gastric ulcers 5
gastritis and stomach ulcers 62, 76
gastro-intestinal tract 62
gastroenteritis 5
genus 9
gingivitis 20
gluco-oligosaccharides 137
Gram-negative bacteria 48
Gram-positive bacteria 156
gum disease 20, 88
gut-associated lymphoid tissue (GALT) 81
gut immune tissues 46
gut microbes 35
gut microflora 35, 139

H

halitosis 18, 88
hay fever 47, 79
Helicobacter pylori 5, 60, 76, 149, 152
helminthic worms 48, 164
HIV/AIDS 96
hookworm infection 163
hookworm larvae 164
how microbes are classified 9
human intestine 25
hydrogen peroxide 36
hygiene hypothesis 47
hypodermis 12

I

ileum 27, 119
ileum microflora 30
immune-malfunction 164
immune system (IS) 40, 96
immunocompromised person 93, 96
infants 46
infection risks 93
infectious diarrhoea 62, 63, 78
infectious diseases 25
inflammation 42
inflammatory bowel disease (IBD) 49, 62, 72, 164
influenza vaccination 91
innate immune system 42
intestinal bacteria 33
intestinal diseases 154
inulin 135, 150
irritable bowel syndrome (IBS) ix, 62, 69, 78, 113
IS malfunction 49
isomalto-oligosaccharides (IMO) 136

J

jejunum 27
jejunum microflora 30

L

L. crispatus 22, 119
L. gasseri 22
L. iners 22
L. jensenii 22
L. johnsonii 119
L. reuteri 119
L. salivarius 119
Lachnospira 33, 127
lactase 105
lactic acid 34, 36, 53, 119

lactic acid bacteria vii, 119
lactobacilli 22, 34, 38, 48, 139, 150
Lactobacillus 9, 21, 33, 76, 77, 82, 88, 94, 95, 97, 112, 117, 118
Lactobacillus acidophilus 9, 57, 119
Lactobacillus bulgaricus 56, 57, 75, 105
Lactobacillus casei 57, 69, 112, 119
Lactobacillus delbrueckii 55
Lactobacillus plantarum 109, 119
Lactobacillus rhamnosus 109, 112, 119
Lactobacillus sporogenes 112
lactose intolerance 62, 74, 78
lactosucrose 136
lactulose 136
large bowel/intestine 25, 30, 31, 119
leaky gut 154
Listeria cytogenes 35
lymphocytes 44
lymph system 44
lyophilisation 106

M

major microfloral genera 127
Malassezia 13
Marshall, Barry 60
Medline 111
memory cells 45
meningitis 5
Metchnikoff, Elie 54
microbiota 131
microbiota hypothesis 48
microflora 6
microflora (prebiotics) 3
microfloral bacteria 11, 46
microflora of the human body 8
microflora of the large intestine 32

milk 105
milk-based probiotics 105
milk products 53
model microbes 122
mouth 17, 87
mouth microflora 20
mucosa 119
multi-strain probiotic 109
multiple sclerosis 49, 79, 159

N

nausea 149
NDOs as food 133
necrotising enterocolitis ix, 98
Neisseria 16
Neisseria meningitidis 5, 17
Non-digestible food 131
Non-digestible oligosaccharides (NDOs) 132
nose 15

O

obesity 158
oesophagus 25
oligosaccharide 132
opportunistic pathogens 11
oral antibiotics 155
oral thrush 89
organ transplant patients 97
oropharynx 16

P

palatinose 137
pancreas 28
pancreatitis 98-9
parasitic intestinal worms 48
Pasteur, Louis 54
pasteurisation 105
pathogenic bacteria 35, 61
pathogenic microbes 40
penicillin 38
peptococci 34
peristalsis 36

phages 161
phagocyte 42, 54
pharyngitis 5
phosphorus 105
pig whipworm eggs 164
plaque 19
plasmid 95
pneumonia 5, 90
polydextrose 137
polysaccharide 135
Porphyromonas 16
Porphyromonas gingivalis 19
pouchitis 74
pre-term infants 146
prebiotic effect 134
prebiotic foods 133
prebiotics 37, 74, 66, 81, 87, 130, 150
prebiotic skin cream 92
pregnancy 100
pregnant women 47
premature babies 47, 98
Prevotella 16, 17
probiotic E. coli 69
probiotic microbes 93, 105
probiotic products xii
probiotics for animals 58
probiotics influencing the IS 80
probiotics for children 146
probiotic yeast 57, 73, 160
product inaccuracies 115
Propionibacterium 13, 16
Propionibacterium acnes 5, 14, 92
protein-degrading bacteria 34
protozoan parasite 160
pyrodextrin 137

R

radiation-induced diarrhoea 158
reduced stomach acid secretion 149
Rettger, Leo F. 56
rheumatoid arthritis 49, 79, 159

risk of overdose 115
Roseburia 33, 127
Ruminococcus 33, 127

S

saccharolytic 37
saccharolytic bacteria 132
Saccharomyces boulardii 58, 73, 93, 126, 160
Saccharomyces cerevisiae 58, 122, 126, 128
Salmonella 123
Salmonella enterica 5
Salmonella enteritidis 35
saprophytic mycobacteria 48
Shigella 5, 123
small bowel/intestine 25, 27, 29, 119
soil bacterium 125
sore throat 90
soyo-oligosaccharides (SOS) 136
species 9
sphincter 30
spread of antibiotic resistance 93
Staphylococcus 13, 16
Staphylococcus aureus 5, 11, 13, 91
Staphylococcus epidermidis 13
stomach 26
stomach ulcers 60
Streptococcus 16, 19, 34, 91
Streptococcus mutans 5, 20, 88
Streptococcus pneumoniae 5, 16
Streptococcus pyogenes 5, 16, 90
Streptococcus salivarius 18, 89
Streptococcus thermophilus 56, 75, 105-6
stress 7, 154
superbugs 94
surgery 160

symbiosis 3
synbiotic vii, 140
systemic immune system 79

T

T cell 44
teeth 19
tetracycline 95
throat and windpipe 15
tonsillitis 91
Toxoplasma gondii 48
traveller's diarrhoea 65
Treponema pallidum 5
type 1 diabetes 49, 79
types of probiotic microbes 110

U

ulcerative colitis 49, 72, 78, 163
unborn child 93, 100
unsanitary conditions 48
upper respiratory tract 15, 89
urinary tract infections 85

V

vaginal candidiasis 84
vaginal microflora 21
vaginitis 82
van Leeuwenhoek, Antoni 54
vancomycin 163
Vibrio cholerae 5
viridans streptococci 16
vitamin K 35
vitamins 56
Vitreoscilla filiformis 92

W

Western diet 32
white blood cells 44
World Health Organisation 94
worm therapy 161, 163

X

xylo-oligosaccharides (XOS) 136

Y

yeast fermentation 52
Yersinia 123
yoghurt 105
yoghurt benefits 75

About the Author

Peter Cartwright has 17 years' experience of working for patient and self-help associations in the UK, as Assistant Director of the National Association for Colitis and Crohn's Disease, Director of the British Stammering Association and National Development Officer of the Self-Help Alliance. Currently, he is a Trustee of the Bladder and Bowel Foundation. Peter has an MSc in Microbiology and an MA in Sociology, and is the author of *Probiotics for Crohn's and Colitis* (Prentice Publishing), *Coping Successfully with Ulcerative Colitis* (Sheldon Press) and *Coping with Diverticulitis* (Sheldon Press). He has given more than 40 lectures on probiotics to doctors in 13 countries.